Brainwashing

Its History; Use by Totalitarian Communist Regimes; and Stories of American and British Soldiers and Captives Who Defied It

By Edward Hunter

Published by Pantianos Classics

ISBN-13: 978-1-78987-018-3

First published in 1956

Contents

Chapter One - A New Word

The new word *brainwashing* entered our minds and dictionaries in a phenomenally short time. This sinister political expression had never been seen in print anywhere until a few years ago. About the only times it was ever heard in conversation was inside a tight, intimate circle of trusted relatives or reliable friends in Red China during the short honeymoon period of communism. The few exceptions were when a Red indoctrinator would lose his temper and shout out, "You need a brainwashing."

The reason the word was picked up so quickly was that it was not just a clever synonym for something already known, but described a strategy that had yet no name. A vacuum in language existed: no word tied together the various tactics that make up the process by which the communists expected to create their "new Soviet man."

The word came out of the sufferings of the Chinese people. Put under a terrifying combination of subtle and crude mental and physical pressures and tortures, they detected a pattern and called it *brainwashing*. The Reds wanted people to believe that it could be amply described by some familiar expression such as *education, public relations, persuasion* — or by some misleading term like *mind reform and re-education*. None of these could define it because it was much, much more than any one of them alone. The Chinese knew they hadn't just been educated or persuaded; something much more dire than that had been perpetrated on them, similar in many peculiar ways to a medical treatment.

What they had undergone was more like witchcraft, with its incantations, trances, poisons, and potions, with a strange flair of science about it all, like a devil dancer in a tuxedo, carrying his magic brew in a test tube.

The communist hierarchy preferred people to believe that there was no such thing as brainwashing. So long as they could keep it concealed, without a name, opposition to it could be kept scattered and ineffective. As explained by Dr. Joost A. M. Meerloo, a psychiatrist of Dutch origin, in his book *Conversation and Communication*, it is practically impossible to fight something until it has been given a name. "To name an object is to bring it within the sphere of human control," he wrote. "Without a name it arouses fear, because it is unknown...Whoever knows the name has power." Dr. Meerloo coined the fine laboratory word menticide — murder of the mind — for this atrocious quack science devised by the Reds to bring about the voluntary submission of people to an unthinking discipline and a robotlike enslavement. The popular word remained brainwashing, for it has a flesh and blood quality which characterizes any expression arising out of real-life experience.

The German-born Sinologue, Max Perleberg, who is fluent in both modern and classical Chinese, told me that the term might well have been derived from the Buddhist expression *"heart-washing,"* which goes back to the time of Mencius. *Heart-washing* referred to the withdrawal into meditation of a middle-aged man — perhaps weary of worldly cares — living in a bare pavilion in some placid corner of his garden, leaving his offspring to attend to his business.

The reaction among my newspaper colleagues in Hong Kong when the term was first introduced in print was typical of the horror, disbelief, and skepticism that it initially aroused everywhere. These newspapermen were human beings like everyone else, part of the public to whom they were reporting, susceptible to the same emotions and holding identical attitudes.

An outstanding foreign correspondent came to me at once and exclaimed, "I knew that word!"

"Then why didn't you use it?" I asked him.

"Because it's such an ugly word," he retorted feelingly. "I never could persuade myself to put it down on paper."

He was telling me the truth. He was a middle-aged man with Latin sensibilities. But making believe that brainwashing didn't exist could not make it disappear. Neither could people wish it away, any more than the witch doctor I recently watched in the interior of Ceylon could exorcise the evil spirits of kidney disease out of a Singhalese cook by all night Kandyan dancing and frenetic tom-tom beating. The patient, after going through this costly nerve-deadening ceremony, really believed that he was a well man again. He felt well, too; he was sure of it for more than a month. Then the old pain began racking his back again, fiercer than ever. Neither can brainwashing be exorcised by any journalistic mesmerism, nor by recourse to the comforting escape of hush-hush.

Another colleague came to me and said, "You beat me to it! Congratulations!" He had first heard the word after the Reds came into Canton when he was taking a course at Ling Nan University. "I still remember how it sent shivers down my back," he said. "I couldn't forget the eerie sensation that I had gotten from that word *brainwashing*. I wanted to find out everything I could about it. I hoped to do a book on it."

"Why didn't you?" I asked him.

"I was constantly discovering new material and could never get my story pieced together satisfactorily." This, too, was typical, especially in academic and research circles, where professors and investigators ordinarily don't dare publish their findings until they have obtained a complete picture of their subject, neatly framed and ready for the judgment of history. They feel that then their reputations are safe, no matter what the future brings forth. Of course, by that time nothing they say can affect a current situation.

One correspondent, among those who had served the longest in China, smiled knowingly when he first heard of brainwashing and asked if I was writing a novel. His was typical of the customary reactions, "Such things can't happen" and "I simply won't believe it." People closed their eyes to brainwashing. How much of this was calculated and how much naivete can be argued indefinitely. What was obvious was that the communists were very profitably exploiting the opportunity this provided.

After the exchange of prisoners of war in Korea, I was asked a number of times by repatriates, now sadder and wiser, "Why wasn't I told?"

"If I had only been told, I don't believe it could have happened to me," they said. Colonel Frank H. Schwable, who confessed participation in a nonexistent germ warfare, and Corporal Claude Batchelor, the impressionable lad who declared he didn't want to come home and then changed his mind, each said this to me, the former in his Arlington residence and the latter in the model guardhouse at historic Fort Sam Houston in San Antonio.

My first acquaintance with brainwashing came from Chinese who had undergone it on the mainland. They were of all occupations, from merchant to teacher, and included some women. During this early period I saw white men coming out of China, across the plank railway bridge at the border of Hong Kong's leased territory, or through the medieval archway at the Portuguese colony of Macao. I remember one in particular because he seemed to symbolize them all. He walked across the boards feebly, his eyes staring ahead with frightful intensity. He looked centuries older than his middle age. He kept on walking until he was recognized and stopped by a fellow Catholic priest, assigned to the bridge for just such meetings. His Leninist uniform, adapted by Dr. Sun Yat-sen for the Chinese and slightly altered by the Reds, gave no hint of his religious calling. He stood and stared at his colleague and barely answered. He could not grasp the fact that he was out — out of reach of the brainwashers. He just stood and stared for several minutes.

Then, suddenly, realization broke through to him. This was freedom. He was in the Free World. This was more than he could bear. He took a few steps to the side of the bridge and sat down! Then he burst into tears. He was a big man, no longer young, yet he wept like a little child. I do not know how long he cried this way, for I felt as if I were intruding on a man's Calvary. I turned away and left him to his co-religionist.

None of these white people would speak to the press during that early period, and very few of the Chinese would, either. They were being blackmailed. This tactic used to enforce silence was not new, but still terrifying. The Reds threatened to severely punish and even kill the closest associates of any man who broke the hush-hush. Before leaving Red China, each person had to designate a hostage who would sign a guarantee for him. This enabled the communist authorities to avoid making direct threats. The hostages did so for them in the new, so-called voluntary method. "Please do not talk; my life is dependent on it," such persons would beg of their departing friend. They had been his associates, perhaps in church work or in business. The nightmare vision of such old colleagues being put to the rack and tortured unto death rose before a man's eyes and gagged his throat when he wanted to speak out.

Every correspondent in Hong Kong came across living proof of Red pressures. A missionary would arrive at the border by rail, or a businessman on a ship from Tientsin. Usually they were in no shape to speak coherently even if they wanted to. They were sick in mind as much as in body. Horror spoke eloquently through their eyes, but the reporters needed specific details to quote. The pro-communists who came out of China provided them; they did not hesitate to speak. They filled the gap left by the silence of the browbeaten.

When a reporter detected a desire in a man to let go with his true feelings and tell what he had seen and suffered, there usually was a representative of the home office or some official to intervene and say, "Let the man rest," or to take him aside and warn him not to say a word, to wait until a later date, "when you will be in better shape," and "after you have consulted your headquarters." The "later date" during that first year or so never came. The hush-hush dragged on.

This was not the first time that the communists had been able to keep a deadly secret from the Free World as well as from the bulk of their own population. The existence of tremendous slave-labor camps in the Soviet Union was kept hidden for many years in this same manner. They were begun as far back as 1920, in the Solevetski islands in the White Sea, not far from Leningrad. A quarter of a century and World War II were to pass before these became fairly wide knowledge. Yet ten to twenty million persons at a time were incarcerated in these forced-labor camps. Untold millions of men and women perished under bestial treatment and merciless overwork. Inside the barbed-wire enclosures enormous industrial enterprises of every kind were set up, from textile production to mining. When vast labor gangs were required for back-breaking work on such enormous projects as the Volga-Don Canal network linking the Caspian and the Black seas, untold hundreds of thousands of slave laborers of both sexes were used like animals, regardless of beating sun, drenching rain, or deadly cold.

The secret police, under whose direction all these enterprises operated, had a simple method for finding technicians and filling managerial posts. All they had to do was to locate a man or woman with the necessary qualifications. They had no labor unions to worry about or problems of negotiation. Once they found their prospective employee, they could pick him up under any one of the numerous regulations that allowed them to arrest anyone, put him on trial, and sentence him to any work camp, without any publicity except what they might choose to write themselves. If the individual objected, they could put the brainwashing screws on him and exact a confession. How many scientific laboratories working on war secrets have been staffed this way by slave labor — and slave professors — is yet to be known.

Normal people in the Free World refused to believe that such barbarities could exist in our civilized day and age. Proof had slipped out years before to a small circle of politically alert persons, but they were stymied whenever they tried to get the facts to the public. Every sort of diversionary and string-pulling tactic was brought into play to keep the operation secret. What is scarcely appreciated even yet is that these vast slave establishments are a vital part of the brainwashing strategy. Communism requires them both as a softening-up medium against minds and as a source of production.

The hush-hush methods that kept slave labor a secret were employed all over again for brainwashing. Actually, brainwashing was first put on display at the Red purge trials of 1936, when the world was horrified by a procession of "Old Bolsheviks" in the dock in Moscow, announcing that they were traitors to the Bolshevism to which they had given their lives. They were the persons responsible for the Soviet seizure of power. Now they were denouncing themselves as anti-Soviet.

Other big show trials followed at short intervals, each providing the world with still another baffling performance in self-accusation, with insistence on personal guilt and whining appeals for punishment unto death. These persons acted as if possessed. After the occupation of such countries as Hungary and their absorption into the communist orbit, such keen brains as Cardinal Mindszenty's broke under similarly obvious but unproven circumstances. This gave the communists and the anti-anti-communists all around the world what appeared to be incontrovertible evidence that what Moscow was claiming was correct. These men and women had confessed. What more could be asked? Until the strategy of brainwashing was brought out into the open, this question could be answered only in the Reds' favor.

Communist Russia was able to keep brainwashing secret by its thorough control of information, which made an isolated island out of every man and office in the Soviet Union. No individual or bureau dared to communicate with any other except through the approved channels. When the Chinese mainland fell to the communists, brainwashing began to be employed in a slipshod and roughhouse manner as a national policy against the whole population. Security was sacrificed in this reckless, unskilled use of it on a tremendous scale. The secret that Moscow had guarded so successfully at its front door in Europe slipped out through the back door in China.

About a year or so after I first began hearing about brainwashing from the Chinese, I began to discuss it with white people who also had gone through the process in Red China. The futility and tragic consequences of secrecy had begun to dawn on the Free World. I had seen some brainwashed Americans briefly after they had left the mainland; then again, perhaps more than a year afterwards, at home in America. They were now capable of analyzing what had happened to them. What struck me most was the similarity of all their experiences, not only to each other but to that of the Chinese whom I had previously interviewed. Later, I met people who had gone through brainwashing in the communist satellite countries of Europe. Except for the change in locale, the details they told me corresponded exactly with what I had heard from these others. There was no doubt about the pattern, this was a uniform strategy, differing only in degree according to the personality and the local circumstances. The strategy was the same everywhere.

The Free World began to hear strange reports from the communist-operated prisoner-of-war camps in North Korea. Broadcasts were heard in voices recognized as those of normal young men of the American, British, and other U.N. forces. The voices belonged to these men, but the language did not. Pro-communist publications everywhere began to carry purported confessions and grotesquely worded statements said to have been signed by these soldiers in support of whatever propaganda appeal international communism was making at the moment. The free press generally referred briefly to these matters, smelling a rat somewhere, but was confused by the problem of how to handle them. Each editor had to determine for himself, out of his own experience and conscience, whether this material was to be treated as straight news or enemy propaganda. Technically, there was no war. That they avoided falling into the Red propaganda trap to the extent they did was a great tribute to their overriding sense of national responsibility and a confirmation in a time of trial of the dependable qualities of a free press, even when faced by almost insuperable handicaps to the exercise of judgment.

The tendency to suppress discussion of brainwashing and to keep it from public knowledge still had the upper hand. The word continued to be generally ignored, even boycotted. People still kept hoping it was merely a novel word for something old and familiar. Indignation, lacking a target, frequently was vent against the purveyors of the information. In olden times, couriers who brought bad news were often done to death.

This state of affairs, it was evident to me, was fast building up to a declaration by the communists that certain U.N. officers and troops captured by the Red Armies did not want to return home, but preferred to stay with the enemy. The dispatches I wrote warning about this were carried by two national news agencies. The editor of one confided in me later how client papers protested against his carrying the story, insisting that it simply couldn't happen, the old it-can'thappen-here delusion. A few months later, Peking went on the air to boast that a group of U.N. soldiers, mostly American, had decided to remain inside the Red orbit and not go back to their respective lands. This, and the statements made by released POW's themselves revealing how they had been brainwashed, tore the lid off the story and forced the facts out into the open. What they said was exactly the same, detail for detail, as what had been related to me first by the Chinese civilians, then by the white civilians put under brainwashing in China, and next by the Americans and Europeans who had suffered the same atrocities in Eastern Europe.

10

The American public had reason enough now for alarm and shock. Never before had the citizens of a rich, ripe land such as the United States, beneficiaries of the highest standard of living that the earth had ever seen, adopted to stay in an extremely backward, dreadfully impoverished country, supposedly out of preference for its way of life. People could sense that there was something very fishy about this, but nonetheless it was a shock to their pride. At the same time. it led the American people to a self-examination into the state of their own character and their moral defenses, which was the last thing in the world the enemy desired. The unbridled denunciation of their own country, obviously manufactured and parroted, by young Americans whom the Reds had carefully picked from widely separate parts of the United States, shook the public out of its cocksure lethargy and created a scare. The danger now was not only from underestimating the effects of brainwashing, but of overestimating them!

These young expatriates spoke and acted as if they were under a hypnotic spell. Colonel Donald B. Peterson, then chief of Army psychiatry in the Far East, told me in Tokyo that he wondered about the role hypnotism played in this process. In an interview, he declared that "the indoctrination technique in certain elements resembles some techniques used in hypnosis. One out of five persons is very susceptible to suggestion and hypnotizes readily, without regard to age, sex, race, or intelligence level." He also remarked how frequently returned POW's told about their utter fatigue and falling asleep at times during prolonged interrogation. Of course they had no idea what, if anything, had transpired during those periods of sleep. The information I had been gathering convinced me that at least some form of mass hypnosis was part of the Red technique.

In their own publications the communists referred to their methods as "scientific." The enlistment of science on the communist side had a terrifying connotation, and strengthened the invincibility-inevitability line, on which they depended for much of their success. They say dialectical materialism is "scientific." I got a different impression from interviewing scores of brainwashed individuals and many ex-communists who had occupied roles in the brainwashing program; from checking what was said, in "study books" for "learning classes," in documents, in diaries, and in their propaganda generally. As I pored over this enormous mass of material, I grew more certain that scientific was a misnomer, a propaganda term. The scientific form was used but not its content or spirit: there was only plenty of heavy argument, repeating and perpetually rephrasing the same original hypothesis for proof of its validity, and the generous use of selected statistics for irrelevant comparisons.

There was not a trace of original thinking or clarity in any part of it; its main characteristic was its soporific effect. The communist approach was clinical, not scientific! What it brought to mind was the clever medicine man who equips himself with modern drugs and equipment for simple injections to add to his ancient ritual.

The case of Malcolm Bersohn was a tragic episode which helped awaken the public to the awful potentialities of brainwashing. Those who interviewed him were bewildered and horrified not only by what he said — Red ranting was nothing new — but by the unnatural way in which he said it. His speech seemed impressed on a disc that had to be played from start to finish, without modification or halt. He appeared to be under a weird, unnatural compulsion to go on with a whole train of thought, from beginning to end, even when it had been rendered silly. For example, he spoke of no force being applied to him even after someone already had pointed out that he had been seen in shackles. He was like a spider driven by its instincts to go on weaving its web. Bersohn appeared no longer capable of using free will or adapting himself to a situation for which he had been uninstructed; he had to go on as if manipulated by instincts alone. This was Party discipline extended to the mind; a trance element was in it. It gave me a creepy feeling.

I had heard about Bersohn before his release from a fellow inmate of his in the Model Reform Prison at Peking — reform being Red semantics for *brainwashing* — and from associates of his at the former Rockefeller Institute hospital in Peking, the world-renowned Peking Union Medical College. Bersohn was described to me as an intense young man, a Harvard graduate, an extraordinary student with an abnormally high IQ, who had become fascinated with China after he was parachuted behind the Japanese lines during the war. He returned to China voluntarily after his demobilization and joined the P.U.M.C. for study and work in cancer research. Those who came in contact with him in the hospital said he seemed selfless, dedicated to helping the Chinese. He was unable to consider communist promises as only expendable means toward a political end. A hospital attendant was present when a small party of security police came into his workroom. As he was being led out, he was heard to protest, "Well, you're wrong. I haven't done anything against the people's government!" His was a very special case that only an institution with advanced facilities could handle.

During his long imprisonment, which dragged on for nearly four years, his treatment varied from the extremely harsh to the flatteringly soft, including prolonged periods of confinement and shackling. The isolation must have been a maddening torture for a mind such as this, like the drop-of-water torture of the ancient dynasties. The irons, making a man lap up his sorry victuals like a dog, forcing him into crassly humiliating postures, must have been unbearable. He was a difficult patient much of the time, but his crack-up, when it came, was pathetically thorough and thoroughly pathetic. He ultimately became a prize patient and was thrust across the border at Hong Kong, along with a woman, Mrs. Adele Austin Rickett, as part of the diversion technique used by the Moscow-Peking Axis to counteract the extremely damaging effects of the publication at that time of an unprecedented forty-one-page white paper by the Ministry of Defence in London entitled, "Treatment of British Prisoners of War in Korea." This broke London's silence on the subject with a bang. The Reds in Moscow at the same time placed the Italian-born atomic energy expert. Prof. Bruno Portecorvo, on exhibit before newspapermen at the Soviet Academy of Sciences. Portecorvo had disappeared from Britain four years before, and London's characteristic insistence that it had no idea where he had gone, long after it was evident he was in the Soviet Union, gave the Reds this opportunity for propaganda exploitation. As the communists could not refute the devastating charges of atrocities and brainwashing made in the British booklet, they resorted to this customary diversion tactic.

The Japanese I met who had returned from Siberian POW camps singing communist songs, shouting Red slogans, and raising the clenched fist salute had similar reactions. They had been captured by the Soviet Army when Moscow rushed into the war in Asia in its last few days in order to have a legal basis for political intervention and wholesale looting of the industrial plants in Manchuria. These returning Japanese fiercely snubbed their weeping, horrified loved ones who had come from far distances to welcome them home. I talked to some of them about a year later, when they had recovered from their frenzy. What all these persons told me was identical, in essential details, to the experiences of all the others.

The Korean War gave the communists what seemed to be a sure thing. They were suddenly provided with thousands of prisoners completely in their power. They put them under an intensive screening process, disguised as normal interrogation, and chose the comparative few who revealed character defects or other weaknesses. These few could then be put under their hideous pressures of the mind. The miracle is that the Reds found so few to answer their purposes. They publicized what they got by every medium of communication available to them, and as nothing was known about the great majority who either saw through the Red strategy or resisted it successfully, the shock given the Free World was understandably grave. Only later could this be put in correct proportion.

On the other hand, I met many men who had stood up marvelously against exceedingly tough blows and who had survived honorably. They frequently seemed at a loss to explain how they had done it. Simple, down-to-earth truths had been their pillars of strength. The fundamental facts were the same, whether related by a civilian or soldier from China or Korea or someone from East Europe.

For example, my research brought me into contact with some of the 14,000 Chinese in the United Nations' POW camps who steadfastly refused repatriation to Communist China. These stalwart soldiers had succeeded in one of the strangest and most heroic struggles for freedom the world had ever witnessed. They had pitted themselves, with only their desperation to support them, against the most cunning and rigorous pressures that obdurate minds could devise to force them back into the embrace of communism.

To be successful, brainwashing depended fundamentally on the subject's ignorance of it. When understood, the worst that the Red laboratories could produce could be thwarted by the character of the free man. When the techniques of communist brainwashing become common knowledge the system will be either shattered completely or made so difficult and costly to the Reds that the game will be hardly worth the candle.

The patterns were irrefutable — for now there were two patterns, one for destruction of the mind and the other for its preservation. The former was sheer evil and decent people were revolted and frightened by the thought that such things could be in this mid-twentieth century. But the other, less sensational, pattern left me without any doubt as to what the outcome would be in this ultimate conflict for the minds of the people of the earth — that is, if the facts about brainwashing could be gotten to the people.

Thanks to the communist blunder of waging a senseless aggressive war in Korea, the knowledge of brainwashing, its vulnerabilities as well as its strong points, can now be made known to all.

Chapter Two - Ivan P. Pavlov

Man and Dog

The name Ivan Petrovich Pavlov meant almost nothing to me when I began to find out about brainwashing. Yes, I knew he had been an eminent Russian physiologist who had performed some interesting experiments with dogs. That was the sum of my knowledge. Dr. Leon Freedom, an eminent Baltimore neuropsychiatrist, whose personal interest had been deeply aroused by these new pressures of the mind and who was well acquainted with Pavlov's work, first drew my attention to the remarkable similarities between them.

Then I remembered seeing the name Pavlov in sections given over to political literature in the main communist bookshops. What had Pavlov to do with politics? I began to read up on him. My main sources were his own lectures, through which I could plod only very slowly, and lectures about him, which were obscured by a mixture of clinical terminology and Red political verbiage clear only to the initiate.

I came across a paper-bound book published in Moscow consisting entirely of verbatim reports on the combined sessions of the Academy of Sciences and the Academy of Medical Sciences of the U.S.S.R. in 1950, when the only subject was Pavlov! The hundredth anniversary of his birth, the previous

September, had been made the occasion for very special observances throughout the Soviet Union, everywhere from collective farms to scientific institutions. On the face of it, this extraordinary attention given to Pavlov about the time of the Korean War, with its unprecedented treatment of prisoners of war by the Reds, was solely a coincidence. The anniversary explained it all. But did it? Was the anniversary only a convenient medium? The more I delved into it, the more connection I found between the POW camps and Pavlov's experiments.

The academies' reports repeatedly insisted that Pavlov had intended his "strictly objective method of investigation" to be applied to man as well as to beast. This included man's "speech activity," too, I read, and the functions of the "first signal system" and the "second signal system." Did this have anything to do with slogans? I found there was a direct relationship here, too. Any doubt I might have had was dispelled by the seemingly innocuous observation made regarding Pavlov's experiments, that "there is a growing appreciation of their value to the philosophy of dialectical materialism." The doctor's clinic here became the politician's study!

Yet there was a vagueness about all this; the facts seemed to slip away whenever I was about to get my hands on them, like the Cheshire cat in Alice's Adventures in Wonderland.

In this state of mind, I happened one evening to visit the home of Frank Wright, who is an important cog in the New York office of the Committee for a Free Europe. His wife was away in the country and he invited me to taste his own robust cuisine — steak and salad. Our conversation veered over to brainwashing and its origins. We talked of the decisive role that confession techniques played in it. The name of Pavlov came up and at once Frank became very agitated. "I saw a movie on his experiments while I was in college which made such a vivid impression on me that I still have a peculiar feeling when I think of them," he exclaimed. He shuddered as he spoke. "Maybe that's why I'm working where I am today," he added thoughtfully.

I had heard of a full-length popular feature film about Pavlov's life. "I suppose that's what you mean," I said.

"No," he replied. "What I saw was a short film lasting about half an hour. It was intended for training purposes in the U.S.S.R. Its field was medical research, yet there was much more to it than that. I took a medical course myself, but didn't finish it, and my uncle was a doctor. Perhaps that helps to explain why it affected me so deeply. There was one horrifying scene with a young man. I saw it by chance in 1928, and went back three more times. The picture first fascinated, then revolted me, and finally made me angry."

This, of course, sent me on a search for that film. At first I thought I would never locate it. Then I found what seemed to fit the description and arranged for a special screening.

When I went to see the film, I took along some friends so we could discuss it afterwards. One was Ayn Rand, who was extremely pleased when I told her

I considered her powerful novel *Fountainhead* a political book. "Of course it is; that's why I wrote it," she replied. She is a passionate exponent of clear-cut thinking and uncompromising convictions, and her book was one of the first to expose the machinations of the communist network. She came with her husband, Frank O'Connor. The subject of the film intensely interested her because she had written, before Orwell's *1984,* a little book Anthem, in which totalitarian society makes the thought or use of the pronoun *I* the most grievous of all heresies and crimes. She had detected the evil in what she had been taught as a little girl in her native Soviet Russia and had managed to get out of that country.

On the basis of what Frank Wright had told me, I also persuaded Dr. Freedom and his wife to make a special trip from Baltimore to see the picture. The film had the unattractive title *The Nervous System,* but most of it was an exciting and beautiful display of nature, with turtles and bees, tigers and monkeys, snakes and birds doing the acting.

Every amusing episode had a bit of "learning" to go along with it. "One form of behavior is the instinct," a caption read, and another declared, "Instinct is inborn." Baby ducks tottered awkwardly into a lake for their first swim. A fox feigned sleep while crows pecked at the grass near by. A few recklessly came up close and one even stepped on the fox which, in a twinkling, snapped it up.

"Instinct is blind," said another caption. We all laughed at the bird which was desperately trying to hatch wooden eggs, even a square one! A pathetic little hen tried to sit on a big ostrich egg. The hunger, protective, maternal, and reproductive instincts were all shown in this fascinating way.

In more formal scenes, a Russian trainer put a dog through familiar tricks, making it lie down and roll over. We saw a white rat in a maze trying to clamber over a corridor wall, not knowing how to get out. We saw it after training, going the shortest way through the labyrinth to the exit, where a biscuit awaited it as a reward. "Individual training makes behavior more complex," the caption explained. Thus, gently, the film proceeded toward its main point.

A lion, advertising a "learning meeting," stalked about carrying a sign that read, "Joy through Study." We now were in the classroom, where the students were monkeys, and a particularly pompous monkey was the teacher. It was very amusing to watch the serious way a monkey turned the pages of a book as if he were reading. Any ordinary person who saw anything sinister about such good-natured fun would have felt ashamed of himself.

But obviously this was no simple study picture for mere entertainment. In another scene lions were whipped, and the caption read, "Pain method of training." One lion straddled its trainer, the yawning chasm of its jaw nearly covering the man's face. Instead of swallowing his head in one bite, the lion licked his nose with its tongue. Lions and trainer followed this up with a dance, all in one happy circle.

Even yet, it seemed far-fetched to seek any connection between this film and a purge trial. A lion lay down and rolled onto its side. Its trainer sat on it while two other lions came up and they all posed together in harmony. What could be more innocent than a lion trainer posing with his beasts? The wrestling match with a huge Arctic bear was much more exciting.

The central theme was indicated by a scene showing a dog in harness, standing on what looked like an operating table, in a room full of mechanical gadgets and curious meters. What immediately attracted attention was the glass container inserted into the side of the dog's lower jaw. This was supposed to have been painless; it did not seem to annoy the dog. Unsmiling doctors busied themselves with the experiment. One held the bulbous end of a rubber tube. By squeezing it, air pressure moved a circular tray bringing a bowl of food within reach of the harnessed canine. As soon as this happened, a light flashed. The dog hungrily eyed the approaching food, and its saliva began to drip into the test tube attached to its jaw. Each drop was counted and carefully tabulated on a graph.

The dog at first paid no attention to the light. Sometimes the rotary table brought an empty bowl to the dog's mouth, but whenever that happened, the light did not go on and no saliva flowed. A routine was now established. When the light flashed, food appeared and saliva appeared. When an empty bowl approached, the light did not go on and there was no saliva.

After a while, the dog hardly glanced at the bowl. It had identified the light with the food. The light was sufficient sign; it had "learned." The crucial point in the experiment was now reached. A white-gowned doctor pressed a push button, the light flashed, but this time the round table did not bring the dog any food. Its saliva dripped just the same. The light had replaced the food in the mind of the dog, the way a slogan or label can replace a thought in a man's mind. The caption merely read, "Reflex caused by flashing light."

The portion of the film showing this experiment was illustrated by a pen-and-ink cross section of the dog's head. Rows of little gears, a significant touch, connected its eyes and mouth with its brain, and traced the path of the messages that came to it from the outside. Another row of gears traced the path taken by the brain's reactions — its reflex — by which it sent an order to the salivary glands in the jaw that food was on the way and to prepare to receive it by secreting saliva. Finally, when only the light flashed, without food, the gears went into motion anyway, and the same message was sent by the brain to the salivary glands. An attitude had been created! A caption explained this as "the pathway of the arc of the conditioned reflex."

Conditioned, in Pavlov's experiments, meant "induced by man, or by outside influences." By unconditioned, he meant "natural," or "instinctive," such as the eye's involuntary blinking when an insect flies close to it. Conditioned-reflex action can be brought about deliberately, and this is what the communist hierarchy now relies upon to make a basic change in human nature, to give birth to the "new Soviet man" in whom the conception of the individual *I* is to be replaced by the *we* of collectivity. In short, what the totalitarian state strives toward is no less than the insectivization of human beings.

One scene showed a puppy that had not yet tasted meat. When red meat was put in front of its nose for the first time, it showed no interest and no saliva flowed. It had to learn that it was food and only then did its glands go into action.

Another scene showed a baby. The caption that went with it was severely unemotional and read bluntly, "The new-born has no conditioned reflexes." We saw how it had to be taught to feed. The food reflex was illustrated by its learning to drink out of a bottle. Its grabbing instinct was illustrated by the extraordinary vigor with which it grasped its mother's finger in its tiny fist.

Man not only has instincts, but also possesses reason conditioned by his social environment, the film pointed out. But the similarity between the baby and puppy scenes was startling and at the same time confusing. Were instinct and reason really so close, or only superficially so?

Except for the extreme seriousness with which the Russian physiologists and doctors went about their experiments, the film did not appear to demonstrate anything not already known to any dog fancier. The Soviet Government surely would not have engaged in such intricate and costly rigmarole if only to confirm something that anyone with common sense knew.

What we saw didn't nearly match Frank's description. His description was much more incriminating. He recognized it as the same film, but said there had been more to it. This aroused my suspicion that there had been cuts made.

There must have been more to it, and I made a persistent effort to trace the complete film. Months later, I succeeded. The crucial, tell-tale part was in it! As soon as it came on, I experienced a twinge of horror. The twinge was involuntary, what Pavlov would have called an unconditioned reflex.

I arranged to see the completed film myself. What we had seen before, everyone has seen in real life or circuses throughout the world — but not the tell-tale scene. When this was included in its original context, all the previous scenes then began to uncover, startlingly enough, the message that the communists wished to convey to their hospital interns and to their police practitioners, particularly in the MVD training schools.

The incriminating scene began with a young man sitting in a chair, attached to it like the dog in a harness. The switches and push buttons were to operate a combination of gadgets identical to those used for the dog.

A rubber suction tube was stuck into the boy's mouth to measure his saliva. Pills were given him to chew to induce its flow into a glass receptacle. A small cake was waved in front of his eyes, stuck under his nose, and thrust into his mouth. All this was done with grim seriousness. At the same time the light flashed on and off as it had with the animal.

The next scene showed the lad stretched out on a hospital cot like a patient awaiting an appendectomy, except that he was fully dressed. The rubber tube was still inserted into his mouth, its other end projecting into the thin glass receptacle.

A fat cone, with its narrow end open and pointing downwards, was attached to a hinged arm above his head. It was swung over until it hung directly over the boy's face. A push button was pressed by one of the doctors and a few small biscuits were released from the cone into the young man's open mouth. Some of these he caught and chewed, others fell down the side of his face. The light flashed each time the biscuits were dropped.

The scene shifted again, and the light flashed without any biscuits falling from the cone. The boy's saliva flowed just the same. He was reacting exactly as the dog.

This was the part that made the film of such vital importance to the training laboratories operated by the Soviet secret police. Conditioned reflexes could conceivably be produced to make this youth react like the dog that rolled over at its trainer's signal. Only instead of a light, the Kremlin could use words as signals — any words would do — *imperialism, learning, running dog of the imperialists, people, friend of the people, big brother,* without any relationship to their actual meaning. The Kremlin's plan was to make these reflexes instinctive, like the reactions of the animals — and boy — shown in the movie. When we appreciate that this film was produced in 1928, the long-range planning of the communist hierarchy becomes frighteningly evident.

An ordinary person in the Thirties who insisted that the reason the Kremlin produced this film was to teach the use of such practices on mankind would have been accused of being ridiculously obsessed by communism. But we now know well enough that the Kremlin actually was making just such plans for the future.

The purge trials burst into headlines in 1936. The brainwashing strategy by then had been developed by constant clinical experimentation. The world probably will never know how many unfortunates in the U.S.S.R. were guinea pigs in the dungeon laboratories of such prisons as the Lubyanka in Moscow before the technique was sufficiently advanced for Stalin to make a public display of its victims.

The scene with the boy was in the middle of the film. The first reel had given the impression that it was a simple lesson in naturalism, and put the audience in a good mood for the second reel, which was the shocker. The last reel relieved the tension with amusing episodes, but all that really mattered was the dog-man sequence.

Nobody who has ever seen that sequence can possibly forget it, nor can any normal person fail to be revolted by this entire process of mind attack. Without the sequence, the film was easily disguised as a non-political study of animal behavior. It was not intended for general circulation even in the Soviet Union, but only for those already hardened by communist "learning."

One caption explained that the experiments were made on "the isolated animal." In the POW camps in Korea, in the early 1950's, it was "the isolated man" who received the brunt of the pressure. The scene with the harnessed boy could have warned the Free World that these experiments really had human beings in view.

Another caption betrayed the communist determination to go all out in the use of this strategy once it had been sufficiently developed. "A conditioned reflex can be worked out to every stimulus," it read. Such calm laboratory language didn't sound as if it could possibly have any application to everyday living. What it meant to the indoctrinated was plain enough. Any human activity, from the flow of saliva to an embrace or a murder, could be clinically predetermined in politico-medical laboratories by connecting it with a shouted or written slogan, a hand signal, a smear word, or the color of a man's skin. Anything could be made into a trigger, or what the Pavlovian doctors called a stimulus. This was what the caption meant. What they had learned from animals could be used to intrude into the mind and soul of man, to warp and change his brain. Brain-changing was the culmination of this whole evil process, when actual damage was done to a man's mind through drugs, hypnotism, or other means, so that a memory of what had actually happened would be wiped out of his mind and a new memory of what never happened inserted.

Just as Hitler had done, Stalin was proclaiming openly his basic principles and ultimate objectives. He was making no secret of his intent. By shouting it from the housetops, he made it easy for his followers to carry out his instructions, while he could rest confident that others would not see through his machinations. The few who managed to do so, he was sure, would be neutralized and hushed up by the ridicule and attack to which they would be subjected by collaborators and dupes.

The Popular Version

At my first opportunity after viewing the missing scene from the Pavlov training film, I went back to Dr. Freedom to discuss it with him and to hear his clinical analysis. We had settled upon a routine long before. After I completed an interview or a piece of research, I would visit him and we would go into every phase of it. He would make his clinical analysis, and his amazing wife, Virginia, whose hobby was geopolitics, would help to simplify what he said in everyday language. We talked for hundreds of hours, upstairs in their home, above his clinic. I introduced him to several of the refugees from brainwashing and former POW's, and he studied their cases individually.

After relating my reactions to the complete film, my first question was, "Do you really think that the part with the boy in harness could really have happened that way?"

"Of course," he promptly replied.

"Do you mean to say that if you turn on a green light each time you feed candy to a kid, one day you can just switch on the light, without giving him any sweet, and his mouth will drool just the same?"

"Certainly," Dr. Freedom answered. "With grownups, too."

"What if the person doesn't want to react that way?"

"He can't help it! Nothing he can do can stop his salivary glands from working."

The political inference sounded horrifying. "Does this mean that when everything is said and done, a man is no more than a dog?"

"Of course not," he replied. "That is the point at which communism is bound to fail. I know this is true as a surgeon and as a psychiatrist."

He explained how an animal could possess, in greater or lesser degree, the same senses and feelings as a man, up to a certain point. Beyond that, the man had something in addition that made him Man. This was his reasoning faculty — his reasoned judgment and reasoned free will. This was what was meant by the divine in man, that differentiated him from all else that lived. So long as reason could be kept healthy and free, man's future was safe.

"There's one more question I want to ask you," I said. "Did the scene with the boy mean that some unscrupulous power group might succeed someday in inducing a whole population to react to its wishes in the same unquestioning way a dog can be trained to obey its master?"

Dr. Freedom did not reply as promptly as before. Much more grimly, he explained that insofar as a human being allowed the divine traits in him to be overcome and his reasoning power — his judgment and free will — to be atrophied, he could be made into a demon, a puppet, a sick man psychologically, just as sick as an athlete who has allowed his body to be run down by dissipation until he easily contracts some crippling disease.

Moscow produced several full-length feature films about the Pavlovian experiments for popular consumption. In these, the harrowing scenes of the original laboratory film were made palatable in the Hollywood manner. During my travels, I was fortunate to be able to see them. They proved how thoroughly the Kremlin was going about its task of creating the "new Soviet man." Whereas the short film was intended for training purposes, the full-length pictures were part of the softening-up program for the public. These movies confirmed the callousness with which Moscow was absorbing medical science into its control-expansion strategy.

At the same time, Moscow produced a series of films about foremost figures in Russian history. Together, these outlined the Red pattern for world conquest.

Peter the Great was the first of these historical pictures. When first shown abroad, it was acclaimed as fine theater and exciting biography. Critics exhaustively discussed it as entertainment. Actually, it revealed a new and favorable interpretation of the brutal careers of Russia's early rulers. Previous-

21

ly, no denunciation had seemed strong enough. Now, they were suddenly glamorized as great leaders. The complete subordination of all media of communication to policy under communism would have made this basic change in line unmistakable to any who had analyzed it from the Kremlin's standpoint. Unfortunately, this was done only by a heroic few whose voices were smothered by the communist propaganda machine.

The full-length movies about Pavlov and his conditionedreflex experiments were merely popularized versions of the brief film, with new symbols chosen in accordance with the different types of audiences to be influenced at home and abroad. One film was a highly dramatic biography in which Pavlov's theories were presented as a scientific basis for the acceptance of brainwashing as a natural stage in man's evolution. Instead of merely glamorizing incidents in his life story, the Soviet rewrote history for political reasons.

In the beginning of the film, young Pavlov, who had only recently become a doctor, felt a wealthy patient's pulse and bluntly informed him that he was going to die. Infuriated, the landowner — he had to be a landlord to provide the film with the approved stereotype villain — ^jumped out of bed in a manner strangely virile for a man supposed to have one foot in the grave. He dashed to his big French window. Staring avidly at his property, he swore that what he couldn't take with him, he would destroy. He ordered all the beautiful trees on his estate to be chopped down. His serfs rushed forth with axes to fulfill this last mad wish. Giant trees came crashing down. Pavlov, at this point, vowed that the heritage he would leave behind when he died would be knowledge and achievement. This incident was written into the story to indoctrinate the audience with contempt for property and, indirectly, with scorn for a decent wage scale.

Pavlov's earliest interest was in the digestive processes. He once noticed that his dog began drooling although there was no food about. When he investigated, he found that the servant who usually fed the dog had just passed on the other side of the corridor. The footsteps of this man had the same effect on the dog as the food itself. This, according to the film, was the great inspiration of Pavlov's life. Intrigued by the effect that a sound could have on a dog's salivary glands, he changed his specialty from digestion to reflexes.

Here his difficulties began. Old friends and colleagues warned and even threatened him against it. They complained that his stubbornness was making a laughing stock of them in scientific circles. Even his faithful old servant quit him in a tear-jerker of a scene. Pavlov paid no heed, but pushed forward purposefully on his chosen path. The film portrayed him as a ruthless dialectical Marxist, which he never was. Indeed, if Pavlov knew his simple findings were to become the modem basis of brainwashing, he would have recoiled in horror.

His finances dwindled away. He couldn't afford to pay for the dogs he needed in his experiments. Obstacles faced him wherever he turned. At the opportune moment, a girl presented herself. She was also a dedicated scientist and worker. She sought no affection, no recompense except to work more and more, without any thought of pay. She worked eagerly fifteen hours a day.

Pavlov accepted her sacrifices as natural. The only warmth that the film showed in him was once when he grabbed his wife and danced about with her in great glee over a successful four-hour operation on a dog. He told her about a litter of beautiful pups he had seen on the way home. He wanted so much to buy them. His wife promptly returned the pay check he had just brought home so he could buy the pups, not to keep as pets, but to put on the operating table for his experiments.

Pavlov's wife was presented as a weak and trusting female, symbolizing the masses, in contrast to him, the dialectical master, whose will she never questioned and whose reasoning she could not understand.

The Red script writers made Pavlov a sort of master magician with occult-like powers over men's minds, the Merlin of dialectical materialism. According to the film, he set himself a goal. "The task of physiology is to learn to direct the human brain," he was supposed to have said. His objective was just the opposite. He conceived of physiology as mankind's servant, not its master. Nothing he ever said indicated that he entertained any such hideous concept as mind control. His purpose, as he always insisted, was to make use of animals to discover basic laws in physiology which would help medical science heal the afflictions of the human body and work toward the avoidance of mental disorders. The Kremlin exposed its own objective by this distortion of his actual purpose.

The film quoted him as saying that, unable to experiment on people, he would begin with dogs. This alone should have warned the world of Moscow's goal.

Another caption had Pavlov saying, "The brain created science and now will be subordinate to it." In a brazen admission of communist intent, the film declared that a person's individuality, his *I*, was derived out of his environment. The inference was drawn that by altering a man's surroundings, his inner nature could be changed as well.

"We are seeking new ways of dealing with the brain," Pavlov was made to declare. "We already know the basic laws of the brain," he was further quoted, following it with the ominous statement that these laws had "nothing to do with human nature."

A scene laid in London was a dead giveaway of the Soviet goal. Pavlov went there to attend an ultra-swank session of England's highest scientific society, at which he was to be presented with its most important award. His speech was the high light of the ceremony. In it he presented on the stage an actual experiment on a dog, the same as in *The Nervous System.*

To have followed this up in a popular movie with the experiment on a human being would have been far too revolting. The Reds thought up a conspiracy. Three sinister figures staged a demonstration against Pavlov, to accomplish the same end. The three plotters, symbolizing obstructionist and non-communist elements, replaced the young man in *The Nervous System.*

Soon after Pavlov took the rostrum, catcalls and hooting started. The conspiracy against him might just as well have been against the state. The pattern was the same. But the state, or rather Pavlov, was supposed to see all. He strode to the front of the stage and pointed to the three "counter-revolutionaries," as they would have been labeled in the communist language. They had been edging forward without being noticed by the rest of the audience of scientists and socialites. Pavlov interrupted his analysis of the dog's brain to explain what was going on in the minds of this trio. He diagnosed their crime. They were about to create disorder in response to a conditioned stimulus. The camera showed the three men standing transfixed in their tracks while Pavlov informed the audience that they were halted in their plotting by the law of inhibition.

He had already shown how inhibition worked on the dog. Its saliva stopped when he created a counter-stimulus. As soon as this inhibitory process ceased, Pavlov continued, the three would recommence their plotting, in the way the dog's saliva resumed flowing. So they did. The three "enemies of the state" recovered from their temporary immobilization, and a scene of utter disorder and hate erupted inside the dignified old chamber. This was finally overcome by Pavlov's convincing demonstration and by the timely support of a youth group in the audience, which constituted a victory for what the caption said was the "materialistic understanding" of the brain.

All that was lacking to make the picture truthfully realistic was a scene showing the three diversionists being taken from their homes late that night by the police authorities, and another showing them some time afterwards, contrite and confessing. That is how it would really have happened in the U.S.S.R.

These films about Pavlov and his experiments exposed the hideous strategy of mind attack that the Kremlin was building up. If these movies had been taken seriously and properly interpreted when they first came out, along with the *Peter the Great* series, the world might have been spared many tragedies.

The Secret Manuscript

Pavlov was already sixty-eight years old in November, 1917, When the Bolsheviks seized power from the Kerensky government. The Czar and his family were slain on July 16, only four months after his abdication. Pavlov had already completed the experiments for which history would remember him. He received a Nobel prize way back in 1904 for his unique experiments which clearly demonstrated the functioning of the digestive mechanism. The twentieth century had been only two years old when he began his research into the workings of the animal brain. His findings on conditioned reflexes and inhibitions had been made before World War I.

He was now an old man who had endured much deprivation because of his persistence in keeping to his chosen work instead of earning the high income his pre-eminent standing as a physician would have assured. The maintenance of his kennels and the normal overhead of his laboratory kept him impoverished.

He lived in an isolated village called Koltushy, twenty miles north of Leningrad, in a plain wooden building where he performed his involved research on living animals. This had been one of his pioneering contributions, experimentation under conditions as nearly normal as possible, instead of on dead animals. It greatly complicated matters and multiplied costs, but it gave immensely better results. Fortunately, he had inherited an iron constitution to go along with his iron will, and his mental vigor seemed to belie the weariness that was creeping over his once active body.

Pavlov's entire life had been identified with Mother Russia, and he loved her soil deeply. His father, a poor priest in the peasant town of Ryazan in central Russia, had to raise his own food the same as neighboring farmers. Ivan inherited a kinship with the good earth, and felt content and happy when he could dirty his hands tending it. He had suffered much on Russian soil, but he was born of it. He was a stubborn man who well knew the impracticability of starting over when the Biblical threescore years and ten were already his, or very nearly so. He made up his mind that he would stick it out whatever the communists did.

Old friends strongly urged him to leave while there was yet time. He did not need their urging to know how dangerous and chaotic conditions had become, or how many per« sons around him were escaping while they still had a chance. These were not only the rich, who could go in comfort, but ordinary intellectuals and the middle class. This was the period of the great White Russian exodus. The pathetic efforts of the idealistic provisional government to accomplish its ends strictly within a democratic framework were being exploited on all sides.

Plodding patiently ahead, the new republic gave promise of settling down. If abnormal pressures had not been put on it from abroad, it might have succeeded. But that was the moment chosen by the German military planners to sneak a coterie of political extremists called Bolsheviks through Germany in a sealed train from Switzerland, directly into Russia. This was the real beginning of twentieth-century psychological warfare. It changed the whole direction of contemporary history. The long-overdue Russian revolution was kidnaped by the unprincipled machinations of the new arrivals and twisted into the extremism of world communism. The German people were ultimately to pay heavily for this maneuver of their diplomats and warlords. This last desperate measure of the Junkers, heartlessly undermining the sort of regime for which the Russian masses had yearned so long, brought the pillars of civilization toppling down on friends and foes alike.

A Ukrainian named Michael Korostevetz, whose estate was not far from the Pavlovs', was among the last to join the trek abroad. Before escaping with his kinfolk and whatever they could carry, Korostevetz made several visits to the home of the physiologist. A close friendship had existed between the two families. Years later, in London, Korostevetz revealed what had transpired at those conversations.

Korostevetz strongly recommended that Pavlov escape, pointing out how hopeless conditions were becoming and warning him that the time when people could still get away was growing very short. Pavlov's only reply was that he could not bring himself to leave. His whole life's work was rooted in Russia. He loved his country too much to bear the thought of living anywhere else. Furthermore, he saw no reason why any government would want to interfere with his purely scientific research. He could not imagine any regime — red, pink, green, or white — suspecting that there was the least political connotation in his undertakings. Nothing could be further from politics than his experiments with animals. No, he told Korostevetz firmly, he would remain.

His friend went to England, where he settled down and became a part of that cosmopolitan society. Pavlov struggled on at home against deprivation and sorrow — he had lost two sons. After the elapse of only a few years, his name began to be mentioned flatteringly in dispatches from the Soviet Union. Yet he was no communist. He had made that very clear. Nevertheless, he was coming more and more into favor. The Soviet Government gave his experiments extraordinary support. The Reds built new laboratories for him on a scale he had never dreamed of and provided him with all the animals for his experiments, as well as with whatever scientific and clerical staff he required. The Kremlin made this a priority matter at a time of great shortages everywhere, when the state was not sparing a ruble for anything it did not consider absolutely vital to its own survival.

A dacha, or summer villa, was built for Pavlov, and as the years passed, the equivalent of a college town was constructed at Koltushy. Doctor W. Horsley Gantt, director of the Pavlovian Laboratory at Johns Hopkins University in Baltimore, went to Leningrad with the Hoover famine relief commission in the early 1920s, made Pavlov's acquaintance, and became one of his collaborators for nearly five years, from 1925 to 1929. Dr. Gantt translated a collection of Pavlov's lectures into English. In the "Introduction," he refers to his great astonishment when he revisited Koltushy in 1933 and found that "a new city of laboratory buildings had arisen, dominating the village and hiding the forest."

Pavlov's frequently expressed dislike for communist ideology was obviously being brushed aside, ignored as if never uttered. Pavlov maintained what Dr. Gantt described as an "attitude of bold animosity" towards the Soviet Union until about 1930. The Kremlin turned its head in a peculiar exhibition of what appeared to be amazing tolerance. What would have brought the heaviest penalties of the state on anyone else was allowed in his case. Indeed, high honor and great flattery were bestowed on the aging man. He was permitted to make brief journeys abroad for lectures that became triumphal tours. He went to the United States in 1923, France in 1926, and London in 1928. He would have been less than human not to identify the acclaim that was his with the Soviet regime that made it possible.

Moscow had no worry about Pavlov not returning. All that had meaning in life for him, his family, his work, his laboratories, were at Koltushy under government protection — and surveillance. Purge trials and brainwashing were still in the future. A certain tolerance for dissenting views within the party framework still existed. S.M. Kirov, Politbureau member and Stalin's close collaborator, had not yet been assassinated. The summary execution of so-called suspects and the killing of thousands for sheer terroristic reasons were still a decade away.

Pavlov lived until February 27, 1936. By a strange quirk, this was the very year of the first spectacular trials of Old Bolsheviks in Moscow which mystified the entire world but which Pavlov certainly would have seen through. The colossal purge and the sensational treason trials that followed Kirov's assassination on December 1, 1934, must have deeply worried him but without seeming to be related in any particular way to his own specialty, for the Kremlin's reaction was principally the traditional use of terror in the old-fashioned manner. This charged environment could not have been without any effect on him, since it virtually monopolized the press and discussion.

The old man probably died before he even suspected the double game that the Kremlin was playing on him. After all, Pavlov lived in splendid isolation among his family, co-workers, and dogs. The only contacts he had were discreetly but thoroughly screened by the authorities. He was living in the same controlled environment which he had devised for his experimental animals. Comprehension of the bestial use that the Kremlin was making of his life's work inevitably would have led him to denounce the horrible perversion of what he had achieved, and he would have done so in his usual unmistakable language.

Pavlov would have been repelled in the same manner as another great old man I saw at a communist mass meeting in Paris in the early 1930s. He was the famous French writer Andre Gide, who was featured as the principal speaker at a tremendous Red rally. The enormous auditorium was packed with people attracted by his name. The audience fidgeted through the speeches of one French communist agitator after another, from 6 p.m. until just before midnight, when Gide was led to the rostrum like a prize exhibit. I sat in one of the front rows so I could catch every detail, and noticed how pathetically leaden Gide's eyes were, although he was only in his early sixties. He raised his right arm weakly in the communist clenched fist salute, and uttered a few spiritless words of comradely greeting which, from his once eloquent mouth, sounded wholly out of place. His appearance, for which we had waited the whole evening, lasted a couple of minutes and then he was led off the stage. The callous exploitation of this once great mind was nauseating.

Gide himself, to his everlasting credit, broke through this false facade when he was taken on a tour of Soviet Russia long afterwards. He found that he could not even express appreciation for his trip in a telegram to Stalin without using a forced adulatory salutation which smacked of religious quackery. This experience aroused Gide's old critical faculties, and he began to look about him with awakened eyes. Horrified, he possessed the strength of will to oppose what he now realized he had been deceived into praising. In order to make his voice heard, he had to wait until he was safely outside of the U.S.S.R. Perhaps if even Pavlov had so much as whispered such pointed opposition after Kirov's assassination, he would have been permanently silenced.

Those were the last months of Pavlov's life. They were strangely coincidental with the experimentations and rehearsals being conducted in the secret-police chambers to extract the weird confessions that were to stun the world during three major trials. The settings were already being planned for the liquidation of all the Old Bolsheviks within the Kremlin's reach, except for one — Stalin. Each of the defendants in those three gigantic trials was held, like "the isolated animal" of the training film, for from six months to a year, while his public performance was being rehearsed in the Pavlovian manner. The chief of almost every branch of government joined in his own indictment, pleading for his own prompt extermination. This shocking exhibition of Pavlov's own handiwork, undoubtedly stage-managed without his knowledge, began six months after his death.

The preparatory period, in the year before Pavlov died, saw a marked change in his own expressed views regarding the Kremlin. In those final months of his long life — he was eighty-six years and seven months old when he died — Pavlov underwent what Gantt refers to as his "conversion." Gantt insists that this "was as complete as it was sincere," declaring that "Pavlov's change of heart was in no sense a recantation such as was forced upon Galileo by the Inquisition." The comparison was inescapable, Gantt notwithstanding. The only difference was in the improvement of the technique.

Pavlov, in spite of his advanced age, had a dangerous operation for gallstones in 1927. He resumed his strenuous life after a short convalescence. The Soviet Government spurred him on by heaping additional glory and work on him until almost the day he died. "Help me, I must dress," were his last words. His Institute of Experimental Medicine had been only recently renamed Pavlov Institute in his honor. Outside traffic into the area was forbidden by the authorities, increasing Pavlov's isolation. Koltushy village, which he loved, was renamed Pavlov village. The government's subsidy for his laboratories was constantly raised and new workers added to his staff.

Pavlov, in this last year, wrote a letter for the Kremlin praising the Stakhanovite movement in labor. The old man had no conception of a slave-labor camp, never, of course, having gone near one. The unmerciful speed-up of labor in factory and mine became identified in his own mind with the delightful working conditions in his own privileged and comfortable laboratories, where it was a joy to work.

This was the final cruel brainwashing jest played by the Communist Party on Pavlov's own mind. There can be no doubt that he was the most protected and privileged character in the Soviet Union outside of the Kremlin. Greater favors were showered on him than were accorded even to the writers and dramatists who wrote the Communist Party's propaganda. There could be no question that if the Kremlin had not felt a critical need for his services, it would never have tolerated his biting criticisms for so long. Others, in every sphere of life, from the textile workshop to the medical clinic, disappeared into slave-labor camps and the grave for voicing much milder disagreement.

Pavlov himself provided the explanation for what happened in his case. He told it to a few former friends, such as Korostevetz. Those two old neighbors met again in London in 1928 when Pavlov went there to be made an honorary fellow of the Royal College of Physicians. They had a great deal to say to each other, the man who had gone abroad and succeeded in picking up the threads of his life, and the man who had stayed at home and reaped great benefits. Pavlov told Korostevetz all about what had happened in those early days.

Conditions were almost unbearable the first few years. Pavlov explained how his animals, on which he depended for his experiments, succumbed to starvation and the freezing cold. He himself sometimes had to stay in bed under blankets when he should have been up and at work, because he had no fuel to make the cruel Russian winter bearable. When he did get out of bed, he was often so hungry he could hardly think. The days were wintry short and there usually was no electricity. Even when he had light, he had no supplies and no money to pay the costs of the simplest experiment. Life was indeed miserable, and he had nowhere to turn in all Russia for assistance.

Then he received an astonishing summons. He was informed that Nikolai Lenin himself, the most important man in Bolshevism, wanted to speak to him. The head of the state had heard about his experiments and had indicated a keen interest in them. Pavlov was brought to the Kremlin for an interview that was to be decisive in history as well as in his own life. He was received as an honored guest. Lenin asked him at once to explain what he was doing, and when Pavlov began to give details, Lenin indicated that he was not interested in his early work on the digestive apparatus, nor in his study of blood circulation. What he wanted to know was what he was doing with all those dogs of his. Lenin listened carefully while Pavlov told him, and then said yes, that was all very fascinating. But what he was interested in were human beings, not dogs. What had Pavlov learned about people during the course of his experiments?

This was largely in the realm of speculation, and Pavlov tried to avoid giving answers for which he did not have sufficient physiological basis. He expressed confidence that his findings on conditioned reflexes and inhibitions, which resulted from his experiments with animals, would be a blessing to mankind someday in its struggle against human ailments.

Lenin persisted in his efforts to pin Pavlov down on people and, finally, gave him an assignment. There was no question whether he would accept or not. Pavlov was told to stay right where he was, inside the Kremlin, until he finished his task. He was Lenin's personal guest, given every possible comfort. The assignment was to write a summary of his life's work on dogs and other animals; only, he was to apply this knowledge to human beings. He was to relate in precise detail exactly where and how his research did or could affect the human race.

Pavlov told his old neighbor that he occupied a room in the Kremlin for three full months. He was a free man so long as he stayed where he was and voluntarily kept working on his assigned task. His surroundings couldn't have been more impressive. Who could tell? Here, perhaps, was an opportunity to convince a man of immense power of the great worth of the physician's traditional approach. Could this do otherwise than good to the human race?

Pavlov told Korostevetz that he completed a 400-page manuscript. This was a book, a priceless book. He handed it to Lenin.

Pavlov saw Lenin a day or so after the dictator had gone over the manuscript. Lenin was in high spirits. He shook his hand warmly and told him to return to his laboratories and get to work. He would be given all he needed. Lenin's last words to him were uttered in a tone of greatest enthusiasm. He told Pavlov that he had "saved the Revolution," and that his findings guaranteed the future for world communism.

What Lenin, the remorselessly practical dictator, did not tell Pavlov was that he had come to realize how impossible it was that he would ever obtain the people's willing co-operation in changing human nature and creating the "new Soviet man." He saw in Pavlov's discoveries a technique that could force it upon them. Marx had expected communism to change human nature. Lenin had found out that it would never happen naturally. Now he saw in the Pavlovian technique the ferment which could bring it about despite the opposition it naturally aroused. As he read through Pavlov's book-length report, he felt sure that he had discovered the means to bend free will to the Party will, to his will.

This was what Lenin thought Pavlov had given him. But Lenin, far from showing gratitude, had already betrayed Pavlov. He used the knowledge that he had obtained from Pavlov against the aged physiologist himself, in its smoothest and most relentlessly subtle form.

Pavlov's manuscript, which became the working basis for the whole communist expansion-control system, has never left the Kremlin.

Chapter Three - Brainwashing in Action

Total Means "Everybody"

The newly devised pressures of the mind — mind atrocities called brainwashing — were as modern and as devastating an advance in war as nuclear fission had been only a few years before when it made its unannounced debut with a hellish flash and a gigantic mushroom of pallid smoke over the luckless city of Hiroshima.

The form this brain warfare took was totalitarian, meaning just that — total! Civilians and military alike were sucked in indiscriminately, in front and rear, in peace and war, exactly as communist ideology implies. The civilians who came out of brainwashing prisons in Eastern Europe and Red China and the soldiers who came out of brainwashing camps in North Korea told me the same stories, similar to the smallest detail.

Although this totalitarian approach was easily grasped in theory by the nontotalitarian countries, still they could not bring themselves to face the harsh, cruel facts in reality; to believe that human beings of any color could really be so debased. Otherwise there would be no explanation, no excuse, for the unpreparedness of our fighting men taken prisoner by the Reds in Korea. They and their civilian colleagues on the Chinese mainland became guinea pigs for a big-scale ideological mind warfare, a brainwashing campaign in which no weapons were barred.

Few in the Free World fully realized that the Reds had erased the line between war and peace, that for them peace merely called for a change in tactics. Few could conceive that the missionary in a prison in the Chinese interior, the businessman in an interrogation center in Eastern Europe, and the military officer in a cave in North Korea were being asked the same questions, were subjected to the same humiliating pressures, endured the same tortures, and suffered alike in the same gigantic war against men's minds.

Few could understand that the success of this unified Red strategy depended on the people within the communist-bloc countries acting their parts as puppets on a string. An actual instance of this, which in essential details was acted out again and again and again, was the germ-warfare hoax. This, like Hitler's big lie, depended on its all-inclusive character to carry conviction. This was the big lie acted out in real life.

Many other instances of the big lie and the travesty of responsibility used by the communists can be cited. The persons who were forced to enact these fantastic performances told me the details. Let me tell you of some such diabolical shows as they were related to me by the leading men. You have to see a play in rehearsal as well as in its public presentation to fully appreciate its completely sinister plot.

"What a Scoop!"

A small select group of reporters for the press of Communist China and North Korea stared at the white prisoner. They looked him up and down in the professional manner of newspapermen all over the world, silently appraising his character and instinctively checking their findings against his words and the way in which he presented them. Did he have the real goods? Or was he a phony?

There had been a big change in journalism since the Reds had taken over. News was now a weapon. The reporters knew, from their own experience on the job, that the new authorities didn't hesitate to alter details according to what they wanted to prove, and even to cut the news out of whole cloth when it suited their purposes.

They had pleaded for this interview for a long time. The first meager reports that had come out about germ warfare in Korea were a year old. Since then it had been made the main topic of official and semi-official pronouncements, sometimes the exclusive subject. The accusations were backed up by every conceivable form of proof. Peasants had been brought in to tell how they watched the germ containers fall. The reporters were shown the shell cases, too. Hadn't epidemics broken out in those areas? There were glass slabs on which anyone could see, under the microscope, the guilt-proving swarms of bacteria swimming about. There were actual flies and rats — plenty of them — enough for exhibits all over the country. The Red officials appealed to a man's common sense. Seeing was believing, wasn't it? Well, here were bugs and rats — germ-laden bugs and rats, the Reds said. They brought in biologists to agree. Who could refute this weight of circumstantial evidence? Only the confession of the guilty party had been lacking to make the case airtight.

The American appeared worn out by the strain that came when he finally comprehended his great crime. In his tense state, half an hour was all the newspapermen could ask without taking advantage of him. He spoke earnestly and contritely. He said he hoped the Chinese and Korean peoples would forgive his misdeeds, and explained with disarming frankness how he had engaged in germ-warfare attacks against the simple peasantry. His eyes looked infinitely sad. The fast flow of his answers removed any skepticism.

The reporters' pencils raced fast. He was obviously sincere. He was an American officer, a pilot in the U.S. Air Force. Everything about him had the stamp of authenticity. The six questions they had thought up in a collective manner were simple and to the point. What they did not know was that the prisoner had been thoroughly rehearsed on these same questions before the interview. While the reporters had been maneuvered into asking these pre-determined questions, decided on by the higher authorities, the prisoner was being manipulated into giving the desired replies.

The American pilot — let us give him the neutral name of Marlin, for what happened to him was done to others, too — had been informed quite a while before, casually, that the newspapermen were pestering the government for a chance to talk to one of the men who had actually dropped germ bombs. It was carefully explained to Marlin that holding them off was getting more and more difficult. "All right, let them come," he had finally agreed.

"They've consented to limit the interview to half an hour," he was told. One never knew what a newsman might ask, and so they suggested he be prepared for anything.

"The best thing we can think of is for you to figure out ahead of time what the reporters will ask, and decide how you'll answer," they advised. So Marlin and his Chinese confidant, an American-educated fellow named Ling, sat down to figure out what questions these troublesome newspapermen would throw at him.

They went about this in the "democratic discussion" manner, even though there were only two of them. Marlin and Ling kept hammering at a point until they both reached agreement on it — this was the new principle of una-nimity. Once they had agreed on a question likely to be asked, they figured out the reply to it.

"I'm not supposed to be helping you prepare for our reporters this way," Ling confided one day. "I'm only supposed to question you. The last thing we want is for you to think we're trying to influence what you've got to say."

"You're a swell fellow, Ling, and I'm terribly thankful how you're helping me out," Marlin hastened to reply. He was deeply impressed by Ling's thor-oughness. The two worked together intensively to determine just the right wording for each answer, and Marlin repeated it often enough to never for-get it. He almost dreamed it.

He felt so tired that his mind did tricks on him. He wished at times Ling wouldn't be so terribly thorough. They repeated each question again and again, with Ling taking the part of the reporters, until Marlin felt as if he were talking in his sleep. He shook at times, as if possessed. He was deadtired. This was the one complaint he had against Ling — he kept him so dreadfully tired all the time. Marlin remembered reading somewhere in the far, far distant past — ages ago — about the subconscious. This seemed at times to change places with his normal, conscious self, and to be directing his actions and speech. This new Marlin was a strange being, so loosely tied to him that sev-eral times lately, when he had fallen asleep dog-tired — God knows how little sleep he got — he woke up feeling as if some part of himself had been detached and was floating about in the ether, and had to come back, and go back into him, before he could arise out of his bed and be whole again.

Marlin was thankful for all this rigorous preparation when he sat waiting for the reporters to come in. He felt thankful that Ling stayed in the room, so he could steal a glance at him whenever he felt the need.

How could he miss a beat? He had repeated the answers so often that they had become part of him, and he couldn't forget them if he tried. He believed them himself now, explicitly. He had long before stopped thinking about what was actually true or not. What was truth, anyway? Nobody knew. Sure he believed what he was saying. Yet there were moments when in the back of his mind he knew that he was uttering falsehoods. Or was he? What was false? Could anyone understand what was false anymore, now that he had been taught that truth was an unknown factor?

Others had confessed the same as he. Everyone couldn't be wrong. Could they? What of it if someone else had done the actual dropping of the germ bombs? They, too, had been Americans, hadn't they? They couldn't all be lying. His buddies had done it. Well, he was one of them; he represented them. Weren't they all one team, as his superior officers had told him? A collectivity, as the communists expressed it. Wasn't it only a difference in terminology?

Enough of this nonsense; he'd go crazy if he kept worrying his head about it. He sometimes felt daffy. "Am I going mad?" he wondered at times. His job was to keep sane, to retain his balance. This was his priority job now. The war was over for him. He had to be clever and keep his skin whole.

Yes, he had been given a little help from that Chinese interrogator who kept sticking to him like a leech. There he was, still standing where he could not miss him. He couldn't take his eyes off that yellow, spiteful face. How he hated him!

He was a pest. He'd like to strangle him. For a moment the desire came over him to walk over and take his scrawny neck in his hands and shake it like a chicken's until all life had left it. Why did he look at him that way? Ling didn't seem able to take his eyes off him. Or was it the other way round? All Ling wanted was to help him. Marlin knew this well. Hadn't Ling often told him? "You're your own boss," he always said. He kept telling Marlin that he didn't have to make a move or open his mouth until he wanted to, until he believed it himself. That was the right way, the new "people's way." Ling had told him that, too. Ling told him everything. Good old Ling! He was always so patient, and he always tried to do just what Marlin wanted, even to anticipate his wants. Marlin had never met anyone in the U.S. military service who was that patient and thoughtful.

After the fateful interview was over, thinking about it to himself, Marlin recalled with a glow of elation how he had held those reporters in the palm of his hand. He had been ahead of them all the time. He felt high, from smoking marijuana. The Reds had told him not to, but he did. He foxed them; the stuff was growing all over the place. Funny, if they were so anxious to keep it out of his hands, why didn't they uproot it? He was glad he had taken that puff. Ling wasn't so foxy as he thought.

The reporters were just as satisfied as he. The interview was a success, from any angle. What particularly impressed them was the frank way Marlin answered their toughest questions. He showed no hesitancy. Now they had the final proof that America had engaged in cowardly and loathsome germ warfare against the poor peoples of Korea and China. They had the details from the mouth of a man who had done so. This was the incontrovertible proof that they were seeking.

What a story! Every newspaper in every city in China ran their interviews, in full, too. They were copied by hand, for wall newspapers posted on countless house fronts in every city street and village lane. They reached incalculably more people than the daily press. Farmers were approached in wet paddies where they worked by "able Party members" who told them the news.

The radio, with an emphasis all its own, repeated every detail. The routine discussion meetings, held daily in every school, office, or factory, were given over to this news by order of the authorities. The interviews were read out loud during lunch or after work, by group chairmen who asked, in the "democratic manner," for each person present to express his frank opinion about this "unspeakable barbarity perpetrated by the imperialist Americans." The repressed burdens each man carried within himself could find vent here.

Everybody in China, within the space of a few days, heard about this dramatic spontaneous interview at which a group of reliable Chinese and Korean reporters spoke face to face with an American germ-warfare pilot. Every person was given the feeling of being an eyewitness. Everyone in all of China was called on to swat flies and squash bugs. The authorities explained that there was no telling how many innocent people had been infected with the "American plague," as they officially called it. A minimum quota was set for insect slayings, and each family had to send a bundle of the tiny corpses to neighborhood leaders. Schoolchildren had to deliver their quota to their teachers. All these were then passed on to the police for listing, so that nobody could evade his responsibility to the state.

The news was radioed and cabled around the world, so it could reach the quiet folk of India and the hot people of the Argentine, the sophisticated gentry of England and even the guilty Americans themselves. Everywhere, from New Delhi to London, from Djakarta to Mexico City, numerous editors, who said they were being objective, informed their readers that such disclosures could not lightly be brushed aside. After all, hadn't it been a group review? For doubting Thomases, there were movies made of the interview, so all could see and hear with their own senses. So people abroad would know, the films were shown to selected groups of officials and ordinary citizens at parties given by Red diplomats.

This was no make-believe! This was war! This was how the communists were waging war in the mid-twentieth century. Some called it psychological warfare. A better name would be *brain warfare*. The only difference between it and the conflicts of the past was that formerly weapons were aimed principally at bodies, to incapacitate and destroy them, whereas now they were aimed mainly at minds, to subvert and control them.

What had altered was the type of weapons used. The discovery had been made that behind each gun there had to be a will, and that whoever could manipulate this will was able to determine where the bullets sped — to friends instead of foes, or whether they were fired at all. The discovery had been made, too, that in brain warfare ultimate victory lay in the conquest of attitudes and feelings. In this arena, anything that achieved this objective, that hit the target, was a weapon.

Sam Dean

The Build-Up

The first time I heard about Sam Dean was at Hong Kong. Refugees from Red China, who had come by ship, told me about an elderly engineer who had tried to persuade his escort at Tientsin to let him go to the police station because he remembered some points he had failed to include in his confession. Poor, saintly Sam Dean had felt the full weight of the confession technique. Within the next couple of weeks, mutual friends told me how Dean sat at the table, staring over his plate, never blinking, not seeing what was in front of him, seldom speaking. Ruth, his courageous and devoted wife, filled the gaps in the conversation.

Although I very much wanted to see him and hear from his own lips what had happened, I knew this would impose too great a strain on him. The couple sailed for home soon after. The probability that I would never meet him was great.

Yet the chance came, nearly two years ago. The interval was fortunate, for the Deans were now living in the Navajo Indian territory in Arizona, where he was teaching and helping operate an electric power plant in the large compound of the Ganado Presbyterian Mission. Aided by the wide open spaces and the naked, hot sun, renewed with a sense of accomplishment and a job still to do, he had worked the poisons out of his mind. This was what was most important in his story. He was now able to appraise what had been done to him in Red China.

Sam could not have been sent to a more favorable spot for his recovery. He was in the United States, yet in an environment that reminded him of China, especially the northern part where he had spent so many years. The similarity in the appearance of the people was striking. The Indian trading post where the bus stopped, which sold rough turquoise and chipped ruby gems, hammered silver bracelets and buckles, might have been in Kalgan, near the

Gobi Desert. The horseman who came up, wearing a fancy vest, sitting on a sunbright saddle, heralded by a tinkling harness, could have been coming down the rust-colored road from Mongolia.

Sam said he sometimes had the impression he was back in China, teaching Chinese students, especially when he heard the Indian dialect. The Navajo language has tones like Chinese. While we chatted about this mutual interest, I noticed that Sam, six feet two, looked the Western type for whom sincerity is a faith. I could easily imagine him, in his younger Texan days, thrusting a leg over a bronco and riding into the horizon.

The Deans put me up in the comfortable Mission rest-house. Petrified rock that had captured the rainbow tints of the sun was scattered on the ground outside. I stayed several days, so we had plenty of time to talk.

Sam's father had taught in a freedman's school for the Negroes after the Civil War. Both his grandfathers were Presbyterian ministers. Sam, now in his sixties, had taken up railroading before obtaining a degree in mechanical engineering and at middle age went back to school to get a degree in architectural engineering. A short while before World War I the Y.M.C.A. was recruiting young men to serve in the schools of China and Sam volunteered. This was how he went to Asia in 1914.

Sam discovered that education and work didn't mix in Chinese minds. He determined he could contribute most by teaching young Chinese to learn by doing, to get proud people proud to dirty their hands doing a job. He often got his own hands full of grease, setting the example. He watched carefully for young people with good brains and fine motives who were not afraid to pitch in and work. He trained them to teach night classes of apprentices and craftsmen. His objective was to develop Chinese students who would build up their own country. He had nothing to do with politics. His trust was in people of character who did things for themselves, who believed that God's greatest gift was a brain and two hands, and that these went together.

He gathered around himself a circle of his former Chinese students who, like himself, believed that a hand dirtied by honest toil was the most honorable badge a man could wear. They designed and supervised the construction of modern buildings all over China. Schools, hospitals, and churches went up from Canton to Peking, usually at no cost whatsoever to China, in a style that retained Chinese motifs while adding modern facilities.

World War I came and went. Yenching University eagerly took over Sam's engineering school, asking only that the ideals of its founder and his methods of instruction be retained. World War II came and went. Sam was building a faculty that was bound to exert powerful influence in every corner of the land. He now had Chinese instructors who had completed their training with first-hand experience abroad in everything from constructing bridges to erecting power plants.

People remarked to Sam that the Reds were nearing Peking. He believed that any human being who had dedicated his life to education, something always respected in China and who, in addition, was turning out increasing numbers of men to dirty their hands in the sort of labor the new China so desperately needed, could never have any political difficulties. He felt that any regime, even a Red one, would consider what he was doing an asset to the government.

Fighting went on north of Yenching. Afterwards, when friends mentioned that the Reds had come, he said, "Oh yes, they have, haven't they? So they have," and just kept on with his job. He was dedicated to his task and to his objectives for the Chinese people — all of them. He simply wasn't interested in politics. He had never voted anywhere or joined any political faction; he had never mixed in politics.

"All around me I heard talk of it being just an agrarian revolution," Sam said. "That there was any communism in it was pooh-poohed. I had lived through more than twenty big and little civil wars in China and was led to believe this was just one more. After all, politics wasn't my subject, and people who kept up on those things kept telling me that this was really just a reform movement."

Chinese faculty members, on behalf of the new communist authorities, came to him and said, "Carry on! Everyone here knows what you are doing for China." The university head called in the American faculty members and asked them to continue as before, mentioning guarantees promised by the new government. Soon, however, classes had virtually stopped. Varieties of "learning" meetings were taking up all the time. The students were working on confessions, as were many of the faculty members. The big auditorium was now given over exclusively to these matters.

The university head called Sam in to explain that a Chinese now had to head every department, and while the authorities were most anxious for him to continue his work just as he had been doing, his title would have to go to someone else. "A title doesn't mean anything to me," he replied at once.

As the money for his work came from American contributors, a new problem was created when funds for Red China were frozen. He was asked whether he would accept the same salary as an ordinary Chinese professor. Sixty American dollars a month! This was to be his pay after a lifetime of achievement that was visible in modern structures and skilled people all over China. Sam saw this as a test of his sincerity. He figured out his resources. He had saved some money, and had planned on returning home in a few years. He had no need to buy any clothes for quite some time. He could raise vegetables in his garden. He was residing in a little house on a small island with a lotus lagoon around it. He could stay there. So he willingly agreed. He did so particularly after hints were dropped by Chinese that they would feel safer if someone on whom responsibility could rest, such as himself, remained on the faculty.

He would be less than human if he didn't feel personal satisfaction over this evidence that he was needed. He threw himself wholeheartedly into his work, not concerning himself with anything else. This kept him from heeding certain warning signals. Students and professors, his old friends among the contractors and technicians in Peking, visited him more and more rarely. Soon none came. Later he learned that they were not allowed to visit Americans any more. Old contacts who happened to walk by when witnesses weren't present told him this was not against him personally. They emphasized their respect and affection for him.

Meetings were being held in vacant rooms and open spaces wherever a group could gather to discuss, self-criticize, and confess. The big staff room in his power plant, which he had to pass to get to his office on the mezzanine, was taken over. Meetings were run by his former students and workmen he had known for years. He saw some new faces, of people who had never been to Yenching. Party folk came in from the outside and wandered about, and when they saw him, would ask, "Who's that American? What's he doing here?"

The university head called him in one day and warned him not to continue traveling about on his bicycle. He asked him, too, to let the police — now stationed at the gate — know whenever he went out and where he was going. Sam noticed that this man wrote everything down. The policeman told him to be sure not to go anywhere except where he said. Sam was positive such nonsense would blow over, and didn't mention it to his wife, so as not to worry her. He kept it all to himself. "If the objective of the new regime is to have the Chinese people take over, it is what I want, too," he told himself. The situation became very tense during the Korean War. Classes became even more difficult, and an assistant was assigned to him to do the actual teaching.

Sometimes during the germ-warfare scare he'd overhear exclamations such as, "Watch him; he's probably polluting the well water." Could this mean him? Sam couldn't believe it. But everyone was talking as if there was no question but that the U.S. was engaging in a germ attack.

They started building walls around the workshops and the power plant that he had constructed, and banned him from them. Loudspeakers were strung up on the water tower and on the gables of various buildings. These were busy blaring out the proceedings of constant meetings. Accusations, self-criticisms, and confessions were on the air until late at night. The atmosphere became heavier. Something was cooking, he knew, but he could not believe it could possibly involve him. Then one day he got an order to attend a meeting in a small auditorium.

The Inquisition

When Sam came into the hall, he was surprised to see it fitted up like a courtroom. The stage was taken over for extra seats. Sam sat in one of the front rows facing several desks and a blackboard in the open space in the center. He was in the dock. A returned student from America, now heading the department of journalism, took charge. This lad had been in the communist underground long before the Reds came in, even while studying in

America. Another returned student, a geographer who had studied in England, sat at one of the desks.

Several cases were handled before his. Sam felt sorry for these people — both the accused and the accusers — as he watched the same scene repeat itself each time. A student instructor was called forth and informed that his confession was "not frank" and that he had to do it over. The chairman and co-chairman discussed its contents publicly, and the audience, composed of students and faculty, joined in. Everyone seemed to have a suggestion, and the accused had to satisfy them all. Everyone acted as judge, but the chairman had final say. His role appeared to be to guide the verdict of the audience into the strict pattern. Sam got the impression that each had already rewritten his confession several times. The accused were not given their old confessions back, but had to write them entirely new. These were then compared for contradictions.

He was still wondering about this when one professor stood up. His face reddened as he glanced toward Sam. He seemed to be reciting something he had rehearsed. "I heard him pronounce my name," Sam said. "He was accusing me! He said something about me and my relationship to Leighton Stuart, founder and former president of Yenching. What this professor was saying, it dawned on me, was that Stuart had picked me specially to start a school of engineering to train subversives to sabotage Chinese industry. He said Stuart's appointment as American ambassador to China proved he had been a spy and a saboteur all along. Mine was a school of sabotage, he said."

Sam was not called on to speak. After the accusation, the chairman stood up and angrily ordered him to leave. He did so, not knowing what it portended. He was left to worry about it. Posters appeared all over the campus accusing him of all sorts of "imperialist crimes."

Nothing was said directly to him until one afternoon when his wife called to him, saying, "Sam, what are those people doing over there on the lagoon?" He didn't notice anything unusual at first, then saw someone walking about, as if searching for something. His wife pointed to another part of the encircling pathway, where someone else was doing the same.

Then they saw one of the campus policemen from the gate approach. The Deans went out on the porch to greet him. He didn't greet them, only curtly ordered them not to leave the house. His wife asked why, as everyone knew they stayed at home all the time now. Somebody was coming to question them, the cop said.

Others joined the people circling the lagoon until there was quite a crowd. The Deans saw someone else approach, whom they recognized as a workman. He didn't return their greeting, but went into their house without a word and yanked the telephone off the wall.

Suppertime came and the Deans ate as usual, except this evening they didn't draw the curtains. They sat in front of the window, so everyone could see what they were doing. The date was March 20, 1952.

Nobody came until 8 p.m. Then three Chinese in faded yellow uniforms entered, while a crowd milled around outside the house. The three proceeded to make a methodical search. One was an American-educated faculty member who made believe he didn't speak English, but Sam saw the shame in his eyes. The couple were ordered to sit on the couch and not talk. "We felt foolish, like bugs on a log, sitting this way for a couple of hours," Sam said. The Reds put the things they wanted in a heap, including a scarlet silk banner, embroidered with golden threads, that had been given to Sam in appreciation for what he had done for China. They went through his Bible page by page, to see if anything was hidden in it. They took most of his personal photos, especially if Chinese were in them.

When they finished, they stopped near the door, holding the loot in their hands. 'You are a very bad man," they said to Dean. "We don't know what we are going to do with you. We haven't decided yet. Meanwhile, you can stay here." He was given a receipt made out for "sundry articles" and instructed to show any letter he might write to the communist official in town.

A few days later the Deans received formal permission to keep their servant, who alone could go to market, and to use the water and electricity in their home. The ban against receiving visitors was repeated — as if anyone would dare be seen talking to them now!

This was house arrest, after a month of virtual campus arrest. Sam knew he had to stay put.

"For five days we sat and worried over what would come next," Sam said. "Then, on March 25, I was summoned to the Bureau of Public Safety. This was the police station. I was sent upstairs and seated in a chair in the center of a room. Police officials sat all around me. They had prepared a long page of accusations. They told me I had been accused of a great many crimes and that many persons had given them evidence of my misdeeds. I felt a sinking feeling as I thought of the pressures that must have been put on my former students and associates. I now saw why they had made sure I stayed home and didn't go into the college buildings. They had rifled the files for material to go with what they had seized in the raid on my home.

" 'We have been investigating you for a long time,' they said. You should know you have made many enemies because you treated people badly.' This gave me a shock. I couldn't understand why anyone should be my enemy or how I could have treated anyone badly. 'The teachers and students have told us all about your misdeeds,' they continued. 'You might just as well confess these things right now. We know all about the subversive activities in which you've engaged and the spying you've done.'

"I sat stunned, not knowing what to say to show them how wrong they were. Of course, I was foolish to think they believed the accusations themselves. They started asking questions right after this, from the long page of accusations and a pile of notes. I answered as honestly as I could. They insisted I speak only Chinese. I spoke it well, but couldn't understand what they meant. They spoke a new kind of language, using a lot of political terminology I had never learned. My language was the Chinese spoken by the people — by the workers, students, and contractors.

"They were terribly angry over my ignorance and insisted that everything be expressed in the new political jargon. 'You claim to be a Christian, don't you?' one suddenly asked, sneeringly.

" 'Yes,' I replied. 'I don't claim to be a very good one. I only try to be.'

" 'Do you think it's good for a Christian missionary to live in a fine house and get a big salary?' I was asked. 'Did you ever live better than your Chinese associates?'

"I tried to explain that the house I lived in was part of my salary, and had been built by the mission with money from America. Actually, it was a very simple home. I didn't want a big house, and told them so. Their only retort was, 'Don't tell us a lie like that. You're an imperialist. Why don't you provide a big house like that for your Chinese associates?'

" 'I'm a poor man,' I said. 'I have no money to build a house for anyone, even for myself.'

" 'Then why didn't the mission?' they said.

" 'The money it sends to China is contributed by poor people, too,' I replied. This quibbling went on for hours. Lunchtime came and I wasn't given a chance to eat. Only once that day was I allowed to go to a toilet. Groups came into the room to question me in relays. As soon as one group got tired, a fresh batch came in and got to work on me.

" 'You've told us nothing but lies the whole morning,' one group said. 'You've confessed to terrible things, such as living in a better house than your Chinese associates, but you don't admit it's a terrible thing. So we'll let you sit here and think about it.' Then they left me all alone.

"These questioners made a big thing out of my designing and building the Peking Language School, where Chinese was taught. British, Americans, all the missions, and the Rockefeller Institute gave funds to help pay for it, so they insisted it was a training school for American subversives and headquarters for a cultural invasion of China. My construction of it was interpreted as a disservice to China. I admitted my part in building the school and the source of the funds. They insisted this was a confession, although I denied their conclusion.

"My mistake was in taking this seriously, thinking they actually believed what they were saying. I tried hard to express my viewpoint truthfully. They made something evil out of my friendship for Mr. Stuart and Sidney Gamble of Ivory Soap, who contributed a great deal of money to Yenching for its School of International Affairs. The schools of Journalism, Sociology, and Political Science all were incorporated into it. They said it was all done to create subversives and espionage agents. You sent teachers and missionaries to engage in a cultural invasion, to wean the Chinese away from love of their country,' they shouted at me.

"I had conducted a survey for Sid Gamble in connection with a fund appeal for simple industrial projects, such as a dairy farm, that could have enabled the Chinese to pay for their own schools, hospitals, and churches. A Chinese girl studying engineering did an extensive survey for me. All this was now hurled at me as accusations. My mind was reeling. They let me go home only after dark. 'We should put you in prison for all these crimes, but we won't,' they said. 'We are going to let you go home. But we want you to show your penitence by writing your confessions. You are to spend the next few weeks thinking about all the crimes you've committed and confess them in writing. One of our representatives will visit you every so often to see if you are doing as we've ordered.' "

This was as far as we could go with the interview that first night in Arizona, for Sam was working the late shift at the power plant. His wife stayed behind, deeply stirred by her husband's recital. She remembered how low he had looked when he came home after that grilling. "He was so very, very unhappy," she said simply. " 'They want me to write down everything I've done against the interests of the people,' he told me. I could tell from his voice how seriously he took it. He could not believe human beings would be so evil as to make such horrible accusations against a person if there wasn't some truth in them. He couldn't understand how he had been doing wrong.

"He began writing confessions right after breakfast the next morning. As he had nothing to confess, he only tortured himself. He probed and probed into his motives and his past; whenever he thought of something he jotted it down in a notebook. He filled entire notebooks that way. This was all he did for a month. I tried to argue with him, saying, 'Sam, you know there wasn't anything wrong in this,' pointing to a paragraph. 'What you did was right.' 'But, this is what they now say is wrong,' he'd reply. He'd lay his pen down and look at me with deep sorrow in his eyes.

"He knew his old students and associates, now scattered all over the country, would have to denounce him to stay out of trouble themselves. They would have to confess the same as he. He just couldn't believe it, and kept thinking it was something he had done. Then he dug deeper into his soul. He became terribly depressed. My heart was torn because I couldn't do anything for him. He wracked his brain a whole month this way, trying to find where he had sinned, sincerely trying to do as they had instructed."

He kept working at his notebooks, copying and rewriting. "This is not quite right, is it?" he would ask his wife, reading it to her. "Is this true?" he would inquire, and pray over it for guidance.

"I was able to get him to work a bit in the garden now and then," she said. "I tried everything, but usually he just sat in his corner, thinking and thinking, filling those notebooks. The communists now had the only copies of the letters he had written, and he was trying desperately to remember them so he could explain them and admit any errors."

On April 24 they summoned him once again, and once more he left at dawn and returned only after dark. This time he took with him a heap of notebooks, written in tragic sincerity and with real agony. After going over them, the inquisitors turned on him and screamed, "You're lying. You're not being frank. Confess! You're not telling the truth. You're hiding much more."

Again teams of fresh interrogators came in relays, hammering at him every minute. Once more he had not a bite to eat all day. "I was by then a little out of my head," he told me. "That month at home writing my confessions had been a greater strain than I had realized. I remember finally breaking down and saying I would confess to anything that was true, but that I was a Christian, and couldn't help wishing they were Christians, too.

"When I said this, they all got up immediately and left. This was late in the afternoon. I blacked out. I was practically nuts, I suppose. After what seemed a long while, a big shot came in. He brought paper and a Chinese brush. He said, 'You've confessed this and that, and the other thing; now write it all down.' There were nine or ten points. I had lived in a big house while other Chinese didn't. I had a bigger salary than others. I had built the Peking Language School. All this was true, but lies the way they were written. I was very hungry, terribly tired, and dreadfully worn out. The official dictated what he said I confessed, and asked me to sign it. As soon as I did, he grabbed the paper from under my nose and stalked out. I hardly knew what was happening. I was like an automaton. Only now can I talk about those things without going into a daze."

He said they returned in a group and read him the whole list of his supposed crimes, including the charge that he was a spy, which they said he had admitted, too. "I remember them saying I was an old man now who couldn't do them much harm any more," Sam went on. "They said they ought to put me in prison but because of my age they would let me leave China. They said I had to quit Yenching at ten A.M. on Sunday, taking the train from Peking to Tientsin. They said they had arranged where I would stay until the first ship left for Hong Kong. They warned me to hurry to get my documents in order for leaving.

"I was in such a fog that I don't know how I got home. I had only two days in which to complete arrangements. My wife went with me to the government offices. I don't really know how I got from Peking to Hong Kong. I now realize that for several weeks at Hong Kong, while arrangements Were being made for me to come home, I just stared ahead when I sat at table for meals. I remember that my eyes were always open, while I hardly noticed a thing."

This gentle, conscientious bridge-builder and housebuilder, man-builder and soul-builder, had passed safely through his undeserved purgatory. We took a walk into the red hills where the Indians built huts called hogans. I couldn't see them until Sam pointed them out for me, for they were blended into the landscape like camouflage. We talked a bit about Indians, and on the way back we discussed his experiences again. He said he now understood how the Reds had laid their trap for him and how he hadn't noticed it until he was caught in it. "The communist tactic, when they want a certain action taken, is not to say so at all," he said. "One by one, they make every alternative move impossible. They put you in a position where you have no other possibility but to do as they wish. They never say. Do so and so. That, they insist, is not the 'democratic' way. They say you have to act voluntarily. They don't tell you what they wish, but wait for you to find out by yourself, no matter how long it takes. You're trapped like a rat. You've perfect freedom to choose, they say. You try one way and find it's impossible because perhaps money is lacking. You try another method, and it doesn't work for some other reason. They make sure of it. Finally, you have to take the line they've wanted all along, although nobody told you."

Sam realized, as much as anyone, the critical blow dealt him. Soon after returning to America he set to work, in his characteristic manner, to pull himself out of the doldrums into which the Reds had put him. He took a radio and television course that forced him to concentrate. "I felt that as I had been a student so many years, if I could select a new subject and master it, I would regain my faculties," he told me. "It wasn't easy. At first I read and read and got nowhere. Five minutes afterwards, everything left my mind. I was only able to keep up with a simple routine. I kept making silly mistakes because I couldn't remember instructions. I was a very slow student. A little fatigue knocked me out. It wasn't me at all. I'd sit at the table nervous from exhaustion and suddenly blank out.

"The most painful task I ever did in my life was this job of forcing myself to remember again. By keeping doggedly at it, I've been slowly getting back into shape. It's taken a long time."

John D. Hayes

Encirclement

The one thing that John D. Hayes never could have imagined happening to him was to have a hallucination. He was the last type of individual one would think of in this connection. He possessed everything that should have made it impossible in his case — a clear, strong-willed mind, a fine physique, an excellent education, and deep convictions. He had always been able to reason clearly, to separate fact from fancy. Yet he had a hallucination, with all the trimmings, and it was the climax to his brainwashing.

That made him confess to what never happened and, what is more important, convinced him at the time that he was telling the truth. When he told me about it, I felt that here was the key to the inner mechanism of a whole chain of baffling confessions that had stunned the world, from the early Moscow trials to Cardinal Mindszenty's pathetic breakdown and the germ-warfare performance put on by the Reds in Korea.

Hayes was a highly educated man who was capable of objectively studying his own case, putting the details into perspective, analyzing what had been done to him and what 'effect it had on his mind. He had studied psychology and knew of Pavlov's theories, although when arrested, he didn't dream that the physiologist's experiments could have any possible relation to his case.

The first time I met him was at his home in Washington, about half a year after his release from the communist prison in Kweiyang, in central China, where he had undergone an intense siege of brainwashing. He was able then to give me only a smattering account of what he had gone through. He was still too near this mental hell to be able to stand the strain of thinking back on it deeply. When he searched his mind for details, it was like probing into a still unhealed wound. It hurt. The agony that brainwashing imposes on its victims was still in his eyes.

We next met more than a year later, on the other side of the world in Singapore, where he was stopping briefly on his way to Indonesia. We took up where we had left off in our previous discussion. Points which previously could not be analyzed because of the mental anguish they caused could now be logically pursued.

He was now able to present an integrated account of how he had been led by subtle and brutal pressures to believe and admit what had never taken place. What was evident when I first met him was doubly evident now — the most important part of his case was that he took all the Reds dealt him and yet beat them in the end. This was the thrilling finale of the Soviet extravaganza, an act they hadn't written. The Reds were never able to achieve their primary objective with him. His mind kept slipping away from them.

The communists had been able to do anything they wanted with Hayes except what they most wanted. He had something in him they couldn't take away without destroying his mind or body. Either way, he would be useless to them. He left them self-defeated. His experiences exposed the fatal limitations to brainwashing.

Hayes had a big frame and was bearded like a sailor. In spite of his age — he was about sixty-five — he retained the athletic contours of his youth, when he played basketball for Princeton and rowed at Oxford. His high scholastic attainments won him honors and degrees from both universities.

He had been born near Chefoo in North China of missionary parents, becoming a missionary in turn. He was perfectly at home among the Chinese. He had thoroughly mastered Mandarin, the national language. They often told him they considered him as one of them. The Chinese mind seemed part o£ him.

His inquisition really began when he saw close friends and old colleagues arrested and executed. The authorities already were irritated because a cast of seventeen of his students had put on the *Merchant of Venice*, with its dangerous thoughts about the quality of mercy. A Chinese official whom he considered one of the noblest of men was taken out one day and shot. The Red student group in his class pointedly called on Hayes right afterwards to ask his "opinion" of it. He frankly said, " No civilized country ever shoots a man for his political views."

When they put this into the papers next day, Hayes felt the cords tightening about him. A couple of days later, when the news spread that General MacArthur had been dismissed, he felt even more sure of it and figured he had only a very little time left as a free man. Peking would now be even more cocksure in its hate-America campaign. So next morning he told his classes, "I'm proud of America. For the first time in history a nation has cashiered its winning general for fear of offending the sensibilities of a friendly people."

The following day the authorities informed him that he had "committed the sin" of attacking the new government, that "there was probably more behind it, and the law would now take its course." He was ordered to go home and consider himself under house arrest. As his wife had left shortly before the Reds took over, Hayes was alone in his home for the next six months, subject to a whole chain of strange pressures. A hard-core communist named Feng, who headed the neighborhood ten-family group, came at any hour of the day or night, staying for hours at a time.

He kept up a continuous conversation to which Hayes was obliged to listen and answer. He obviously had received instructions on what to say, for he mixed his talk with curious "advice" and snap questions. He was especially interested in what friends showed up. No Chinese dared come any more. One American friend came for a chat regularly once a week. This was noted and Hayes's hallucination nine months later was directly connected with the insistence that he remember every word they had spoken.

At the end of the first month, the police informed him that as "no overt revolutionary activity" had been traced to him, he could leave his house but must use discretion when doing so. From then on Hayes did his own marketing once daily. One of his rooms was taken over by a local adult literacy class whose instructor obviously helped Feng in his surveillance. He was married to Feng's sister.

When meals were prepared, Feng's habit was to invite himself to share them. Hayes was much tempted to buy extra food, but what he already had learned of Red subterfuge warned him against doing so. This continual drain on his mental and physical resistance brought his weight down considerably. He was lucky he had deprived himself, though, because in prison he was accused of "entertaining" Feng and when he denied it, they checked up with his cook. Otherwise, he would have been trapped into another "crime," the very serious one of "bribing a communist officer." The need to think ahead every moment to avoid falling into such traps was an extra strain.

One day Feng blithely announced he wasn't coming back and that Hayes was free to see anyone he wished. The Reds hoped that others whom they hadn't uncovered would take this opportunity to visit Hayes under the impression that the heat was off. Hayes himself was led to believe this and asked for an exit permit. Instead, at dawn of October 29, 1951, he heard a terrific racket at the gate. The next thing he knew revolver butts were being pounded on his bedroom door. When he opened it, he stared into three revolvers and the first words he heard were, "You are an imperialist spy!"

"I'm not!" he retorted, although he knew this sounded childish. They manacled him and pushed him out into the cold in his pyjamas. They spent an hour ransacking the house, seeking a gold cache which they insisted he had hidden to finance his "operations." They then called him back into the house, sat him down at his desk, and photographed him beside an unfinished letter to his son, then in Princeton, saying this was proof of his spying. They ordered him back into bed, so they could photograph him being arrested. For more realism they unlocked one wrist and ordered him to hold up this unmanacled hand. The photograph posed the police officer so the picture would show him pointing his pistol at Hayes. The cop glared realistically.

What gave all this an insane rather than a silly complexion was that the room was dark and the photographer had no flash for his commonplace camera. The negative couldn't possibly show a thing and everyone knew it, yet they all went through the motions. This was only play-acting. If it weren't for the fact that so much suffering and killing accompanied this sort of thing, nobody would have taken it seriously. The deadly consequences gave it importance. Anyone who denied its reality would be quickly and fiercely disabused.

From his lifelong knowledge of and intimate relations with the Chinese Hayes knew he had to take the chance and deflate them a little bit. Otherwise they would consider him too much the sucker and take even greater advantage of him. If he told them in so many words that the picture wasn't going to come out and why kid themselves, they would lose so much face among themselves that they would be sure to revenge themselves on him. So, in a knowing voice, Hayes asked the cameraman, "What aperture are you using?" He thought his head was going to be cracked open then and there! They got the point at once and all turned on him!

But such things tire a person's mind! Who was fooling whom? Must everyone go through the entire make-believe for the crazy pattern to work? Where did fantasy begin or end and realism come in? A man couldn't help being affected by these acts. Actually, they ultimately led up to Hayes's hallucination.

This particular diversion gave him the opportunity to grab his fur coat on the way out, which served him for the next four months in prison as bedding and blanket. He was put into a cell already occupied by three Chinese. His initial reaction, after being taken unawares in spite of so many months of cat-and-mouse play, was defiance. Everything now took on a political slant. His conversations would be misinterpreted to involve his friends. Hayes decided not to talk. No, they could pound the table and threaten all they wished, let them do anything they wanted to him, he would not talk! What right did anyone have to ask a man about his personal conversations with his friends? No, he told them, he would be making no statements.

They had a very simple and effective way of dealing with such an attitude, for it wasn't the first time they had come up against it.

He was blandly informed that as he was a spy, all his friends were now regarded as espionage agents, too. The report made by the security police alleged conspiracy. If his conversations were so mysterious that he didn't dare divulge them, they must indeed have been criminal. They would have to act accordingly.

Hayes now realized that his silence put his closest Chinese and American friends in grave jeopardy. He knew that the new authorities would not exercise patience. Some of the former, at least, would be tortured bestially and even done to death. Yes, he could adopt the martyr's role himself. He wasn't young any more and the prospect of this was not especially harrowing to a missionary. But unlike the persecutors of the past, they made all his friends hostage for him. Had he the right to force them into martyrdom, too? That was his first agonizing problem.

He decided, while he still retained some of his mental stamina, to change his tactics. He had already been informed his friends were being questioned. He had no way of knowing what they were saying. If he evaded questions, he would only be involving them more. He decided that as he was innocent of any wrong-doing and the whole spy story was make-believe, he would follow a policy of strictly telling the truth. Yes, he would talk, if that would save those people, but he would confound the examiners by never lying. They had the names of all the persons with whom he had been in contact. Feng and his brother-in-law had done their work well. Their names could be cleared only by Hayes, he was told in no uncertain tones. He must recall every conversation he had had with each of them. They gave him a form to follow, "When, where, what did you say, who else was present, and why did you say what you did?" This last point proved the most wearying, for it led into such trivial channels. Yet the penalty for forgetfulness could be the destruction of any one of these persons.

Hayes felt that as a missionary, he could be more himself by speaking the truth; it was the weapon he had been trained to use.

Once this point was settled, the next hurdle appeared very minor, indeed. A man obviously was bound by the laws of the country where he resides. "You must remember that you are in our country, now," the indoctrinator told Hayes. "Our laws are what you must obey. We have to learn your laws when we go to your country. You should know ours." This sounded reasonable and Hayes readily agreed. Of course, until the closing years of World War II, foreigners in China were liable in criminal cases only to the laws of their own country. This extraterritoriality was abandoned by the Western Powers as an expression of trust in the Sun Yat-sen republic.

China's laws were now Red. Part of the reason Hayes accepted the communist position was because his Chinese church organization now would also be held responsible for his acts. That put him in still another spot. He sensed the danger in it but saw no alternative without causing hurt to others. He decided to look on this as a challenge, in the manner of a warrior agreeing to his opponent's choice of weapons. The battle was now joined.

Responsibility

At the outset, Dr. Hayes came up against the communist interpretation of responsibility. "You are responsible for everything you said or did," they told him. But what they meant was not at all what those words meant to him. He had been brought up to consider responsibility within the framework of his individual personal life, and of his own conscious efforts. His responsibility was like an island, his own alone, and so was the responsibility of his neighbor. Where there was mutual responsibility, this was conscious and equally binding. There were definite limits. But no such limits existed in the Red concept. Where no borders existed, how could he locate any? His instinctive efforts to do so added to his mental fatigue.

He was told by the communists that he was completely responsible for what anyone else did on the basis of what he had said or done. As the Reds phrased these things, a man either "thought through" to his new position, and adjusted his judgments to this new "standpoint," or rejected it and held onto his own. The Reds gave him no choice in the matter; he was going to play their game whether he wanted to or not.

He thought it out in his cell. "There was plenty of time to think," he said ruefully. He decided to take refuge in his convictions, which he believed equipped him to fight and survive in any company. He decided to trust in the invincibility of his faith.

"Under their interpretation of responsibility," he told me, "if you are in the army and your officer tells you to shoot someone, you must not allude to the officer in your confession but you must write, *I shot him.' If the officer is questioned, he has to accept responsibility, too, and answer, *I ordered it.' What this did was to extend responsibility indefinitely. Yet this theory of responsibility was basic to the whole totalitarian concept of life and its control."

From three to nine hours a day for forty straight days, Hayes was worked on in prison by relays of interrogators and indoctrinators. The strain of the long preliminary sparring had already rubbed his nerves. Now physical pressures were added to the mental.

Hayes was constantly hungry. A rice diet, with perhaps a couple of spoonfuls of vegetables added once a day, was calculatedly insufficient. He felt drugged from lack of sleep, especially in the beginning. Later he was allowed to take his rest at night without being called in for brainwashing. "Otherwise I would have been sunk!" he exclaimed to me. "Each night I went to America and woke up in China." Humiliation was another corrosive influence. "I felt humiliated that my affection for the Chinese people was not getting across and that I was being accused of being a spy in a land I loved," he said.

The brainwashing chamber was a downstairs room in the prison, about twelve by eighteen feet, where he faced anywhere from one to seven people. Their functions, like brainwashing itself, ranged all over the field, from examiner to indoctrinator, prosecutor to judge, inquisitor to torturer. Brainwashing victims from East Europe have described similar courts to me, with hypnotists and psychiatrists on the staff!

The court simply informed Hayes he was head spy for all Southwest China and demanded he fill in the details for them by confessions. "Confess!" was as strange a refrain as the raven's "nevermore," only without the poetry. "Confess and all will be forgiven," they would say. But plague it all, how was a man to confess when he couldn't grasp what he was supposed to have done wrong? They gave him peculiar titles, such as "sub rosa American consul for Southwest China," and insisted he explain how he "operated." They insisted he reveal his connections with the F.B.I. They provided what they called proof and spent ten steady days pounding on this. They had a church calendar listing J. Edgar Hoover, the F.B.I, chief, as a member of the Board of Trustees of the National Presbyterian Church which had sent Hayes abroad. They insisted it meant he was an F.B.I, agent in China. When he asked for details of these charges, they kept repeating, like a mad chorus: "You know what you did wrong, so confess it!"

They would vary this with a sudden order, "Think!" When they released him from the day's grilling, they frequently did so with the injunction, "Now go back to your cell and think what you did bad. Confess it!" They had a trick of telling him to think about some specific point but ignoring it next day, going on to some other will-o'-the-wisp.

They gave him thinking assignments on which he had to write or report. The tension of daily going through these same points was like a drill piercing his mind, "Worse than physical suffering," Hayes told me. Each day he was called and each day the accusation was gone over in minute detail, from every conceivable angle. "I'd rather be whipped than have this questioning continue," Hayes cried out to them one day.

Questioning was rarely ordinary questioning. The correct term for it would be "suggestive interrogation," with the desired answers implied in the wording. The brainwashers alternated this with a barrage of denunciation and accusation to make their victim cringe. Then they would make their statement in question form and expect Hayes to agree to it. When the accused or the witness failed to agree, it took on the appearance of defiance of the court.

This type of questioning went on for a month without Hayes appearing to give way, although he felt thoroughly fatigued all the time now, as if drugged. "If I could only have eaten one square meal!" he said to me. "If I could only have had one day's break!"

He still had enough clarity left to refuse an offer which in Korea had much to do with edging men into treasonable acts. A "nice Chinese" came to him and said he knew that in America a defendant had a lawyer to help him. "We don't allow that here, but I would be very willing to assist you, so you can have the same privileges as at home," he told him. Hayes's China background instinctively put him on guard. He thanked the man for his "services" but rejected the offer. This man he later found out was the top prosecutor! He would have helped Hayes like the two renegades, Alan Winnington and Wilbur Burchett, "helped" POW's in Korea.

Hayes had to be on his guard all the time. He had to watch out against specious arguments which led to pro-communist conclusions. He developed a counter-technique. The indoctrinator would begin with ideals on which they could mutually agree. By deduction, he would go on from there to try to inveigle Hayes into a false conclusion. Hayes accepted the idea and watched for the opening in the Red argument, when he would suggest another line of thought. This frequently nonplussed the court. Hayes was able to get away with this because it was not a defiant action. "My objective was not to anger the judge or win the argument but to win the man," he said. Hayes made it even more difficult for them to refute him by nailing down his replies with a Chinese proverb. This is an old trick in China. He felt he was in a Chinese market, where the buyer traditionally wrestles with the merchant over prices. "The difference now," Hayes said, "was that we wrestled over the truth."

They tried to destroy his lines of defense, saying, "Forget about the white wall; concentrate on the black dots. We know all about the white wall." They tried to get him to concentrate only on his purported political sins.

Hayes was given plenty of homework to do in his cell. They gave him some of Mao's books and urged him to write any questions that might arise as he studied them. Hayes filled pages with questions that were never answered — neither did they give him any more such dialectical literature. They had him write a long autobiography, summaries of long past conversations and, as he was known as a liberal, a paper on the third-party movement. They pressed him for a self-criticism, making it obvious they sought criticism of missionaries as "tools of the State Department." He got around this by criticizing the mission organizations where they fell short of their own ideals, shifting the blame to himself under their own theory of responsibility. This enabled him to write sixteen pages of Christian doctrine, with a different point stressed in each paragraph. He would explain each point, then end up with a personal confession of his failure to live up to it. Red doctrine inferentially was torn to shreds. This had a laudable end but nonetheless contributed to wearying him down.

They were constantly putting stress on some very inconsequential detail and harping on it interminably, jumping from one detail to another with dreamlike inconsistency until the whole matter would be abruptly dropped and something else, equally irrelevant, leaped upon. One time the inquisitor insisted he name the shops around the market place. Hayes thought hard and named each store. The insane exchange then went like this:

"Did you say there were two electric shops?"

"Yes."

"Did you buy from both shops?"

"No."

"Which shop did you buy from?"

"The second."

The inquisitor's voice became sharp. "Why did you buy at that shop and not at the other?"

"Why ... eh ... I don't know."

"There must be a reason. Think now and be frank I Why did you buy at that particular shop and not at the other one?"

This began to have implications! The brainwasher looked hard at him. "I just liked the looks of the place more, I suppose," Hayes said hesitatingly. "The store looked sort of friendly. Yes, it looked friendly." Then, to relieve the tenseness that had suddenly developed, he added, "I almost always try to make friends of people I buy from."

"Oh!" exclaimed the judge. "So that was it! Did the shopkeeper smile when you bought from him?"

"Smile ... ah ... smile? Why, yes, he smiled."

"WHY did he smile?"

"Why? ... Why did he smile? I don't know why he smiled. He just smiled because ... well ..."

Hayes, his body and mind thoroughly tired out, remembers thinking to himself, "That's a fool question," but he had to put on a serious mien, otherwise he would have been accused of showing "contempt for the court," resulting in much trouble; it was easier to take it all seriously.

Taking it seriously because its consequences could be very serious, although at the same time it was silly, had him upset. The brainwasher could see it. Hayes looked very puzzled over that final question of theirs. That was the moment the indoctrinator selected to adjourn the court and quickly stalk out, leaving Hayes sitting, still puzzled.

Hayes had gone through many, many such trivial interrogations, and they hadn't flustered him. But the cumulative effect was achieving the Reds's purpose at last. "Now I know that their aim was to becloud my clarity of mind," Hayes told me.

"They were chiseling away at my memory. Yet I could still look back and tell them exactly what I had said or done, and was equally positive on what I hadn't. The struggle settled now on one main point. The Reds insisted that the American who used to visit me, and whom they had already put into prison, had a transmitting radio set which he used for sending my messages. I had successfully refuted this. In order to do so, I had summoned every ounce of my retentive powers. This uninterrupted use of my memory every moment even made my mind clearer. That was very strange. The court noticed it, complimenting me for a 'dependable memory.' They encouraged me to keep concentrating."

Now Hayes knows why! They knew that he was critically overstraining his brain and that it couldn't indefinitely stand such unnatural pressure.

Hayes went back to his cell, thinking ... thinking ... thinking. "You got into its swing and couldn't climb out. Your cellmates were waiting to call you to order if you were just idling. They gained merit that way, at least they escaped some punishment, for each was responsible for everyone else in the cell." Inwardly, as Hayes referred to this, I shuddered. The Reds had thought of everything, it seemed, to make each man the hostage of his comrade, to set each man spying on the other, on pain of immediate heavy punishment if any evaded this Red "responsibility." Agents provocateurs were slipped into the cells to test the occupants.

"Why should I suffer this way?" Hayes asked himself. "Here you've made a clear and frank confession of all you've done against the regime. You've told them the whole truth. You can't do any more than that. You've brought matters to a head. They'll have to do something definite now, kill you or free you! Your conscience is clear. Now it's entirely up to them. Stop worrying!"

Hayes told me that as soon as he had spoken this way to himself, a change came over him. That puzzled spell that had enveloped him in the courtroom dropped off. He felt relaxed. This whole incident — the foolish questioning about the shopkeeper and why he smiled — was forgotten and he felt relaxed and slightly exhilarated. How long it had been since he was last relaxed! He felt good now. He felt airy. Dr. Hayes didn't know it, but under the strain he had become light-headed, too. Then it happened!

Hallucination

Back in his cell, stretched out in his usual corner, despite the brilliant overhead lighting that was on day and night. Dr. Hayes breathed deeply of this curious new feeling of relaxation that coursed through him. Now that he had cleansed the slate, he had no further concern over what the morrow might bring. That was the Red worry now!

He had successfully maintained his guard every wakeful second since that first day when the new college head, a Communist Party official picked by the Reds, told him to go home and consider himself under house arrest. How long ago that seemed! He was still on the alert against any outside trickery. He recognized full well that there was a devilish consistency and persistence about the Reds.

That recent scene in the brainwashing chamber where they had got him all wound up and bewildered over nothing at all and then, having reached that stage, abruptly got up and left, seemed something far remote.

Actually, for the first time, Hayes left his guard down, inside himself rather than outside. That was even more dangerous, although he had no reason to know it. The mind can play tricks itself as well as be twisted out of focus by the Commies. He hadn't anticipated that.

Lying in his cell, light-hearted and light-headed, as if a tremendous weight had suddenly gone from him, he couldn't be expected to know that there was something peculiar about this. If he had, he might have kept his guard up inside himself.

In his mind, comfortably void now, placidly comfortable, a stab came from somewhere within him, A lightning stab of memory, all the more brilliant because he felt so airy. The release of strain let go an unknown energy that hit him like a bolt of lightning. The scene came back to him as if it had happened that same day. How could he have forgotten it? He saw it all now in his mind's eye, all over again, exactly as it had happened. Indeed, how could he have forgotten! The time, that is, when his friend came to him in his house while he still was only under detention and they chatted and this man remarked in a worried way, "By jove, I better get rid of that transmitter!" He heard the words distinctly.

Hayes remembered, too, how this remark had astonished him, and all he could answer at the time was, "Oh yes, you better had." Even his own casual intonation returned.

He remembered it all very clearly — only it never transpired. We discussed the phenomenon at great length this time in Singapore.

Under the uninterrupted demands made upon his mind in that grotesque environment, it appeared to me that Hayes had attained a clarity very much like that of a hypnotist's subject, who can recreate from deep within his subconscious some exact memory of a long past incident which he had believed gone entirely from him. This relaxed feeling, too, was something that subjects of hypnotism experience after they have come out from under the trance. I asked Hayes whether he had suspected any hypnotism in the treatment given him in prison. He was quite sure he saw no evidence of it and did not believe it was used — at least not in the form customarily known. Whether the effect of it could be duplicated in some long-drawn-out torture such as in brainwashing was another matter entirely. He just couldn't say.

What he did say was: "Under that persistent striving to remember every forgotten detail, the fog had been receding from the scene as far as all matters of fact were concerned. But regarding the transmitting radio, which had never existed and on which they were continually harping, there was a curious confusion between fact and fancy."

The brainwasher had refused to accept Hayes's amazingly clear memory on this point. Until that evening, he had stanchly adhered to his denial of it. But he had not been able to persuade his inquisitors to leave the subject alone. They kept tormenting him to think some more about it, to focus on it, to try to recall the truth. They worried and teased him with their perpetual insistence that he was not telling the truth, like a cat worries a mouse. They had an irritating habit of ignoring his flat denial and asking some question such as, "What was the transmitter's color?" as if he hadn't been telling them all along there was no transmitter. If only he had been allowed to laugh over it, but that would have been contempt and hostility. He forced himself by conscious effort to retain a firm grasp on that whole period of his American friend's visits to his home.

He had succeeded until this night, until after that strange scene in the brainwashing chamber that left him puzzled and confused over something extremely inconsequential.

Now, so soon after that, he was remembering very vividly a scene when his friend had referred to the radio machine. He sure had something critical with which to tussle now! The old worries, the chronic uncertainties, that he had been so sure were lifted off his back by his integrity — all returned to him now, much heavier than before.

"When the hallucination came," Hayes said, "I was faced with the ghastly choice of telling the whole truth, with its untoward consequence for this other man, or giving up my own compass — the stubborn attachment to truth that had kept me going. I was also deeply concerned over the effect it would have on my Chinese church. I took recourse in the communist version of responsibility, which would enable me honestly — inside that framework — to take the whole burden to myself, relieving my American colleague of any disastrous result of his continued denial, because I was sure his actions would be recognized as based on loyalty to me."

Fretting in the cell corner, he made up his mind to remove that last impediment to a clean slate and in that way regain the exquisite joy of the blissful, relaxed state he had experienced for such a short time. He desperately clung to his early resolution. With faith, it would see him through somehow. He understood that he probably would be given a ten-year prison sentence for the crime he was confessing. Well, that was only two years longer than his present mission contract for work in China! The work wouldn't be what he had anticipated, but he would trust in his Faith that its purpose would be achieved somehow better that way if this was how it had to be.

He called for the guard and asked for paper. So certain was he of himself now that when it came, he went at once to America in his sleep, as was his habit, and woke up in the morning ready to begin the full confession of this incident, which was now so crystal clear. He didn't dare tell his cellmates what he was writing. "I was lucky they didn't ask," he said. He feared they might put him off the track, making him lose some of this precise recollection that had finally come to him. He mustn't allow for any distraction.

I could see some of the old strain returning in Hayes as he repeated this now painful procedure of delving into the past, this time for the purposes of record. The facts had to become known! Any deliberate effort to lean on his memory was now a strain. He had always preached extemporaneously, depending on his memory. Each time he spoke now, even in some new locality, he drafted a sermon anew because it was less of a task than remembering one he had delivered previously. His memory was still very sensitive.

He worked for three days on that new confession. His reward came the morning after its completion, when he woke up fresh for the first time in his prison experience. He had awakened from a drugged sort of sleep.

He was summoned to the courtroom that evening. The whole panel was waiting for him. They verified the details in his confession, going through the items carefully one by one. His memory was sure.

A few days later, the examiner said he wished Hayes to identify some of the messages he had sent over the transmitting radio. Hayes saw a small pile of them on the desk, probably twenty to thirty. The interrogator picked up one and read it. "Did you send this?" he asked.

"No," Hayes said. "That's not mine."

No nasty pressure this time! The examiner patiently put it back and took another seemingly at random and read this, too. This routine went on for some time. Hayes would have liked to have looked at the messages himself, but the indoctrinator held them at arm's length, but close enough for Hayes to recognize his friend's handwriting.

The first three messages were purely military. Such data never came his way; it was too far-fetched for his interests. He was able to deny these at once, although the dismal thought came to him, "They still must think I'm some sort of a head spy to have anything to do with that kind of information."

Unperturbed by Hayes's denials, the indoctrinator picked up still another message and read from it. This one was about the structure of the youth organization. One phrase in it, "youth very well organized," rang a bell in Hayes's poor mind.

"Did you send that message?" the inquisitor asked quietly. The roughhouse tones used against him before his final, all-inclusive confession were absent now. Hayes appreciated this thoughtfulness. They were doing nothing to upset him!

Hayes remembers how startled he was by that message when he heard that phrase in it. He even recalls the reserved tone of voice in which he replied, saying only, "Yes, I recognize that message."

At once the inquisitor brushed all the others aside and exclaimed with finality, "Yes, that's the wire you sent. The others aren't yours."

Sitting in that narrow room, with all the memories it had engraved on him, Hayes distinctly remembered the words in that message. Of course he had given that message to his friend. He had no doubt of it. Wasn't it in his handwriting?

"I now saw myself responsible for a transmitting radio and consequently for a whole series of telegrams sent over it," Hayes told me.

"Was there any radio? Were there any messages?" I asked him.

He shook his head. "No," he said. "None of any of that existed except in my tired head. The brainwashers, of course, knew it was all a fake. Even the handwriting was forged. They must have worked very hard the preceding week or two on that pile of messages, duplicating the penmanship and figuring out the wording. They had no problem in quoting me exactly in matters that were really of common knowledge. The people whom they questioned about me had remembered what I had said."

If Hayes had only been more himself, he would have been able to see through the Red sleight-of-hand in a flash. In other times, his penetrating brain had been able to quickly see through intricate parlor tricks by entertaining magicians. This Red piece of trickery would have appeared far more transparent than any of those tricks if his mind had been fairly normal. After three-quarters of a year of uninterrupted, intensive drilling away at his mind, he was in no shape to reason things out.

He had sat by the hour and chatted with his friend about everything of any significance that was happening around them. Of course they had talked about the role that the Reds had given to the youth. Of course they had discussed the youth groups being organized by the political commissars. Hayes must have used the very words "youth very well organized" which sparked off this new clear-cut recollection. He probably used them several times. That was a world of difference from making a telegraphic message out of them. Of course there had been no such thing.

The message would have been silly, for the Reds organized youth groups wherever they went; it was standard procedure. What possible use could such information be to anyone anywhere? None of this logical reasoning could go through Hayes's head at that time. He had never anticipated the indoctrinator quoting his own conversations this way. He went back to his cell befuddled, letting the acceptance of this new guilt sink into his subconscious.

Actually, the Reds had used no great skill, had resorted to no original thinking, to bring this hallucination about. They had only been devilishly persistent, inhumanly patient.

Victory

Dr. Hayes was warned by prison mates that when a man, out of desperation or hopelessness, said to his indoctrinator, "All right then, go ahead and shoot me," the Reds considered this relieved them of responsibility and were likely to go ahead and carry out his wishes. Hayes knew of this happening in Kweiyang prison while he was there.

Until his hallucination, except for those few early days of defiance, he had been careful not to give the Reds an excuse to lower the boom on him. The combat of minds was still being fought. But in his hallucination, believing that he had told the whole truth without them being able to capture his mind, and that there was nothing more he could say, he became wholly unconcerned over what the Reds would do to him.

In this moment which had all the exterior marks of defeat for him, Hayes felt positive that he had won the fight. He just did not care what would happen to him physically from then on. He was sure they had failed to win his spirit, and this was the fort he had been defending all along. From there he made his sallies. The Red objective was to "convert" him, to indoctrinate him into their ideology, actually to win his loyalty, on the firm conviction that environment, if the pressure is sufficient, will not only break a man but remake him.

Although he had abandoned his natural defense works — his own normal approach to logic — for the offensive advantage that went with accepting theirs, infiltrating their positions, he was now content, certain that their siege of his mind had failed. Indeed, whatever tolerance he had had for communism when the Reds first arrested him had now been eliminated by the demonstration they had given that their smiles and their reforms were only tactics — means to the political ends of totalitarian domination.

The next session was decisive, when the brainwasher went back to the spy charges reinforced by Hayes's admission of responsibility for the telegrams. He had also accepted complete responsibility for having given advice on how to dispose of the radio transmitter and of providing the information for the telegrams. Intent was extraneous under Red law. By accepting full blame himself, Hayes hoped to relieve his friend of it.

The brainwasher went onto a new tack. "We find that you are not an American spy but an international spy," he exclaimed, leaving Hayes to puzzle that one out. "You have the best espionage system we've come across yet. Friends? Bah!"

Then, after letting this news sink in, he asked, "What countries have you been in?"

Hayes carefully listed the countries, knowing that exactitude was required in this sort of interrogation, which was meant as a trap rather than as just questioning.

The brainwasher listened carefully. He had evidently memorized every facet of information on the case. When Hayes ended, he asked simply, "Is that all?"

"Yes," Hayes said.

"You're a liar!" he roared. "You haven't listed all the countries you've been in."

Hayes went over the list again very carefully. Doing so, he recalled staying a few days once in Sumatra. He had forgotten to mention it. He put it in this time.

"Is that all?"

"Yes."

Again: "You're a liar!" Hayes thought carefully. No, he had given them the complete list. Then, instead of going back over all of it again, as was the required routine in such circumstances, never leaving a subject until the interrogator was satisfied or changed it himself, Hayes exclaimed, "All right then, go ahead and shoot me!"

This time it was the brainwasher who was stunned and puzzled. "He gave me a curious look," Hayes said. "I thought he was going to order me shot. I only realized afterwards that this was confusion in him. I turned the tables on him at the moment he was most certain of his prey.

"He didn't order me shot. In the interval, while the indoctrinator was figuring out his next move, I said:

" 'If you can't believe what you can check at any port of entry, how are you going to believe what is in my heart?' "

This was another of those small verbal shots which deal such major blows in mind warfare. Trivial scenes come back to a man years later, from his boyhood perhaps, and prove to have had a determining impact on the whole direction of his thinking. So it is in the whole realm of attitudes. Hayes's challenge to them to go ahead and shoot him and be over with it was not the decisive point, as developments showed, but the latter statement that came from the depths of his feelings, out of his integrity.

The brainwasher's first reaction was to rise from his chair and walk from the table. He said an amazing thing then. "We are all beginning to think that!"

Hayes, not grasping it, replied, "Really!" in a bit of an angry tone, then asked, "Think what?" Instinctively, he was driving home his advantage.

For reply the brainwasher broke into a loud laugh, a horrible guffaw. Hayes, not knowing what to make of this, felt alarmed.

"You didn't put China in your list," the indoctrinator turned to him and said.

"I caught what was in his mind at once," Hayes told me, "and he knew it! They couldn't accuse me of being a spy now, for it was obvious to them that I had not listed China because I considered it almost my own country and could not think of myself as a visitor to it."

Whether this was so or not, the brainwasher was visibly nonplussed by the turn events had taken, and the spy charges obviously had not served them as fully as they had hoped. He looked at Hayes again curiously, without smiling, and only said, "Go to your cell!" Every insight that Hayes possesses into the Chinese mind and his feeling for human nature convince him, he said to me, that the brainwasher couldn't take any more. Working for an ideology that did violence to the true character of human beings, certainly of the Chinese, he had reached the end of his tether. He exposed himself, for all his thick veneer of communism, as vulnerable!

Others, too, have told me equally revealing experiences of momentous significance. Students from the Communist Party's own universities have told me of Party functionaries, men who had participated in purge trials and indoctrination campaigns, themselves being sent back for a brainwashing. The Chinese communist prisoners of war I met who had refused to return to the Reds included a startling proportion of Party members, some of whom fit into this category. That is why the purge must be permanent in any Red society!

His release — or execution — was now only a matter of formality, Hayes was sure. He was released on September 20, 1952, and put across the border at Hong Kong exactly two weeks later.

Sitting back on a rattan chair in Singapore, he analyzed his little battle in the brain warfare that was being waged around the world. "The more I think of it," he said to me, "the surer I am that the mind is influenced to a great extent by its environment and training, but that the really decisive, controlling factor is the spirit. You can't crack that if it is sound."

I thought back over the cases I knew of the many brainwashed in the POW camps in Korea, those who had broken and those who hadn't. Without doubt, this additional force — spirit — had been the most important weapon for those who had successfully resisted. For the lack of it, others had miserably broken.

Hayes called this a "crusading spirit" and sometimes a "sense of mission." It was inextricably bound up with his Faith. He agreed that other elements were essential for mental stamina, too, and could see a man through to victory. But in a situation when the odds were piled highest against a person, his experience had proven for him that the fort which can hold out longest was a man's spirit. If he had it, he possessed the strongest possible weapon. "One phrase kept ringing in my ears all my time in prison," Hayes said. "It was, 'taking captivity captive.' In that spirit, I determined to go on the offensive, not remain on the defensive. I was going to win the enemy!" This win-the-enemy idea became an obsession to him.

He went on: "The mind, the tool of the spirit, is remarkable! There was my mind, sadly damaged. Somehow, with my mind damaged, I was still able to unsettle the court."

He discussed this with medical men in America. A San Francisco doctor told him, "Your mind gave way when you had your hallucination. That is what saved you. You were still intact, only your mind had cracked. The Reds couldn't do any more to you. The indoctrinator gave you the curious look when he saw that. He realized then they had not got you — that your spirit had escaped them."

This is what made the brainwasher feel beaten.

This was a medical man's analysis, uninfluenced by elements outside his field, certainly uninfluenced by any missionary thought. Yet on this field of battle of the mind, these two men saw eye to eye.

"The spirit never went into real action for me until that last, critical skirmish," Hayes said. "When the turn came, I was able to deliver the decisive blows. This was after my hallucination, when I found in myself the opportunity to be expendable for the lives of others, and with perfect composure I was able to say, 'All right then, go ahead and shoot me.' At that moment, I surely saved my life, probably literally, certainly all that gave it meaning."

With all the rest of his weapons knocked from his grasp, his crusading spirit held him up. He went into that last fray not concerned with defense but with offense — "to win the enemy." Whether he did so or not is anybody's guess. But he obviously rattled the foe and saved himself.

During this conversation, Hayes had let slip a remark of the utmost significance. "I knew I wasn't a spy but that I was framed by their laws," he said. I now reminded him of it.

"You've been telling me about your hallucination," I said.

"You were convinced your false memory was the real thing. Did you have any suspicion it was a hallucination before your release?"

"Exactly!" he replied at once. "I believed I had had a hallucination and I believed I hadn't."

He went on to explain that while he did not doubt the hallucination, at the same time, he also had this other belief in the back of his mind.

Perhaps this was a contradiction, but if so he hadn't noticed it. The brain apparently does not always follow the rules set down for it in books of logic.

"Is that what psychiatrists call ambivalence, the division of the brain into separate compartments?" I asked.

"I suppose so," he said, smiling.

If truth can linger in the mind in spite of the strongest hallucinations, and the evidence I have accumulated indicates it can, the reason is clear why the Reds cannot be sure of even their completest victories, their Mindszentys. They never capture their minds completely!

Chapter Four - The Negro as Pow

The Korean Miracle

In the prisoner-of-war camps in North Korea, the dark-skinned American was put on his mettle racially because the communists insisted on appealing to him as a Negro. The color of his skin was constantly emphasized as his all-important characteristic. He was pitted against his country, symbolized in the person of the white man. Every humiliation, every indignation, every betrayal of the Bill of Rights was stressed to him by the Red indoctrinators. But they failed miserably in their efforts to impress him and to gain the great propaganda victory on which they had counted to win the minds of the non-white peoples of the world.

I heard rumors about this Red propaganda setback almost as soon as the first prisoners began to be exchanged. The stage was set for the communists to drop their usual political bombshell. Editors all over the world focused on the lonely spot called Panmunjom, where "Little Switch" was taking place that cold April day in 1953. These first returnees were supposed to be only the very ill. The Reds made it a propaganda show, carefully selecting prisoners from as many different parts of America as possible. As was to be expected, the first man out was a Negro. Six out of the first group of sixteen released were Negroes, and eight out of the second batch of thirty-five. The Red emphasis was unmistakable.

The bulk of the prisoners were exchanged in "Big Switch," which took place in chilly August and September of that year, yet little was heard either time to give more than token satisfaction to the Red racist propagandists. Out of the thousands of Negroes taken prisoner, only three were among the twenty-three cowed and mentally upset lads who said they did not want to return home to America.

The communists had started publicizing pro-Red statements by dark-skinned POW's soon after the first were captured. They evidently expected these to grow into a crescendo that would reverberate throughout Asia and Africa. They were positive that the Negroes caught in the Korean fighting would be putty in their hands. Believing their own propaganda, they had every confidence that this would be the case. Instead, the blare that was started up in the beginning faded away into a few lone squeaks. I had paid little attention to this at the time because so much else was happening.

I thought of these developments one day when a newspaperman just back from the Korean front remarked that the communists were obviously disappointed over the failure of their efforts to exploit the American Negro. "How did the colored man come out in comparison with the whites?" I asked.

'Tine," he replied right off. "Some say he came out better, proportionately speaking."

Statistics were unavailable, of course, but others who made it their business to keep their ears tuned to what was going on in the POW camps told me the same thing. I did some investigating on my own, and what I discovered was incontrovertible. The Reds had dismally failed in their attempts to squeeze racist propaganda out of their colored captives. Our boys just weren't buying any of that stuff! Talking to repatriated Negroes, I found that they had seen through the enemy game right from the start — they could detect racist cheese by its smell no matter how it was camouflaged.

The communists exposed their own biased thinking soon after the POW enclosures were set up by segregating the non-whites as firmly as the most rabid anti-Negro would desire. "What for you putting us by ourselves this way?" a colored American told me he asked them.

"You're being sent to get higher education," was the cynical reply.

"Yeah man, I see!" this man exclaimed. He saw, all right — he and his buddies saw clearly enough. Those who had any doubt about it were later convinced by people such as the communist doctor in a Chinese hospital.

He thought it great fun, when he came across a Negro patient, to look baffled and say, "Tell me, are you really black, or is your face just dirty?" This bit of crass humor was considered a great joke by the Red Chinese hospital attendants, but it rapidly became known throughout the Negro compound. The effect can be imagined.

I made a point of locating returned colored prisoners so as to get their own feelings on what had transpired. What I learned from them made me very proud of the human race. None of these men, any more than any others in the U.N. forces, had received even a hint of what they were coming up against when they were sent into battle. They had not been warned about this new communist trickery. Of course the Reds had every reason to anticipate easy propaganda pickings among their captives, particularly those, such as the Negroes, who had any cause to resent their treatment as a minority.

Yet the Negroes refused to fall for this Red bait. Evidence of the enemy's hypocrisy was not the main reason, I found out. The colored people did not expect others to be angels. The real reason was twofold. First, the Negroes had them selves witnessed too much of the dreadfulness of race bias to want to have any part of it, particularly a communist variation. Second, when the chips were down, what seemed to be more decisive, the Negro realized the United States was his country and he wasn't going to do anything to hurt it. His attitude came to the surface under Red prodding; it wasn't so much a case of his belonging to America as America belonging to him, and only a fool damages what is his.

What soon became evident to me was that the U.S. had a great deal to learn from its Negro citizens faced by adversity in the POW camps. The colored man was stripped down to his naked character. This was hurled into the hottest crucible that sly, subtle minds could devise, the tortures of hell brought to earth. He came out of this test whole and with plenty to teach others. The Negro retained a far greater capacity than the white man to keep his mind focused on fundamentals. He was far more difficult to lure off the track than his white brethren. The stories of what took place in the Korean POW camps substantiate this generalization.

He had an additional quality that stood him in great stead in this supreme emergency. This quality is exemplified in Negro songs generally. They are without bitterness and without hate. I know no other people in the world of whom this can be said. Bitterness and hate are negative reactions, and sour a man. They contain a certain drive potential, but they can run away with a man and be used against him. In the long pull, as in the POW camps, the prisoner's primary objective was to protect his own faculties. He had to keep his hope up. When this was lost, so was the mind. That was why the Reds kept chiseling away every moment at his hope. He had to be totally deprived of it so he would have nowhere to turn but to the Reds. A people to whom hope — optimism — is second nature, is the toughest nut of all to crack.

The Negro had resources for survival to which he turned when most desperate. These were usually simple in nature, down to bedrock, not involved in sophistry. There was the case of a young colored boy stripped and hung head-first from the rafters in an effort to make him accede to Red demands. His body was then beaten in its most sensitive parts.

This failed to crack him. "How could he continue resisting?" I asked, for the pain must have been excruciating. Buddies of his quoted his own explanation. "When the pain got real bad, I thought of religion, and then it didn't hurt any more," he had said.

This was all he remembered, for he lost consciousness. Nature came to his rescue when the torture became unbearable. In the critical moment or two between the time when he might have been forced to agree to the Red demands and the surcease that unconsciousness gave him, the religion he had been taught as a boy monopolized his mind, crowding out everything else.

Perhaps as revealing as any other aspect of the Negro's heroic resistance to brainwashing was that he came out of camp without any idea that he had been doing anything special. He had just been himself.

Simple Things

The name of Roosevelt Lunn, of Baltimore, was given to me as that of a Negro POW who could tell me a lot about what kept a man going under adversity. People knew the neighborhood where he lived but not the house number, and it took a lot of doorbell ringing to locate him. Finally, in desperation, I stopped a man crossing the street and asked him if he had ever heard of a returned POW named Roosevelt Lunn.

"Sure I have," he replied. "I'm Roosevelt Lunn."

He took me to the home of relatives and we sat in the parlor. He was a tall, earnest man who had been a prisoner for thirty months. He was captured after an all-night fight when his detachment had run out of ammunition and came up against a roadblock. He tried to make it into the mountains but was shot in the hand. His captors marched him back downhill, making him slide on the snow, and it froze his hand.

He saw buddies to the left and right being clubbed and murdered as the Reds marched them to the rear. "That's when I got my determination I was going to live," he said. "When I saw other guys being beaten up and killed for stumbling, I said to myself, 'If it's God's will, I'm going home.' I kept this faith all the time."

They marched him for a couple of months, stopping only a few hours during the day to sleep. Then they stayed put for two or three weeks before marching again, all night and every night, and part of the day. They started out with 700 men. Two hundred made it. The other 500 were left behind as frozen corpses.

"I never had the feeling I wouldn't make it, as I always had that faith with me," Lunn said. "When I began getting a little doubtful at times, I quickly forced it out of my mind. I wouldn't let anything get the best of me."

Men died fast in his first camp. "Lice ate us up, fever burned us up," Lunn said. "They fed us half-rotten food, and after a while said to us, 'Would you like to eat well? Would you like good medical care?' Who wouldn't? They improved the chow a little, and let us play some basketball and baseball. They had a lot of sports equipment sent in and took photographs of us using them.

"Then they started talking to us, chummy like. Right off, they asked us why we were fighting. 'Because we're Americans,' we said.

" 'Your color is different, so you have no reason to fight us,' they replied.

" 'We are Americans and we believe in democracy,' we retorted.

"Then they brought us newspaper clippings about American Negroes badly treated in the U.S. 'What's happened, has happened,' we'd answer. 'We're not worrying about the past. We're looking forward to a better way of life.'

"They tried to wear us down with stories about how all Americans were supposed to be first-class citizens, while we were treated like second-class citizens. We answered back with proof that our position was getting better fast, and that there was a wonderful future ahead for both us and the whites. It was tug-of-war between their minds and ours.

"They put their educated blokes working on us, who had studied in mission schools and colleges, some in the U.S. All spoke English. Some spoke it fine. They brought us communist papers and gave us lectures. They called us out by groups and said they wanted our opinions. What did we think of their peace drive? Wouldn't it be wonderful if we all were at peace and everybody could go home? What would we suggest? Most guys just gave no opinion. Some did, and then the Reds had something to start on. They worked on those guys to break them down and to pick the men they wanted from among them.

"The best defense was to have no opinion about anything. You would say one thing out of place and they'd start messing with you right off. You had it bad from then on.

"The Reds were on the lookout for any fellow who showed signs of weakening. He was called to headquarters and they'd strike up a conversation. They'd ask some more of his opinions, this time on how the others liked it in camp, how we were acting, thinking, talking. They wanted to know everything. When this fellow came back to us, he'd be scared and shaky, but he'd let us know everything that happened.

"This was when we had to act, right at the start. We'd have a little get-together, a little conference. We'd tell him how anything he said, out of his mouth, would hurt any of us and him, too. We used a lot of proverbs in talking to him, because they're simple and plain. 'A man's most dangerous weapon is his tongue,' we'd say. 'Silence is golden,' we'd say, explaining how it could keep a man out of trouble. We wouldn't preach too much at him, just enough. Then we'd change our tack, and this was the important part.

"We'd go all the way back home with him. We'd bring back his home life. We'd do it naturally, and show a sincere interest. We could do this because we were all in the same boat. Someone among us was sure to have lived his kind of life, maybe even been his neighbor.

" 'If you weaken and break under their pressure, there'll be no way of getting out,' we'd tell him. 'If you weaken, right then and there it's going to hurt us all.'

"We learned to listen to the communists in a way that went into one ear and out the other. We learned how to do this as soon as we saw what they were up to.

"We showed those fellows examples of others who had gotten messed up by the Commies. They'd make the man their flunkey right away, and his buddies would regard him as an outcast. We used those men as examples, and we went to work on those fellows at the same time! This was good for us, too, for it kept us busy, so we wouldn't be obsessed with the Red talk.

"Someone remembered or got somewhere a copy of Kipling's poem, 'If.' We read it to each other all the time. This helped a lot, because the Reds always kept preaching this second-class citizen stuff at us. Little by little, you could see some fellow weaken, just from the awful monotony of it. He'd be pushed along by punishments. One man would be made to stand at attention for hours, holding up a heavy iron bar until he was totally exhausted. Another would be stood on the Yalu River ice with his shoes off. They'd tie a man up and let him swing from a rope while they beat him with clubs. They'd stick a fellow into a hole in the ground. They'd do anything to a man.

"We either learned to think ahead of them, watching out before getting into trouble, or take the consequences. By thinking it out, I found that I was fighting to save my life and that of my buddies, and that I was also fighting to save my country. Those were the two reasons I fought in any battle in the war.

"I learned that you can weaken a man either physically or mentally, but if he's got the determination to survive, he'll likely walk out okay. When the going got tough, no matter where, I switched my mind to the things I had back home, and I'd think about my mother. I kept living because I kept thinking about how much I had back here to live for. I learned pretty quickly, from being under the communists, that I had a democracy to live for.

"None of us had ever gone through any such experience before. We tried not to let it get the best of us, watching out for each other.

"The Reds first mixed up all the races and nationalities, thinking the men would fight between themselves," Lunn said. Then they outfoxed themselves by segregating the Negroes, exposing communist hypocrisy. "This threw us on our own resources," Lunn went on. Segregation defeated the Red scheme of depriving each individual of ties in any group that was not communist-dominated. The Negroes now were strengthened by a sense of belonging in their own organization, where the color of their skin was the sole requirement for membership.

The Reds divided the prisoners in this camp, known as No. 5, into five companies. Besides the colored, there were sections for white Americans, "special Americans," Turks, and British. "Special Americans" meant Puerto Ricans, Filipinos, Hawaiians, Japanese and Mexicans, Australians, French, and one Greek. The English, Irish, Scotch, and Welsh went into the British company. A mixed company was formed later of recently captured personnel. The set-up differed from camp to camp. The communists apparently experimented with different approaches, as all the POW's were under a co-ordinated control, with main headquarters at Pak's Palace.

"After they separated us, they began working on each group, giving each something that was supposed to be special for it alone," Lunn said. "Some say the Negroes got it best, but this wasn't so. They did the same to all in turn, taking everything away and then giving a bit back to make us think they were being kind.

"Most of all, the Reds tried not to let anyone have anything to think about except communism. That way a man lost every bit of self-confidence and went out of his mind. The only way to prevent it was to stop thinking about them. We soon realized that our main problem was to get our minds off the Commies. They tried to keep us thinking about them, worrying about what they'd want next, worrying what we should do.

"The heat was on us day and night, and they never let up a second. If we kept thinking how powerful they were and how weak we were, we'd lose hope and end up saying, 'What's the use? They'll have their way with us anyway.' We had to think hard and fast to beat that, and we couldn't be choosy. We had to use anything that would do the trick,

"You'd see a man sitting beside you. Maybe he'd been sitting that way for hours. You knew what he was thinking about, because the only comments he made were about the Commies. Maybe they had called him in for a brainwashing and told him he wasn't frank and to go out and think, just think how wrong he'd been, and to come back in a couple of days and confess. Confess! Confess what? They were always insisting on confessions, and on what they called self-criticism, and they wouldn't tell you what crimes you were supposed to be guilty of. You were supposed to figure that out yourself.

"You'd see that fellow, like I see you sitting here, and suddenly he'd go off the beam. He'd crack. Just like he was smashing up from the inside. He'd be all gone.

"He'd first look off into space for hours, and then he'd do crazy things. He'd walk out of the camp in broad daylight, going toward the river, and not have a chance in the world. We'd stop him if we saw him in time. Sometimes we had to sit out all day and night watching one fellow when he got into that state, because you never knew when he'd try to kill himself.

"When we saw the Reds were driving men crazy that way, we decided two could play at that game. I did it once myself, and helped save myself. I felt myself passing out from weakness and decided that I wasn't going to get weak for nothing. The next time they came, they found me sitting up staring into space. When they said something to me, I just kept staring. I knew how to look, because I had often seen the real thing among my buddies.

" 'The most they can do to me is kill me,' I thought to myself. 'Okay, if you want to kill me, I know you can,' I said to myself. 'If you don't want to kill me, don't mess with me.' That's the way a lot of us guys learned to take it.

"You can't just tell yourself this. You have to be in the mood. You have to face it like a soldier. You'd be surprised how often that saves a life.

"A man was in the groove when he knew that if it was in his power and was God's will that he'd be coming home, that's what he'd be doing. That's how I figured it out, and stayed by it all the time. I never let it leave my mind. I clung to it."

A minute later he added: "You have to have faith in something to make that work. If you don't, how can you get the will power to survive?

"A lot of us went on a crazy bat to get the pressure off. We played as if we were in another world. We just had to get out of our surroundings. We had to keep one step ahead of them because they had us, and we didn't have them. We had to think.

"Sometimes, when the Chinese came up, a man would get up and grin and then start laughing. He'd do so no matter what they said or did to him. He'd grin and laugh hard, for he was doing it to save his life.

"You did simple things like that to outsmart them. A man might walk round and round all the time, in an aimless way. You did the first thing that came to your mind, crazy like.

"We had to think hard to see through their tricks. We had to fall back on what we had learned from life. We had no leaders. It had to be every man for himself."

Every man had to accept the responsibility for his own survival, and at the same time had to help the next fellow, the same way as the next fellow had to help him. They had to think for themselves and for each other, not the collective way of the Reds that buried individuality, but the democratic way that broadened a man.

"We'd get our heads together when we were sitting around and pool ideas," Lunn said. "We'd do this when we went to the river to wash, or anywhere else we had the chance. We've learned from life how things meant to hurt you can be turned into a blessing. The Reds gave us only what they thought would crack us. We had to turn this to our own good. Marijuana, for instance, was growing all over the place. The Reds officially banned it, but weren't very serious about it. If it would demoralize us, they knew it would be easy to get stool pigeons among us. We had to put a stop to that. We saw what marijuana was doing to white folks. Nice fellows brought up in fine families took it because they were feeling hopeless. The marijuana completed the job for the Reds.

"Our spirits were way down. We had no medicines, no sleeping pills. We were like men with the DT's. Instead of seeing pink elephants and purple ants, we saw Reds, until we were ready to screech.

"One day we saw a fellow coming from the brainwash er looking like a ghost. He was on his way back to his hut, where he had to 'study.' He was on the verge of cracking, and when he did, he'd hurt others. He knew our secrets. We had to do something quick and it had to be good. One stool pigeon was all the Reds needed in a group.

" 'You got to get groovey,' we used to say, and, 'Get on the ball and blast.' Those words had special meanings. The Reds tricked us by using words differently than we, so we did the same. The Commies had their eyes on us and were listening. *Blast* meant to smoke marijuana. If we could get him to smoke a bit of it right now, before he cracked up, not after, it would save him from the Reds. After would be too late; it wouldn't be medicine then; it would be dope. We had to keep our timing just right.

"That's when someone first put those words into a song, like this:

> " 'In this society you got to be in class.
> You got to get groovey.
> Get on the ball and blast.' "

The tune sounded quite catching. "The fellow caught on," Lunn continued. "He carved out a bit of time for himself, free from worry over the Reds. He didn't think about a thing. He was in his own world at last. The pressure that had been put on him night and day was taken off him for the first time, and it saved him and us. The pain pressing on his brain gave way. He didn't crack."

I doubt whether any moralist could condemn this. If there had been a doctor among these POW's, he would have prescribed a sedative for a man in that condition. Nothing was available except marijuana, and the physician would have had to use that. Thrown on their own resources, this is what the men did.

Marijuana, growing all around them, was too great a temptation for men driven almost mad by mind attack. The whites, more susceptible to formalized codes of behavior, usually abstained until it was too late, so that it helped in their demoralization. Almost everyone smoked it in that pitiable group of U.N. soldiers who said they didn't want to go home.

The Golden Cross Club

Several released POW's had referred to an organization that the Negroes had formed while prisoners of the Reds. This sounded almost unbelievable, for the communists had ruthlessly ferreted out and smashed any group that wasn't a part of their network.

Yet an organization called the Golden Cross Club Against Communism was formed right under their noses. I was told it had been started by a fellow named Robert Lee Wyatt. He had been married only a week when I located him, in a small house he shared with a chum, Russell Freeman. There was nobody home except the bride when I knocked, and I waited until both men came home from work.

Freeman arrived first, wearing high rubber boots and rough workman's clothes. In the lobe of his left ear I noticed a tiny golden cross. I had seen the same in Roosevelt Lunn's ear. Freeman was a hard-chested, broad-muscled man. He and Wyatt had been buddies since 1948, and they had gone to Korea together, where they were separated. Wyatt was captured while Freeman was in a hospital. Two and a half months later. Freeman was caught, too, and they met unexpectedly in a prison camp after not having seen each other for nearly two years.

I talked to Freeman while waiting for Wyatt. He said he wore his emblem in memory of his buddies who died in camp. "What you see isn't what we had in Korea," he said. "We wore anything there, from bits of straw to a piece of tin. When we got home, we decided to keep the club going. We were very thankful for what it had done for us and didn't want to let it drop. Some of us had a small cross of gold made up. In camp, we made crosses out of anything we could get, and we knew what they were, even when they didn't look a bit like a cross. This helped us fool the Reds.

"We all pierced our ears at the same time. That way, we felt the pain less. One man did it himself, if he could, or for someone else. We used anything available, such as a rusty nail or a piece of sharpened tin. The club had no officers and no meetings, nothing the Reds could pounce on.

"The Commies only saw what was stuck in a man's ear lobe. They couldn't understand it, but we knew they represented crosses.

"We formed the club to keep up our spirits. Anyone who wanted could join. Some Filipinos and white Americans did."

Freeman was at the front six months and a prisoner thirty months. He was beaten for an hour when caught and then marched twenty miles the same night. He marched from February to May, 1951, when he contracted yellow jaundice and had a high fever. He was then thrust into the "death house."

"I prayed every day," he said. "I wouldn't let anything stop that. I based my strength on the Bible. The night I was supposed to die, I lay on my back praying and praying that the Lord would come and touch me and make me holy. He did come that night, and He was in the room with me, and I know it, and next morning, instead of being dead, I felt good, and I felt happy. I felt like I didn't have a worry in the world, and from that day on, I knew I was going to make it and come home safely."

This is as he told it, as I scribbled it fast into my notebook.

"You have to take the first step forward," he went on. "You have to have the will power and the faith. I've always had pretty good will power. When the chips are low, I never give up."

The Reds used flattery, browbeating, and their best arguments on Freeman. "Weren't you affected by what the Reds told you?" I replied.

"I never doubted my own side, from beginning to end," he replied. "They pitted men with fine educations against me, and I had to do some fast thinking. I decided that I could not believe a word they said because I couldn't trust them. That was good reason. I couldn't trust them because we were fighting them. My country was at war with them. We wouldn't have gone to war if we didn't have a good reason."

Other returned POW's told me how shaken they were by talks given by Lieutenant John S. Quinn, an Air Force officer who was taken on a tour of the camps to confess germ warfare that never happened. Quinn spoke convincingly, and had a starring role in a Red movie on the subject.

"The first time I heard him was over the 'bitch box,' " Freeman said, giving the loudspeaker its slang name. "Right off, I doubted if he was an American. They said he was an American, but how could I be sure? Then, when he was brought to us, I still couldn't know for sure. I never had any doubt that his germ-warfare talk was anything but lies. If I couldn't be sure who he was, how could I know why he was talking this way? You wouldn't believe some stranger who came and accused your best friend of something horrible without proof, would you? Then why believe such accusations against your own country? That doesn't sound like it needed much brains to figure out."

Freeman recalled some of the ways the Reds used men like Quinn to disturb the minds of their fellow Americans, sometimes even letting them chat with the other POW's after a talk, as if off the record. The Reds didn't have much to worry about, because once they had terrorized a man, he would see stool pigeons everywhere.

"At first, when they told us he confessed to dropping germs, we thought it was a Chinese who had lived in America, or maybe a Russian who dressed and talked like an American," Freeman said. "Then the Reds brought him around personally to lecture. Some of us fellows booed him, and the Chinese had to calm the boys down and take him away. In talking about him among ourselves, what interested us was what kind of treatment they had given him to make him act the way he did. As for his confession, most of us just took it for hogwash.

"Right afterwards, the Reds came down on us like a sledgehammer, to get us to confess all sorts of vicious crimes. They wanted each of us to confess to something bad. The germ-war talk was supposed to be the come-on. We decided that the way to fight this was never to admit a thing and to be always against whatever they said, no matter what. We knew they weren't interested in the truth, but only in cracking us. They tried to get a wedge into you, and then kept hammering at it until they smashed you wide open. So our line was, 'We ain't seen nothin' and we ain't heard nothin', and how can you tell somethin' if you don't know somethin'?' When we could keep to that, we were safe."

One day the Reds came to Freeman and said he was a squad leader. "Oh yeah?" he said, but he was a squad leader. He laughed, remembering this. "They fired me pretty soon, after warning me to keep quiet and keep my ideas to myself."

Wyatt came in while we were talking. He was wiry and thin, a handsome man. He had a puncture in his ear lobe, but was not wearing the cross. I told him that others said he had originated the Golden Cross Club.

"Not altogether," he replied modestly. "I had heard that there was a club called the Black Diamond. One of my buddies was beaten for being in it. The time was ripe for some anti-Red organization that could be secret, like an underground."

Freeman interrupted to say he had seen more fellows once at Fort Lewis, near Seattle, who had their ears pierced and wore a diamond in their ear lobe. "Maybe that was in the back of my mind," Wyatt remarked.

Sometime later, going over old newspaper clippings, I found an item about Pfc. Walter Chambers of Hornsburg, Pa., that quoted him as mentioning a Black Diamond Society, "an informal group of song-singing, joke-cracking colored POW's whom the Reds deemed disrupters." They used "bop" jargon to confuse the enemy.

Wyatt said that when the Reds saw the men who had been tampering with their ears, they forbade it, but were too late to prevent it. "As soon as the idea came up," he said, "we recognized how good it was. We knew we had to work fast if we were going to get away with it. The Reds just didn't want anything that looked like it might be an organization. Even with all the scrap tin and old needles we could find, we didn't have enough ear ornaments to go around. Some fellows just pierced their ears and let it go at that. Others put in bits of straw picked out of their gunny-sack matting.

"Our ears got sore. Resistance was low, and it was hard for anything to heal. Ears stayed sore a long time."

I asked him about himself.

"I was nearly dead several times," he said. "I didn't know what kept me alive. It wasn't my help and it sure wasn't any help from the Reds. At first I thought maybe I was just over average lucky. Many fellows bigger than me died. After a while, when I saw myself surviving, I felt there had to be a reason. I felt I was being kept alive for a reason. I've always believed in religion."

"Did the Red indoctrination ever make you feel there might be something in what they said?"

"I was never the least bit doubtful. I thought it out. I decided that ideas that people try to force on a man can't be too good. If they were good, they wouldn't have to force them on you. Once I made up my mind to that, and had this to test them by, no matter what they said, it went in one ear and out the other."

Freeman had been close-mouthed and wary when I first introduced myself to him, but he had gradually opened up, and when Wyatt came in, had introduced me with real cordiality. Wyatt seemed hesitant at first, but as we chatted, he became equally cordial. I asked them about this, and the reluctance of former POW's generally to talk about what they had gone through.

"There're three reasons for it," Wyatt said. "They're afraid. The fear that was put into us in those camps don't leave a man easily. They're suspicious of everyone and don't know who to trust. And they're just fed up with it. We're constantly being asked by people who don't understand what we're trying to tell them, and are mostly curious, anyway."

"The subject becomes a pain," Freeman remarked. "It's a pain in my stomach. In our book, what has happened, has happened. We don't want to talk about it if we can avoid it, because we don't want to bring it back to life. Interviews, any interviews, are now hard. After going months and months, for years, being interviewed by the Reds almost every day, any interview is like rubbing an open sore."

Then Wyatt said something that was one of the best rewards I could be given. "The only people we can talk such matters over with are those who were with us, or who had gone through such experiences," he said. "With you, it was like talking it over with a buddy who was in the camp with us."

First Man Out

I climbed upstairs to the editorial offices of the *Afro-American* in Baltimore and asked what they knew about Corporal Robert Stell, who was the first U.N. prisoner of war to be returned in "Little Switch." An editor interrupted his race against a deadline to take me to the library, where a young lady brought me several fat envelopes of clippings. However, the dispatches about Stell and the other first repatriates provoked more questions than they answered. The articles read as if the reporters had been groping for something that kept slipping out of their fingers.

I jotted down significant points about Stell:

All his toes amputated . . . compound frostbite . . . eyes still too weak for him to wear glasses . . . malnutrition from a vitamin deficiency . . . twenty months a POW . . . "The first book I learned to read was the Bible. I'm really a bookworm. My life's ambition is to go to Howard University and study philosophy, maybe become a lawyer." While in the Army he studied psychology, sociology, political economy, "and a lot of other college subjects." Only seven when his father died . . . "We lived like gypsies." He quit school and lied about his age to enlist.

His bungalow home was in the outlying Cherry Hill section of Baltimore. The house had been built for him and his mother by grateful businessmen and other citizens of the community after his old home had been razed for a housing project. He was a broad, good-looking fellow wearing thicli horn-rimmed glasses, and said he didn't want to talk. "I'm back home," he said. "I survived." I told him the reasons for my interest. "I'm through with that deal," he answered. "I don't care if nobody knows my attitude."

He said this too quickly, too neatly, for it to be the whole answer. I felt sure his insistence on silence wasn't his real feeling. I had met many of the boys who have come home from Korea, and civilians from all parts of the world who had undergone tortures of the mind. I had come to recognize a certain look, the wound showing through a man's eyes that exposed the deep injury to his soul, and his disappointment in discovering that people at home seemed not to understand.

Friends and neighbors greeted the home comer like a long-lost brother. They shook his hands affectionately and slapped him on the back. "Tell us everything that happened to you," they begged. While he was groping for words to explain this strange new experience, someone was always sure to interrupt, and with scarcely concealed curiosity ask, "Did they beat you up? Do you have any marks? Let's see them."

The only atrocities in which these people, who now seemed strangers to him, appeared interested, were those inflicted with a club. Yet the atrocities that often hurt the most and caused the most lasting wounds were inflicted without a finger being laid on the man. How was a fellow to explain this? When he tried, someone was sure to say, "Yes, you had it damned tough. I want you to know that we were rooting for you all the time, and we were sure you'd come through with flying colors. There's going to be a great wrestling match on the television in a few minutes. I . . . you wouldn't want to miss it. Come on over to the house and we'll pull up a chair for you."

I recognized some of this in Stell's face. No, it wasn't really true he didn't want to talk. When he did begin to speak — his first details were given to me an hour later — he did so with such feeling and earthly wisdom that I was awed. He had been thinking it out a great deal by himself, reading up on the psychology of it, too. His was essentially a story of how to survive brainwashing.

He said brainwashing used methods found in "mental therapy," and mentioned the simple things that could "bring a man down" and crush his reserve. "I've seen a strong man, the first time he was given a piece of candy, break down and cry," he said. This was the key to how the communists made others envious, craving for the little the Chinese possessed, "this very little that they now lacked." The tactic was absurdly simple. Fellows who had had a comfortable life, never deprived of anything, were given this treatment. They were made poorer and weaker than even the Chinese. All the Reds had to do then to earn their gratitude was to give them a tiny bit of what they had formerly had so much of.

The brainwasher who had brought a man down to this pathetic pass gave him a morsel of something that recalled his lavish past. Tears would gush forth. His gratitude would overflow like a child's.

Men who had lived simple, down-to-earth lives, who weren't afraid of going without comforts because they had done it often before, couldn't be cracked so easily.

We moved from his neat parlor with its shiny new furnishings into the kitchen, where Stell did his studying. A pile of books and notepaper scrawled over with mathematical formulas lay on top of the table. I noticed he had difficulty reading his notes. He used a magnifying glass to read. We talked a little about his hopes.

"The subconscious mind seeks a form of substitution," he said, the heavy thought startling me. He explained by parables or by incidents out of his own life. He had been self-taught by these, rather than by the books with which he surrounded himself. He gave me the example of a child left alone on the street by its mother. Some kids will insist on waiting a long, long time, while others will give up and go along with the first person who asks them. The POW's put their expectations on the return of the U.S. troops to deliver them from the Reds, he said. The fear rose, sooner with some, later with others, that they would never come.

The Reds stepped into the breach, "acting like a smart parent," he said. They used the whip, but not often. "They knew that the American prisoner had to look to them for everything, and that in this way they replaced his mother and father," Stell said. "Everyone had only rags, and nobody would share even these with you. So what did you do? If you were tortured, you couldn't take it very long because of your weakened condition. A fellow would be stood out on the ice a couple of hours a day without shoes. The Reds were devilishly patient. One day the POW would screech, 'For God's sake, don't take me out there any more. Tell me what you want me to do. Anything.' "

The Reds collected people from various walks of life into one group, and then put pressure on them all together to sign a petition or make a broadcast. They would notice the individual who first showed signs of weakening and work on him. "He might have been a stool pigeon at home, too," Stell said. "The Reds start the ball rolling by picking out such men."

Yet many did hold out, a miraculously large number, considering how they were thrown into this wolves' cavern without being given a hint of what they might find there. Sometimes the man who broke had all the advantages in brawn and brain, and frequently in rank. It depends on a man's previous feeling of security, was the way Stell explained it. "If that is still in him, his subconscious knows there is nothing the Reds can give him. The fellow who cracks never got a real sense of assurance out of his previous conditions of life. He saw nothing to live for."

He took recourse once more in parables. "Take two children," he said. "Both face the same trials of life. One is raised with love and affection and has an integrated environment. When he grows up, he already has known the satisfactions in life. Later on, when he meets hardships, he accepts them as the ups and downs of life. His subconscious, confronted with a terrifying experience, has its sense of security to fall back on. It is with him all the time, part of him. He is not a frustrated, envious man.

"The other kid doesn't get love and affection and hasn't an integrated way of life, so when he grows up he blames his hardships on the past. He breaks under pressure."

Some fellows hardly needed to be pushed. "When one type of man is suddenly brought up against political propaganda, he will grab hold of it, for it will seem to be what he's been craving for all along. He will have been waiting and waiting for someone to hand him something he can grab hold of. He doesn't much care what."

He had seen men who gave every evidence of physical and mental strength crack and die while others who appeared sick and weak lived on. Stell expressed this in his homely manner. "There's a sort of individual who dies easily," he said. "He doesn't think that his present circumstances are worth a damn or that they have anything to offer him. He never really felt life. His present experiences don't give him enough to stand up on. So he sees no alternative to his present sufferings. He got nothing firm out of the past or present. He sees nothing hopeful either way.

"He didn't get enough out of his past to make him want to survive, and his present life certainly doesn't seem worth living, so he feels. What the hell? He's ready to die. He doesn't see anything really worth living for."

Basically, Stell said, this was the lack of a feeling of security, and he stressed that what he meant was not just material security. He mentioned a fellow he used to know who had a prosperous family and all he needed, yet who became the friend of people who didn't have half of what he had. "A man can be in fine circumstances, with a big house and cows, and yet all of this might not be enough for him," he said. "The next chap might be in poor surroundings, but if his neighbors accept him and don't laugh at him, he is contented. What counts for the individual is what he considers important. That is what matters to him.

"You start out when a baby forming a condition," he said. He had given this word a special meaning to fit these exact circumstances. By *condition*, he meant an environment which included one's own self, for the human being helped form the environment of which he was a part. He meant, too, attitudes and circumstances together, everything that gives pleasure or pain, inside or outside a person. "When this is put up against other conditions, you have to be made up firm, so you can be competitive and get along," he said.

"You're not married, are you?" I asked. "No, not yet, but my experience in the POW camps, watching what men did under pressure, has given me definite ideas about raising a child." I asked him about this, so we could talk about something less tense for a few minutes, but his answer showed how his POW experiences were always with him. "I'm going to do two things for my child," he said. "I'll be his vanguard. I'll uphold his little world until he gets strong enough to take care of himself. I'll take care not to confuse him. If I said I'd do something, I'd make sure to do it. Otherwise, I would tell him I wouldn't do it. I wouldn't let the child worry, thinking he didn't know what his papa or mama was going to do. He'd know!"

He stressed these points, saying, "I'd make sure to keep from confusing him. He'd feel sure this was his little world. It wouldn't be over there, or somewhere else — anywhere else. It would be right here, where he was. He'd know that this was where he could put his trust, that he could rely on us, that we wouldn't let him down, and that we were pulling for him all the time. We'd never let him down." He said this last with particular emphasis. I had the feeling that this was what he expected of his country, too.

"The worst thing that could happen to a POW was to get the idea that there was nobody at home pulling for him," he then said. "The difference between comprehension and compassion is that the latter is understanding with feeling. The POW can know that the U.S. is where the sun shines best, that it is the finest country in the whole world, and he can know that everybody in America means him good. But unless he also has the feeling that America is mine, that a bit of it is all mine and not anybody else's, the rest doesn't count.

"If he only knows he has his own dog there that still remembers him and is his friend, that is more important to him for his chances of passing safely through hell than all the talks the President can give. It's more forceful for him, too, than the beat of all the drums in America. He has something his, just his, waiting for him to go back to. That's what counted when the chips were down. Those little things are why a man stands up or falls down, although he may not know it himself."

I referred to the disappointment the Negroes had been to the Reds. His race had been a credit to his country and the Free World at a time when the communists were sure they could shape their unsophisticated minds into any form they wished.

"The Negro is able to take a beating," Stell said simply. "He's had to graduate from a hard school — a down-to-earth school, the simple life — and he's learned not to let bad luck break his spirit. He's got immunity. He's immune to normal setbacks, and he's got the capacity to take it better than his more fortunate brethren. The communists couldn't grasp this at all. They felt the Negro was craving for something the white man had, that he wanted to copy the whites. They didn't realize that during all of his past hardships, the Negro had developed something of his own, distinctly his. If the Chinese communists had taken the Negroes seriously, they would have realized that the Negro put his own taste into everything he got from the white man. They would have known that the Negro had his own characteristics and a character of his own. Part of this character is his attachment to little things that belong essentially to him. He hasn't lost the appreciation of the little things that count the most. He can still see their value, their terrible importance."

Then, in a tone that echoed his own wonder over how it was possible for so many souls to have lost touch with it, he said suddenly, "Religion is what anybody can have." Religion was among the "little things" he referred to that didn't have to be bought and couldn't be worn like a hat. He didn't really mean they were little, but that they could be easily shared. He explained that he wasn't referring to these things in their entirety, grand and awesome and too big for any one man to hold, but the tiny share that the small man could grasp to himself. This is what meant everything to him and motivated his actions and ideas. So long as he hadn't lost sight of them, small as they might be, he had something to cling to that was the biggest thing in his world.

"This little thing the Negro has, he can take anywhere he goes, anywhere," Stell went on. "A lot of white people go to the opera, to the swankiest bars and the most expensive cafes, and eat heavy, juicy steaks as often as they wish. But the Negro is used to eating plain food. He even makes up his own songs."

Softly, to himself, he hummed a song that came out of a POW camp. Then he went on: "We all knew that everyone of us was under a great suppression. We were in sorrow, seeing our buddies dying all around us. Men then can't just sit it out, feeling sorry for themselves. They'd go mad. They have to do something about it. The only thing that could make them keep going was their spirit.

"We'd sit around and we'd see one of our buddies being called to the indoctrinator. We knew the hell he was going through. We'd sit, and then someone would start patting his knee, and others would join, and we'd all say different little things. They all added up. We made decisions that way. Little things like that developed the life within each man and among ourselves.

"Sometimes when one man said one thing and another something else, and they made sense together, we'd make a song out of it, singing the words our way. This made it even more difficult for the Reds to know what we were up to.

"I don't know where one song came from, but we'd sing it when we saw one of our fellows acting sorry for himself. We knew that wrecks a man and can kill him. We saw it happening daily. We sang:

> " 'Six months ain't no sentence,
> And two years ain't no time.
> Because me and my buddies
> Got life time here.'

"Somehow, those words cheered a fellow, bucking him up."

He returned to talking about faith. "Religion came as a natural thing, served as a means of entertainment as well as service," he said, sorting out his ideas carefully.

"Religion with the white man was something he found in church. He went to church to find religion, and he had someone teach it to him there. Religion for a Negro is something he can live. He lived it every day in camp. He lived it no different there than at home. He can work hard back home, and feeling tired and beat up, look up at the sky and exclaim, 'Old Man, You sure am working me today.' Or he can look up and say, 'Oh Lord, this am sproutin' time, lighten up, lighten up!' meaning lighten my burden. This can happen any day. There's nothing difficult about it if it's the way you truly feel. That was the personal, man-to-Man religion — each man and his God — that we took to the POW camps. How could the Reds take that away from us? They were helpless against it.

"White men had formal religion. When they felt dizzy from what the Reds were doing to them, they might stop and say a prayer, or even get on their knees and pray, as a very formal thing. You need time and place for that.

"Not so with us. With us, it's all part of life. With the whites, it was something in a separate compartment of their minds, all alone by itself, left there to be taken out for special occasions in nice Sunday clothes.

"Some fellows had crosses and prayer beads with them, but the Reds wouldn't let them keep them and wouldn't let them have religious services, either. When the communists took away their crosses, hymnals, and other religious symbols and aids, and banned their church services, they had taken their religion clean away from them. They hadn't any left."

Those words stunned me and I thought of the instances I knew of white men whose experiences contradicted what Stell said. But when I thought over the details of POW camp life generally, as I had heard them from many lips, I had to recognize that he was largely right. Many times in the future, while interviewing others, I was to think back on what Stell had said, for what these persons said usually checked up with what he had told me. Exceptions were noble and inspiring, but they were for the most part exceptions.

What Stell was referring to was a religious sense that was as natural to a man as his hand, and for which he required no exterior aids whatsoever. I found that the formality of religion and its emblems had replaced the quality in it for a tragic number of people. They lost touch.

Stell went on: "This wasn't so with the Negro. He could be out cutting wood or drawing water and look up toward heaven wherever he was, and have his own private religious service any time he wanted, day or night. If the job was extra hard or the cold extra freezing, he would say, 'Old Man, You sure am acting up today!' When you feel that close to God, you are terribly strong. Nothing on earth can lick you. This close friendship with one's own God was what the white man seemed to have lost, and it showed up in the POW camps."

Again I thought that his generalization was too sweeping, but as I recalled specific cases I felt there was much, much more truth than otherwise in it. I had to admit to myself, too, that I had not met many white men who could chat in this casual, intimate fashion with the Deity. For most, it would have been sacrilegious, for they simply did not possess that close feeling. Stell had hit upon a factor in basic attitudes of the utmost significance.

After a spell of introspective thinking, Stell suddenly said, "Religion is part of the training I'd give my baby. The Negro has always had to rely on God more than the white man. If the Negro had no God, he had nowhere else to go. What makes you appreciate something is your need for it, and you must learn by experience that it is there with you, waiting for you whenever you need it."

He sat meditating a bit again before he said: "It isn't that I appreciate hardships or like to suffer. The average Negro thinks the same about that as anyone else. We wouldn't like to have to call on God as much as we do. But we've learned how to do it from having to, and it sure stood by us in Korea.'*

Chapter Five - Camp Life

Herb Marlatt

Herb — Army Captain Herbert E. Marlatt — was standing at the door of his parents' home in Detroit in his bathrobe when I first saw him. As it was night when I arrived, the house was lighted up like a beacon to make sure I didn't miss it. He signaled my taxi. Then I noted his handsome, boyish face and his natural, friendly look which gave an impression of recovery.

Yet he had been in bed all day at the doctor's orders because his nerves were still raw from his Korean experience and any little thing caused short circuits all over his body. 1 learned this from his father, a short, stocky man who was the type of highly skilled technician around which American industry has been built.

Later that night, when I caught Herb's profile as he talked, I noticed the tenseness in his lips and the look of convalescence about him. The strain and marks of his long POW siege were still on him. I had further evidence of that a few weeks later when I visited him at the military hospital on the enormous Selfridge Air Base at Mt. Clemens, Michigan.

He had gone there to have a lump cut from his back, a souvenir of camp brutality. The army surgeon hadn't known his story, and when he looked at his back, he exclaimed at once, "Looks like you took quite a beating!" He was right. The lump marked the spot where the Reds most often beat their prisoners with clubs and kicked them. They had beat him often, in irritation over his failure to break. The jellied flesh had developed into a tumor. Herb showed his determined character by getting out of his sickbed that noon and appearing, again in his bathrobe, at the Officers' Mess where I was address-ing the local Lions Club.

We sat up until well after midnight on that first visit. Korea had given him a sense of mission. Indeed, the most characteristic trait of men and women of all stations of life, military and civilian, who have come safely out of a rigor-ous brainwashing is this sense of mission. As I came to know him, I found there was something even more specific in it. His own survival could un-doubtedly be attributed to it. Survival for a purpose made all the difference in the world.

He explained how this had come about in his case. He had seen three-quarters of the men around him perish. He was in the Death March under North Korea's "Tiger," when any man who faltered was battered over the skull and shoved or kicked off the road, to become one more corpse among the hundreds. Herb saw men summarily executed for the crime of being sick or wounded. Men marched shoeless, in cotton clothes, so all down the line limbs were freezing and gangrene spreading unchecked.

They were long weeks on the march. "Whether you lived or died became immaterial even to yourself," Herb said to me. "That you would live seemed impossible. Death was a welcome release from those horrors. When a man's knees faltered or he stumbled, he hoped in his misery that the blow would land on his head quickly, as he had seen it fall on others, and put him to sleep, too, ending all those tortures. We never imagined a human being could stand so much suffering.

" 'Why should anyone go on with it?' This thought came to plenty of men. What seemed certain was that you were going to die. Why delay it when each intervening moment would be dragged out timelessly by pain?

"This was the state of mind of the remnants who dragged themselves to-ward the first permanent camp. Then one man spoke up. He was John J. Dunn, who had served in the Burma jungle with Merrill's Marauders. His voice was angry. There was no despair in him; he was all rage.

" 'Those so-and-so so-and-so's!' he cried. 'They're sheer evil' " — the actu-al expletives he used can be imagined. " 'They will never listen to any reason except force! Their kind of viciousness has to be wiped out on a battlefield. It won't ever be solved at a conference table; it can only be cut out, like a can-cer!'

"Then he became silent, and after a couple of moments, as if inspired, ex-claimed, 'By God, men! That's why we're here. When that day comes, and we meet communism on the battlefield, our country will be in need of people who have seen its face and know what it is. Of course that's why we're here! That's why we have to survive, so we can go home and let our people know. We must survive; that's our job now!'

"When we heard that, it was as if we had been given a shot in the arm. We had a purpose now. There was meaning to our suffering. Whereas the moment before we had hoped for death, feeling the hopelessness of our plight, now we knew we had to survive.

"The entire environment was changed by Dunn's words, transformed from a meaningless morass into a struggle in which we were privileged to be a part.

"Many who would have died, lived, for they had been given a reason to survive that was incalculably more powerful than the pains we were suffering.

"The men were now certain that they were in on the ground floor of what was actually a phase of World War III. From that time on, Dunn kept stressing to the men that they must regard their captivity as a tremendously important opportunity to understand and interpret the Chinese communist mind and to find out the most effective ways of reacting to the Reds and their environment.

" 'We can succeed in our job only if we get out of here alive,' he kept saying. Everyone now focused on probing what the Reds were up to, not allowing themselves to be taken in by trickery. Instead of being discouraged by the enemy's pressures and being caught off balance, they met each blow with eagerness. They discounted the Red propaganda right from the start." Herb was positive that those in his regiment who survived did so because of Dunn's inspiration.

"How did this actually save lives?" I asked. For reply, he told me another experience. "More than once," he said, "I've seen a man sit down in front of his tin of boiled corn or washed-out sorghum in the morning and stare at it. He'd just sit and stare. He had perhaps survived better than others. His physique certainly looked better. Maybe some of the others could hardly drag a frostbitten leg across the ground. Perhaps, too, his education was better than those sitting at the table.

"I'd hear him mutter to himself, 'I can't take it any more. I just can't take it.' Before the day was ended, you'd hear the death rattle in his throat and he'd be dead.

"The fellow sitting next to him, weaker and less educated and perhaps even less privileged than he, maybe sick, too, would grit his teeth a little more and take anything that came his way, determined he'd leave alive. Curious, but that type of fellow most often did."

When a man's spirit died, it killed the rest of him! This was what Herb and countless of his buddies learned in the POW camps. Some knew it before and it helped them survive.

"Call it coincidence, call it anything you want, I'm just telling you what I saw with my own eyes," Herb said. Then he related the most thrilling adventure story I had ever heard.

This was the softening-up period when men were perishing everywhere. Death lived among the men, choosing first one, then the other, indiscriminately. The freeze was so intense that no effort was made to bury anyone.

Rivers were indistinguishable from land, and trucks and tanks could cross without impediment at any point. Bodies were just carried out and dumped, already stiff, for it was almost as cold indoors as out.

Herb was a normal young man, as typically American as the frame house in which he had been brought up. The unrelenting mind pressures, after the rigorous Death March, naturally slowed him up. He found he wasn't thinking as fast as before. A fog seemed settling over him. This situation was entirely new to him, but he saw through enough of it to realize that he had to keep his eyes on the ball as never before. He understood one point very clearly. This was that if he ceased being able to distinguish clearly between his interests and those of the Commies, they would use him for their purposes before he knew what he was doing.

The routine was deadly, especially watching the bodies of those he had accompanied in laughter and in horror being carted out like logs of wood. Each man saw himself in that position. One morning Herb did a daring thing. He didn't think ahead on it, but he did it deliberately. When he woke up he saw two more bodies. He had spoken to each of the two men only a few hours before. Now they were bodies. They were dumped by the door and would be lifted out very shortly, unceremoniously, as was the rule.

Herb was not an ostentatious young man. He wasn't the type to make a show of his religion. But this time, as if it were the most natural thing in the world, he walked over to where those two bodies lay and recited a simple prayer over them.

He simply stood over them and, out loud, not loudly, recited the simple prayer. The men knew what he was doing because the room became very quiet. The Reds became furious. Any indication of religious ceremony sent them into a frenzy. Herb's act had been sheer defiance. He had known it. They called his act a crime and thought up a punishment to fit it. They forced him to stand under a corner of the tiled roof while they poured buckets of ice water down its ledge. The water fell over him, a freezing shower.

This was as excruciatingly painful as being caked in ice. The water began freezing almost as it fell. What happened then he never found out. The intervening six weeks were a complete blank to him. All he knows is that he began to come out of his coma about a month and a half later.

If this had been all, it would have been dreadful enough, but it was only the introduction. The first part had to do with a blow he received from the outside. The second part was the struggle waged inside him. He had kept control of himself by keeping his mind off his troubles, by thinking about his family and the lovely times they had had together. He tried to resume this after awakening from his icy shower.

"I found that I couldn't recall the name of an old uncle of mine," Herb told me. "I thought this was peculiar, but I didn't worry about it and went on to some other recollections. That is when real terror struck me. The names of those other relatives had left me, too. Who was the man on whose knee I used to rock? I had known his name as well as my own. Now I couldn't remember it. For the life of me, I couldn't remember it.

"I don't believe it is possible to fully convey to others who haven't experienced anything like this the fright it gave me. If I couldn't remember such simple facts as the names of my relatives, what resistance did my mind have left? This was a time when the Reds were watching like hawks, taking advantage of every slip a man made. They'd have soon caught on that something was wrong with my memory. That's what they were watching most.

"I had been raised, I suppose, like most children. As a little boy, my mother had taught me to recite the Lord's Prayer. I used to recite it before flopping into bed at night. That was my childhood habit, and I had continued it for years. The words were as familiar to me as my own name. In desperation now, unable to remember the names of my closest relatives, I turned to God to help me. This time I knew I was all alone, with nowhere else to turn — except to the communists, who were waiting patiently and expectantly.

" 'My God, help me,' I prayed, and instinctively turned to the Lord's Prayer, as I had done as a boy. This had always been a comfort. I opened my mouth; but the words didn't come out. I had lost them! They were gone, and my mind panicked. Yet I could no more recall them than walk out of that camp to freedom.

"I knew this was my last chance. They could do whatever they wanted to me now. I began the greatest struggle of my life. I fought to recover the Lord's Prayer before the Reds put the heat on me again.

"I'd struggle a whole day to get back those words, and by the time I fell asleep, terribly worn out, I'd have recovered maybe one of them, just one little word. That let me know I was on the road back. I fell asleep content then and woke up refreshed. Although I had only a few hours of sleep, I'd wake up eager to resume the fight. I was desperate!

"This was the fiercest battle I ever fought. I knew what it was to tire out my muscles in a game or a struggle so that they pained terribly. That was nothing compared to the agony in my mind as I struggled to remember that short, familiar verse from the Bible.

"This effort continued for half a month. Then I won the battle. I recaptured all the words of the Lord's Prayer. With them, I got back the names of all my relatives. That victory was my turning point. I now knew that the Reds would never win my mind, never so long as a breath remained in me. I had licked them. I had beaten them in this decisive battle and no other struggle could ever hold the same terrors for me. I could beat them again and again now."

Herb did not minimize the effect of mind attack. "We could no longer think as human beings," he said. "All we survived on were our convictions. As the pressure increased, they boiled down to just one, the religious conviction.

"When the body deteriorates, only the spirit can maintain life. A strong moral structure is essential, and its foundation has to be belief in a supreme being. I know from my own experience that the spirit is real. This spiritual strength brought me safely into port."

The communists used every artifice, no matter how crude, to corrode the spirit. Captives were kept in horribly overcrowded cells, ill with amebic dysentery and other foul diseases, forced to live in their own filth. The guards then taunted the helpless men for being "dirty," and kicked and beat them.

"Unless a man had convictions, this left him completely defenseless, without weapons to fight back," Herb said.

His mother sat on the couch listening intently to every word her son uttered, sadness and pride in her eyes. She might have posed for Whistler's painting. A big shaggy dog brushed in and out, as if on guard, squatting at her feet. Her husband, on a rocker on the other side of the room, with deep, kindly insight, had bought it for her when it was a pup, soon after they heard of their son's disappearance into the emptiness of Red territory. Mrs. Marlatt used to tiptoe downstairs in her nightgown when she thought her husband was fast asleep. He pretended not to notice. The dog would follow, and she would sit up most of the night worrying over her boy, praying for him.

"I was given my convictions by my parents," he told me. "Because of what they taught me, I knew that my sufferings were for a good cause, no matter what was done to me. I believed sincerely, and this faith sustained me."

He had not been afraid to die, he said. The communists had made death a familiar, even a homely figure. People were dying all around him. Dying didn't seem hard at all. Living was much more difficult and took all one's inner strength.

Herb was one of those to whose integrity the Reds gave witness by branding them as "reactionaries," trying to hold them back as "conspirators against peace" when the other POW's were being released.

Some time later, talking to a campmate of his, I asked how Herb was doing. "He's just had a second operation on his back," he told me. "He's okay now — I think. But you can never be sure. The effects of those clubbings keep turning up when no trace is left and you think it's all faded into the past."

Then he told me an anecdote that Herb had been too modest to mention. Herb was out on a wood detail guarded by a Korean Red of about fourteen, in uniform and carrying a rifle. Some Korean gals came by and the boy began to give Herb a hard time, showing off.

Herb took it all patiently until he couldn't stand it any longer. Then he coolly laid down the heavy log he was carrying, walked over to the youth, took the gun away from him, laid him over his knee and spanked him. Just spanked him! Soldiering was forgotten and this fellow became the bawling kid he was. The girls, stunned for a moment, burst out laughing. A Korean officer, hearing the tumult, came over with a mean look, but couldn't help himself. He started laughing, too. This relieved the tension, although it was a time when they were shooting people for no reason at all.

Zach Dean

The cat-and-mouse game that the Reds played with a man's mind was vividly described by Captain Zach W. Dean of the U.S. Air Force. He was an oil-field engineer from Oklahoma, with deep-set eyes. When I asked him how long he had been a prisoner, he said, "Two years and four days." I almost expected him to add the hours and minutes.

"The Reds brought you to the point of death and then they revived you," Zach said. "Then again they brought you to death's door, and when you were about to enter, they pulled you back."

He gazed at me, hesitating to go on. "You may not believe what I'm going to tell you," he said, "but after the Reds did this a few times, you were thankful to them for saving your life.

"You lost your sense of proportion and forgot that they were the ones who had almost killed you by starving you, not letting you sleep, beating you. You only knew that when you were about to die, they saved you. They did this often enough for it to consume your whole thinking process, until you were grateful enough to do anything they wanted."

He stopped again for a few moments, and I could see he was peering into that horrible past, maybe to the hole, into which he and Frank Noel, the fifty-three-year-old Associated Press photographer, had been kept in isolation for six weeks as a punishment for trying to escape.

Dean frequently referred to the way the communists seemed to know everything that took place in the camps. "We could keep nothing from them," he exclaimed, and it was plain to see what terrifying effect this impression had on him. The illusion of knowing everything was one of communism's most powerful weapons. In some POW camps the Reds made it more than an illusion — they did find out everything. A few weaklings or "progressives" made it possible.

The effect was to discourage men from plotting to escape or anything else because they took it for granted that before they could put any plan into operation, the enemy would know all about it. This led them to distrust each other. The Reds publicized enough examples of people betraying their relatives and friends to make everyone afraid to take another into his confidence. One Chinese camp official bragged that he had betrayed his father to the authorities. He was shaven headed, so the British nicknamed him "Head the Ball" — a soccer term for intercepting the ball with one's head. ' As people cannot keep themselves bottled up this way, the Communist Party offered its own broad bosom for these frustrated, unhappy individuals to sob out their innermost yearnings and secrets, coaxing them to "be frank." Everyone heard those two words again and again; they were reiterated constantly at each of the hundreds of thousands of "democratic discussion meetings" held throughout the Red areas. The guards as well as the captives they watched had to attend such meetings, where they were incessantly urged to "be frank." Every variation of appeal, from self-interest to fear, was used for this.

"You couldn't trust a single person," Zach kept saying. "The way the Reds got hold of almost every scrap of information was eerie."

Yet it was evident that the Reds themselves had built up this illusion. They didn't know everything, by a long shot! Zach's own experience showed it! "A small group of Masons remained intact during their own captivity," he told me. "The Reds never found out." The mere knowledge that they were able to keep this group in existence was a tremendous boost to the morale of its members. Zach stressed that these men, strengthened by this proof that the Reds were not supermen, maintained a good record against crack-ups.

"How were the Reds able to keep up this fiction of omniscience when such a startling secret could be kept?" I asked him.

"Curious, but they did," he mused. "Most fellows didn't know the secrets the Reds couldn't find out, but they did hear of the secrets the communists did manage to learn. If we had been able to get a clearer picture, if somehow information of this sort could have been gotten to us, we would have been much more daring. We could have put over some of the stunts we thought up but didn't dare mention to a buddy or try out because we had lost hope about keeping anything secret.

"Come to think of it," Zach went on, "there was another important secret they never learned. Lieutenant Harrison, who was released by them early in the exchange, would have been held back if the communists had known who he was." He was Thomas D. Harrison, the cousin of the head of the Allied team that negotiated the Korean cease-fire! "Many of us knew it," Zach went on, "yet nobody mentioned it to the Reds."

If the communists had not built up this reputation that they knew everything, the Free World would not have ended the war with practically no escapes. Few attempts were made; the men didn't dare. In some cases, Koreans made their way to the POW camps in the north and contacted American prisoners, saying, "Come along with us; we'll lead you back to your own lines." They were afraid to take the chance. Their trust in humanity had been shattered. They were "too smart" to be trapped this way. Some said, "Why take a chance? I'm going to get out with a whole skin." They were confident release would come in time. The others were just hopeless because no hint ever came from new prisoners that the outside world welcomed such daring. Any rescue effort would have electrified the spirits of all the captives.

Zach was one of the ex-POW's who told me, "I never doubted for a second that I would be free again. I didn't know how it would come about, but I was perfectly at ease about it happening."

The Reds were able to break a man's mind only when they accomplished two things, he said. They had to deprive him of clarity of thought and upset his sense of values. Zach saw men give up their lives for a cigarette. "I saw them starving to death," he told me. "Yet they secretly gave away the tiny portions of food they got in exchange for a butt. They must have known they'd die without the wee bit of nourishment they were getting. Yet they insisted they couldn't go without nicotine."

Frank Noel

Press photographer Frank Noel belonged to a profession which possessed a tremendous propaganda potential to the Reds. They persistently tried to use him, but he had learned about communist duplicity in East Germany where he covered the arrival of Gerhart Eisler, the top Red agent who broke bail and fled from the U.S., and in Yugoslavia, before Tito's break with the Kremlin, where he covered the purge trials.

Frank was captured on November 29, 1950, but he snapped his first picture as a POW more than a year later, in mid-January of 1952. In the next ten months, until November, he took 350 photos, 300 of which were sent abroad by the communists. He was kept in a Korean house for the first year and a half, alone except for a Chinese who stuck to him like a leech, sleeping in a room at the side. When Frank took pictures, the Chinese went along. They had to return by nightfall, and Frank was never allowed to talk to a POW except in the presence of this Chinese.

The communists were most anxious that he make composite photos, superimposing one picture over another to give the effect they wanted. Zach was the first to tell me that Frank's continued refusal to do so was what kept him in the hole for forty-two days with him after their futile escape plot. Frank would have been released from the pit the minute he gave in.

"I doubt whether any man knows his wife's attitudes and background better than Frank and I know each other's," Zach told me. "You can't be stuck in a tight earthen cell with another man for that time and not know everything there is to know about him. The Reds tried every sort of bribery on him. The hole in which they put us was almost as dark during the day as at night. Yet we managed to play checkers with bits of torn paper. When we weren't doing that, we just sat and talked."

Both were put into the hole on several occasions, but only once together. Frank received many other punishments, such as being forced to stand at attention for long periods barefoot on the frozen sod.

Soon after his capture, Frank was put into discussion meetings, but these abruptly ended for him after he took advantage of what he had learned about communism to point out contradictions and political errors. He could get away with this because he knew how anxious the Reds were to use him to photograph germ-warfare exhibits. He stubbornly refused to do so, and succeeded in outmaneuvering their pressure until the truce saved him.

The negotiations for him to have a camera were conducted through Wilbur Burchett, the turncoat Australian. Burchett's sly, calculatingly sympathetic approach fooled many POW's. He and the revolting English communist reporter, Alan Winnington, helped edit self-criticisms and confessions which turned innocent men into renegades like themselves.

These two used their credentials as newspaper correspondents in the truce area to act as semi-official communist spokesmen and as Red spies. Their propaganda output for the Red press was rewritten by the Peking authorities at will, and was printed abroad only by the communist press or quoted by others when they wanted to explain the Red position.

Frank saw some of Burchett's articles in the *Shanghai Evening News*, the only English-language paper on the Chinese mainland, which was promptly suspended — the need for it no longer existed — with the departure of the POW's. Frank one day rubbed Burchett where it hurt, for he evidently was suffering from a frustration complex. "Can't you write any better than that?" Frank asked, reading one of Burchett's pieces.

"Sure I can, but Peking changes it," Burchett snapped back.

When a prisoner was in an agony of loneliness, aching to see another white man, or browbeaten so that he felt utterly helpless, Winnington or Burchett would show up, as if by chance. Burchett was more skilled at creating a sympathetic front, for Winnington was unable to conceal the bitterness eating his insides. Burchett would bustle about at once to make the fellow's lot a bit better, offering to assist him in whatever was giving him trouble. Usually he would discover that the difficulty was a touchy point in a self-criticism or confession. "You're not a writer and I am, so I'll fix it up for you," he'd say. He'd fix it up, all right! The poor prisoner would be edged delicately toward treason. Burchett was an old hand at this. No more lying, slanderous books ever have been written than those about America by him and Winnington.

Burchett had met Frank before, while on assignments in East Germany, Yugoslavia, and Chungking. When the Reds started their germ-warfare hoax, it was Burchett who appeared in the truce area and "leaked it" to the newsmen.

He appeared before Frank one day and suggested that "a lot of good could be done for the families of the POW's" if the American cameraman would photograph their captured sons so the pictures could be sent abroad.

The Reds had plenty of their own photographers busily snapping as many propaganda pictures as possible. The POW's had learned to warn each other by mumbling, "Watch out for Desperate Dan the cameraman," whenever one of these would suddenly appear, for instance, at the rare religious service allowed by the Reds for this purpose.

Frank saw through Burchett's suggestion and decided to use it to his own advantage. He could sneak strategic background and other intelligence into the photographs. He was aware of the Red maneuver to suck him into their network. In the resultant tussle between himself and them, he was confident he was the winner.

In his Texas drawl, he told me he was able to get a peculiarly shaped ridge into one photo and a distinctive hill into another that identified camp areas unknown to the U.N. Command. This was a time when the communists were softening up POW's by telling them that their countries were ruthlessly bombing them, while persistent efforts by the Free World to find out the location of the camps were being frustrated in every possible way.

The dickering over Frank's camera lasted about a year. Finally the Reds allowed one to be relayed to him by foreign correspondents at Panmunjom. "I was very eager to get hold of a camera, because I was positive I could do a job for my own country that way," he told me. "But I pretended I didn't want it, and even after I had it I kept telling the Reds to take it away. Whenever they pressed me to take a picture that had a propaganda slant to it, I'd say, 'I told you to take this darned machine away. I never asked for it, and I'd rather not have it.' Actually, I was terribly afraid they might do so.

"Because of this attitude of mine, before the camera arrived, Burchett wrote me a letter saying I would not be forced to snap anything I didn't want, and that everything I did was voluntary. This was Red double-talk, but I beat it by giving it my own slant. That letter became my most valued possession.

"Whenever anyone tried to interfere with the way I was taking a picture, or whenever they tried to get me to take one of their fake propaganda scenes, I'd pull out this letter and say, 'I don't have to do it. Here's a letter from Burchett saying so. He ranks higher than you do in the Communist Party.'" Frank was quite ignorant where Burchett ranked in the Red network, but it must have been high, as his signature was always effective.

"After such incidents, they always laid off me for a while," Frank reminisced.

He figured out that the Reds needed him alive, and gambled on it. When they threw some extra heavy chips into the pot, he knew he had to meet them or give up the stakes. Both sides played for keeps. I do not believe that a gamble such as this can be safely taken in future combat. Backgrounds in photos can be faked, with very adverse results for the foe. The enemy will be better prepared next time to exploit such a channel.

But Frank Noel, who had been with the Marines when caught, and who could have been given the works for having helped these sea-soldiers carry ammunition in defiance of his civilian status, used his brains in a way that kept them from being washed.

Robert Wilkins

Robert Wilkins was given the works, yet he came out intact in body and soul. He was a master technical sergeant, a specialist whose mind was filled with the details the Reds wanted so desperately. They finally had to brand him a reactionary. He wasn't merely a reactionary, he was incorrigible.

He proved it by selling automobiles while a prisoner. Appropriately, he came from Detroit, a city the communists detested because its workers owned their homes and drove their own cars, making them "capitalists," turning the conventional Red language of class warfare into utter nonsense.

Wilkins planned to be a musician, but joined the Air Force instead, going to Europe as a tail gunner. He thought his war days were over when he was demobilized in 1945, and lost little time finding a wife and a job as an auto salesman. They were expecting their second child when he was recalled into service. He helped ferry the first American warplanes to Indo-China. Soon he was flying into Korea, sometimes on four or five missions daily, in B-26 light bombers. These were all low-level attacks in mountainous terrain, without radar or oxygen, with only six hours' fuel.

"This was far more hazardous flying than in Europe," Bob recalled. "Planes that should have been condemned after 1,500 hours were taken out of moth-balls and were still flying after 2,000 hours. We screamed for more new planes and replacements. We got only replacements, and even those were old. We borrowed planes from other squadrons so we could stay in the air.

"They had a right to call men such as me out of the inactive reserve, alt-hough this was poor planning. Others were available, but they had no time to hunt them up. This was understandable. The boys felt, though, that they shouldn't have been put to unnecessary dangers because of inadequate equipment. There was no excuse for this in a rich country like ours. This made men think they were expendable because of a slip-up somewhere else, and it hurt morale.

"Another blow to the men called back was the lack of discipline we found among those in regular service in Japan. You had to go into town to hunt up your crews, who were shacked up with Japanese girls. They were ready to do their duty, but discipline was shot to pieces by the soft life in Japan. When they returned from a mission, their only thought was to get back to their girls. They didn't even wait to clean their guns. These men, flying combat themselves, were not worried about their guns not firing properly in an emergency, and they didn't bother to put them into shape for the next man, either. We screamed some more, and then some of us reserves were put in charge of gunnery.

"What was just as serious, if not more so, was that we weren't told any-thing about the type of war we were fighting. We were just given planes of a sort and told where to strike. We had no idea why we were fighting in Korea, and we weren't told anything about the communists. I had to become a pris-oner of war after fifty missions to realize why we had to fight them.

"Despite all the lies and twisted facts the Reds told us in their indoctrina-tion lectures, we still got a better all-around picture of the world situation from them than from our own people! What we found out from the Reds themselves proved to us that they were our all-out enemy and justified every bit of fighting we were doing against them. What a wonderful boost for morale it would have been if we could have learned that from our own side, instead of having to wait until we were captured by the Reds to find out how rotten they were and how right we were."

Bob's plane was making a strafing run when the hills on both sides suddenly spewed lead and steel from concealed gun positions. Shrapnel gashed the top of his head and hit him in the leg. He bailed out, and while floating to earth heard the nearby village blow up from salvoed bombs. As he touched earth, his plane exploded against a hillside.

"I found cover in shrubs and trees. But as I took off my chute and hid it away, I felt millions of eyes watching me," he said. "I hot-footed it into the mountains and started climbing. Behind me, I heard shouting and jabbering. I caught sight of guerrilla patrols coming up. They spotted me at the same time and fired. I fired back. This went on in American Indian style for some little time.

"A shot came from the side and then another from farther up. I began to feel exposed. A shot hit the rock near where I was crouching. I saw them closing in, coming from the back of the hill. I hadn't thought of that! I gave myself up then, intending to make an obvious escape attempt if they got too rough, forcing them to shoot me. I expected to be shot or killed anyway. I raised my hands as they came up and disarmed me, taking everything I had except my flight suit.

"A big crowd of Korean civilians was waiting in an ugly mood at the bottom of the hill. They tried to grab me, but two Korean guerrillas protected me, although they knocked me down several times. The leader came running up, absolutely infuriated. His face was contorted, and he knocked me down and shoved me about. Finally he pointed his rifle at me and motioned to the crowd to move back. He meant to kill me then and there. At that moment four soldiers came pushing through and started arguing with him. I found out later they were Chinese. After a hot argument, the Chinese got back my shoes and motioned me to go with them, two in front and two behind. They didn't give me my shoes, but marched me barefoot all night to their command post, where a Chinese officer spoke American English.

"I was told they had saved me for questioning, but that feeling was so high among the Koreans who lived in the destroyed village that they might have to hand me back. They would try to save my life by negotiating with them, they promised. Then they started questioning me. Afterwards, they tied my hands and led me back toward the village.

"The Koreans were all out, squatting and standing around a big fire. I was marched through the crowd and made to squat near the flames, with a Chinese guard standing over me. The Koreans started beating their tom-toms and drums. I remember thinking about a Gary Cooper movie in which he is strung up and the Indians are about to execute him.

"A Korean girl stood in the middle of the circle and did a posture dance until she fell on her face, exhausted. A man jumped into the circle and resumed the dancing, chanting at the same time, pointing at me and then at the girl, who was lying prostrate. The crowd became deadly silent. I heard muttering and was afraid it would get out of hand. Whole families were sitting there. I lost all sense of time. Suddenly everything stopped, and the people calmly got up and started strolling away. The Chinese guard reappeared and led me back to the command post.

"The officer there said he had conducted negotiations for me with the Koreans, and they had agreed to hand me over to him after condemning me to death as a war criminal. This saved their face. How much of this was true and how much an act to make me give in I don't know. Probably a bit of both. Anyway, they questioned me for a whole day, and then my shoes were returned and I was taken away.

"After several days of marching, I was put into Bean Camp, a group of long buildings with metal roofs and no markings. This was on the main Red supply route, not far out of Pyongyang, and had been strafed the night before. They had just finished burying a number of American POW's as I came up. Another American and two British officers who had tried to escape had just been brought in.

"Later the four of us decided on a desperate escape attempt. Two others came along, including a young pilot who was terribly depressed. We traveled all night, and hid the next day in a cave during a heavy rain. We had only two containers of water and a small bag of pulverized soybeans that we called bug dust. We had to drink water to get it down. Our first mistake was trying to go too far too quickly, up and down the hills and through the underbrush, forgetting about our lack of food and weakened vitality. We were cold and wet.

"Utterly exhausted, after two nights and three days of this, we broke our resolution not to go near a Korean house. We saw one up on a hill and went into it. Only women and a few kids were in it. We asked for something to eat and I lay down. In a little while a shot came through the wall, then more. We were like six mice in a cage, moving about on all fours with nowhere to hide. I had on my flight suit. I had tried to trade it off to others in the camp, but had failed, although they were in rags. The Reds had aroused the fury of the villagers by telling them that all their troubles came from the American airmen, and they were hot on our trail. The British officer had given me a beret, the private a pullover, and both had briefed me on a Centurion tank, so I could pass as a British tanker.

"Our new captors, who were Korean guerrillas, waited for nightfall and then marched us to a police station. I squatted in a corner, crossing my legs to cover the zippers of my pilot suit. The British officer was the only one questioned and he covered up for me. Just then the town was bombed, and the Korean police looked at us with blood in their eyes. Afterwards, we were taken to an old mine shaft that had been made into a prison. It was so crowded with Korean civilians that we took turns sleeping, a half-hour each. The floor on which we lay was soaking wet and water kept dripping from the ceiling. The Koreans were taken out and worked in the daytime to the point of exhaustion.

"We were kept there a few days until Chinese guards came to get us. We were tied to each other and led along a deserted road. When we got back to camp, the commander said we'd be shot, and made us kneel. He first walked behind us and then in front of us, his pistol cocked. I don't know whether he was bluffing or changed his mind. Still tied, he marched us to a Korean house and made us kneel on the cement floor. The guards from whom we escaped were put in charge of us. If we slipped, they beat us back onto our knees.

"The next morning we were taken to another Korean house where we were bound with ropes that pulled our arms high and tight in back, cutting into our forearms. We were kept like this for three days and nights. We got one bowl of gruel in all that time. Our hands were loosened for ten minutes, so we could eat. I wished they hadn't, for blisters rose at once where the ropes had cut in.

"Then they retied us with a half square knot that drew so tight it straightened out your clenched fist. Our arms were so swollen that the ropes sank almost out of sight. We had to kneel again, and the rope was attached to the roof, so if we moved, we only tightened the knots. If our knees wobbled, it yanked up our arms, almost tearing them off.

"The next morning they tied us as they had the first time, and we were kept this way for two weeks. The ropes were loosened ten or fifteen minutes a day while we ate. This saved our arms from rotting, but they burned like fire all the time. An American officer went out of his head. None of us was entirely rational.

"Then we were separated and I was put in a small storeroom and not allowed out for another week. The young pilot had hardly eaten in all this time. We tried to force-feed him, holding his nose and shoving food into his mouth, but it didn't work. We tried ridicule. I tried to distract his mind by talking autos. He talked about them, but wouldn't eat. He talked about buying a portable bar and giving us all drinks. He said he intended to buy a car when he got home, but that he'd have to bring his father to see it first. He said he never bought anything or made a decision unless his father okayed it.

"Before the week was over, he was dead.

"Immediately after this, the Chinese began to indoctrinate us. They gave us Red magazines and papers and lectured us. After a while, they came to me and suggested that I voluntarily give a talk on 'the indiscriminate bombing of Korean villages.' What they wanted was a confession that they could publicize.

"I refused and they said they would give me until the next morning to 'think about it,' and that if I still refused, I'd be severely punished. Right then I made a decision I never regretted. I decided that I would still refuse, and if they carried it any further, if they put the heat on me so I couldn't bear it, I would then reverse my decision. I won't make a hero out of myself by saying that I would never have agreed under any circumstances, as I think I would. I didn't know then what I know now about the devilish tricks they have up their sleeves. It is easy to say 'die,' but what if they make it impossible for you to kill yourself, while chiseling away at your thoughts all the time, torturing your body at the same time? This is not a matter of 'No, never,' but of how long a man can stretch his endurance, and whether he can outguess and outlast them.

"The next morning I refused again. They told me they would send guards for me in a couple of hours, and that this would be it! Those next couple of hours were awful! I was less worried when the third hour passed without anyone coming to take me to those new, unknown horrors. They never came! I never regretted calling their bluff.

"When they failed to show up, I lost a great deal of my fear of them. From then on I was able to get along much better. I refused to sign anything. If I had given in on that one point, I believe I would have cracked through and through.

"I also learned something that guided me from then on. This was to let nothing be taken from you willingly. This discourages them if they have to do so much work on little things. I noticed that if a POW broke easily on a minor detail, he cracked almost the same way on bigger matters, and from then on betrayal became a habit with him."

Bob didn't realize it, but he was paying them back in their own coin. Communists never give a man anything until they have to. Indeed, this is a clue to their aggravating behavior in international relations. The Reds never concede a single point, no matter how trivial, until they must, and have gotten everything they can in exchange for it. In this way they tire out their opponents who, glad to get rid of this little detail, surrender something of importance.

"If you stall along until you've come just this side of exhaustion, you'll probably be able to keep control over yourself," Bob said. "I had no other rules on how to maintain control over myself and not become a puppet of the enemy, except this simple one. So long as I could adhere to it, everything else fell into place.

"When we had our next lecture, five or six POW's gave the talk they had wanted from me. The Reds had put the same pressure on a lot of us, certain that some would weaken. Those who did weaken spoke on such subjects as, 'How we shot Korean civilians when we took a village,' 'How we burned peaceful homes,' and 'How we shot communist POW's.'

"In those days I trusted every American implicitly. I knew nothing yet about the Commies using American civilians as Red propagandists in China, or how they softened up a fellow and then used him against his buddies. I was ordered to draw an air map of my base and refused as long as I could.

Then I went back to my shed and told a lieutenant how I would go about it, making it ridiculous. He had been in our escape attempt.

"A few days later, after I had turned in the map, I was called back and ordered to redraw it. I was not shown my original. They asked me the same old questions all over again and searched me carefully, making me take off all my clothes. I was asked about escape routes to such and such an underground. I was asked about the anti-Red guerrillas in the area where our plane had been headed. I stalled on the map. I put in a runway, while trying to remember the other map. Finally, they tired of this stalling and took me into an adjoining room where I was stunned to see the lieutenant in whom I had confided. He had told them everything, and all he knew, too. He had shifted the blame for the escape on me, saying I had instigated it, and that I had a flare on me when we left. This was silly, but luckily the Reds grabbed on this point and insisted I give up the flare, which I never had. Finally they said I had to prove I hadn't ever had it. They said they'd weigh my word against his, and severely punish whoever lied. We were returned to our shed. They interrogated the other four and reached the conclusion themselves that it was the lieutenant who was lying. He was the one punished. The British stood up for me.

"I have nothing but admiration for the British," he said. "I saw them give the Reds a hard time while they were being tied up. They swore at them. They had scar tissue still left from the burning by those ropes. Two British officers were in a horrible condition from deep burns. One died."

The men were then shifted to Pak's Palace. "I got brutal treatment there, but found that by lying about things that mattered, I could get by on the rest. Every man in that camp was ordered to turn in drawings of military bases. The Reds concentrated men there whom they believed had the dope they wanted. By playing them against one another, they got a lot of what they were after, including real names.

" 'You are from Detroit, aren't you?' they said to mc. That's where there are a lot of war plants, aren't there?'

"I denied it. 'They're just auto factories,' I insisted. This didn't go over well. When I couldn't stall any more, I drew a long building that I called an assembly line. I drew other buildings that I labeled 'warehouse,' 'machine shop,' and 'railway depot,' and I marked everything else 'parking lot.' I named the place Briggs Body Manufacturing Company. This satisfied them. An Army officer drew something he labeled 'Seagram's Distillery,' and this satisfied them, too. What they had to have was a certain amount of paperwork from each prisoner or they'd get in trouble. When I found this out, it helped my planning a lot.

"They demanded to know how we located our targets at night. After I couldn't stall any further, I swashed a lot of colors over a sheet of paper, erased two spots, and labeled it 'truck lights.' I did the same with a second drawing. In a third, I erased little squares and labeled them 'door' and 'window.' I took a long time and looked very serious doing it, and it satisfied them. They wanted the paperwork.

"The same thing happened when they landed on me to write about aerial gunnery. I repeated myself, saying the same thing over and over, using slightly different language and shifting the paragraphs around each time like they do. I dragged everything out, padded everything, never using one word where a dozen might do, or even two dozen, and gave 'em nothing. Absolutely nothing! They had a nice stack of paper and were overjoyed. This is what their superiors had demanded of them.

"You must be smart," he said. "When you're being worked over by relays of trained examiners, you can't be quick on all their questions and then act dumb on one. Once you act a part, you've got to go on with it right to the end, even when it's ridiculous. I once got the questioning all mixed up because I kept figuring that Japan was off the west coast of Korea. I don't know how I made that mistake. But I kept insisting on the west coast, even when I knew I was wrong. This systematic blunder saved me a lot of trouble.

"I was kept in Pak's Palace two months. We had to do a terrific amount of labor, hauling wood and water for the Koreans. Then I was sent to Camp One at Chungsong, thirty miles southeast of Sinuiju, where organized indoctrination began. Here I met real collaborators for the first time. I saw some of our men leap up like animated puppets and appeal for signatures to peace petitions and urge the fellows to write letters to their relatives and friends, taking the Red side on everything.

"This POW camp wasn't marked, any more than the others I had been in. From the sky it looked like a regular military target, so our Air Force naturally bombed it. A main military road passed through the middle of camp, and a truck with headlights was approaching when our planes appeared. They saw only an obvious war target. One American officer was killed, several Americans and Britons were wounded, and I got a badly burned toe. This was meat for the collaborators. Right afterwards, they drew up protests against the bombing. The officers all refused to sign, except two or three. The sergeants, all Air Force reserves, refused, too. Funnily enough, the men who had been recalled from reserve stood up fine. Rank means a lot in captivity. The effect of even one officer signing was much, much worse than a lot of enlisted men doing so.

"A couple of days after this, they took away all officers and sergeants. They told us we needed 'special education.' That meant worse brainwashing.

"We were sent to Camp Two, which we opened, and where I remained until my release. Between 250 and 300 of us occupied a cold, unheated building. Indoctrination went into full swing and we were forced to go to classes. They gave us Red stuff written by Americans and ordered us to read it aloud. Study started before breakfast, with another class until noon. We then got an hour break, followed by a third class until dark. We had to spend the evening in discussion.

"We were broken into groups at night and put into separate rooms, with a monitor in each who was supposed to record everyone's opinions. Each man had to write his thoughts and sign them. We hung together on those opinions. Some had been stinkers and known collaborators before coming into camp. The influence of the rest of us stopped their ratting, and they went along with the rest. We all stuck together. We handed in a paper either marked 'no comment' or with something against them."

He then added seriously, "I was kept busy, too, selling automobiles."

"What?" I exclaimed.

"I was kept busy selling automobiles," he repeated with a grin. "Here's how it started. We talked a lot about what we'd do when we were free. We thought up marvelous ways of spending our accumulated pay. 'Be sure to come and see me when you want to buy a car,' I said to them at first. I wasn't joking. You don't joke about those matters in POW camps.

We were dead earnest. Either we were going to be alive or not. If alive, there were certain things we intended to do. One was own a car and drive it. A fellow would say to me, 'Sure, I'll buy a car from you.' Then we'd go into a huddle. I'd do a salesmanship job, explaining the points of the various cars, and finally we'd reach an agreed price.

"Autos were a continual subject of conversation in camp. It went so far that I thought about setting up an auto fleet plan for POW's. If I made sufficient sales, it would pay the auto companies to give us a discount. I started taking names and listing the orders. I ended up with 550 sales. I had agents in other camps selling for me. This had a terrific effect. All day, whenever they had a chance, fellows talked about the car they had bought, the places they'd go with it, and the girls who'd go with them. They gave me exact instructions where to deliver the vehicles, which I had to note down on paper. The time we were supposed to be spending in the evening discussing the day's lectures we talked cars. The Reds noted how serious we were and how excited we got and never caught on why. This was just what we needed to rest our minds when some of us, at least, would have cracked from the strain of having to harp on the same Commie talk all the time."

Just before repatriation, the Reds confiscated all notes and papers. They found Bob's list and grabbed it at once.

Wilkins thought this wrecked his project. He couldn't remember all the names and addresses and the car each man had chosen. But after he returned home, he was astonished to receive phone calls and letters from fellow repatriates. "Where's my car?" they wanted to know. They had bought a car in camp and wanted delivery! Bob went back to work right away, without any rest. He drove about with his wife, delivering cars to former campmates.

Such affection for the automobile industry could not go unrewarded. Bob became district manager for one of the major companies. He called for me at my hotel before breakfast and drove me to a town called Plymouth, about an hour's drive outside Detroit, where he had a brief conference with a dealer.

We spent the rest of the day in the Hillside Inn, in front of a welcome fire. A thin, last snow was falling. When evening came, he drove me to his home, which looked like a picture postcard. I stayed until early morning, still discussing his experiences. The POW camps were far behind him. He was able to analyze his own feelings without passion.

Battle of Wits

Almost every POW whom I interviewed brought up, in some manner or other, the need for maintenance of a spirit of resistance in camp. Hope, on which men lived and for the lack of which they died, was intimately linked to such a spirit. The Reds fully appreciated this, and focused their slyest and most vicious pressures in killing any idea of resistance, and with it hope.

They did succeed in crushing it, but never completely, and it had a way of appearing when least expected.

"The first I knew that we were succeeding in creating a resistance group with some backbone was at an indoctrination lecture," one of the former POW's told me.

"The same routine was being played over. The communist speaker tediously described the Red point of view on some dreary issue, and then he pointed to one of us in the audience and asked him to stand up and give his opinion."

The men had learned through bitter experience to recognize this tactic. By it, the Reds found weaklings on whom they could work, screened out dissidents, and subtly managed to induce prisoners to indoctrinate themselves. When a man repeats something often enough, thinking up new ways in which to express it, although he may begin by disbelieving every word of it, he is likely to end up by swallowing a lot of it.

The POW pointed to by the speaker stood up, barked out the two words, "No comment!" and sat down again.

A monitor always was present to take notes, and everyone saw him recording this defiance. The indoctrinator pointed to another man. "What is your opinion?" he asked. "Please be frank."

This fellow got up, repeated the same words, "No comment," and sat down, too.

"I felt someone tug gently at my sleeve," my informant told me. "I knew this had to be some sort of a signal, so I didn't turn my head, only nodded very slightly. Talking out of the side of his mouth, the man at my left whispered, 'Policy is, say No comment; pass the word along.' I couldn't begin to express to you the thrill that went through me as I did so. We were hitting back! You would have to have been in a place like that for all those months and months, in that atmosphere of growing despair and hopelessness, to know what that meant to us. The lecturer tried once more with the same result.

"Then he left the stage in a huff and returned a few minutes later with the camp commander, who himself took the rostrum. This was it!

"We stood firm. Everyone gave the same answer. And that was that. The commander kept on talking and didn't make an issue out of it. From then on, we always expected word on how to respond to Red orders and it always came. We now had an underground in our group."

The POW's had to learn this the hard way, out of their own resources of mind and physique. They learned that indecision and lack of determination were costly and even fatal drawbacks. In the beginning this new clandestine authority issued orders and afterwards modified or reversed them. Usually this left someone out on a limb, to be badly mauled about by the Reds. "The effect on our morale was disastrous, not because of what the Reds did, but over our own lack of leadership," this chap said. "We saw that once an order was issued, it had to remain unchanged until new, positive instructions were given. Halfway measures never worked.

"The success of this tactic depended upon an officer cadre that knew its own mind and had the capacity for resistance. Feelings ran high in the camp when some of our fellows paid the price for orders changed from on top. As a result of our insistence, it was decided that from then on, when an order was given, the whole group would suffer rather than let a few individuals shoulder the blame. This gave the men a sense of destination. They felt they were getting somewhere."

At one of the big meetings when all the units were together, the head of a squad was called on from the platform and asked to stand up and give the opinion of his men on what the lecturer had been saying. He replied that he was not able to answer for his men's views. "Then find out," he was told. The squad leader sat down to consult them, while the entire audience waited tensely. An order was passed from man to man. He stood up again and replied, "They say, No comment." He had relayed this order himself.

The POW's had to learn to adapt their tactics to the enemy's. The only inflexible rule to which everything else had to be adjusted was that the objective was resistance. This was almost lost sight of at first due to inexperience and enemy blows. During the early period of activity, when the Red objective was to soften up the men by striking sheer terror into them, the problem was one of survival. During those months, the Reds were only seeking excuses for mass mistreatment. Isolated cases of defiance, such as defiling a photo of Mao Tse-tung, only brought about collective punishment. Nobody could be permitted to go off the deep end this way by himself then.

Later, when the stick was moved to the background and the carrot brought to the fore, the POW's changed their tactics accordingly. Anyone who could think up a stunt was encouraged to do so, and if it sounded workable at all, the others would say, "Okay, I'm game. Let's try it." They accepted the fact that the Reds probably would jump on somebody, paying little heed whether it was the right man or not. They accepted this for the sake of the morale effect on all. The communists fought back with canaries — the POW label for squealers.

The most popular song in camp at one time was, "I'll Walk Alone." The Reds asked a company to stage a revue, hoping to infiltrate their own propaganda into it. The POW's went to work to beat them at this game. When "I'll Walk Alone" was sung, it was so loudly applauded that the Reds suspected it had political significance. They called in the prisoners in the usual one-by-one manner. **Is this some sort of a national anthem in your country?" they asked. They wouldn't believe that the song had just caught the fancy of the men, and so they banned it. The whole company rose in its defense. "I don't believe anyone outside can grasp the morale boost this gave us," a POW told me.

The Reds were anxious that the prisoners form a choir, hoping to use it for pictures and radio propaganda. The POW 's threatened to break it up and not put on any more shows if the song was not reinstated. "On some things we won our point, but we never did on this," he said. "The Reds realized that somehow that song had become a symbol. But in the interim, we gained a lot of encouragement by sticking together and making a fight over it."

The communists brought in their most important propaganda play, *The White-Haired Daughter,* hoping to follow it up with a regular tour of communist dramas. They put everything they had into it, with heavy curtains, real furniture, a machine to make snow and another to reproduce thunder and lightning. The play went on for four and a half hours. The POW's simply applauded and hissed at the wrong places. In the thriller-diller scene where the landlord rapes the little slave girl, who of course is the daughter of a tenant farmer, the audience clapped wildly. The Reds were infuriated. They stopped the show and the chief indoctrinator took the stage and gave the prisoners a dressing down. Thereafter, whenever the landlord came on, everyone cheered. This was the first — ^and last — propaganda play the Reds brought into camp.

Such unity enabled the POW's to block another Red propaganda maneuver. One day, all were called out and informed that arrangements had been made for them to write home. Everyone applauded, for this had been a major grievance. Many had not received a letter since their capture. A collaborator bounced up and said how grateful he was for this example of the "people's kindness," and he moved that everyone show gratitude by appealing to their families to join the "peace campaign" and write their Senators demanding that the U.N. forces stop at the Thirty-eighth Parallel. He asked everyone who agreed to stand up. He flopped down and leaped up again — ^and still was the only man on his feet. He thought he had been misunderstood and repeated his motion. Again nobody stood up. "Well, you'll not be able to write home," he exclaimed testily, and sat down.

The POW defiance paid off. The Reds needed some mail by the prisoners for the record, and had tried to insert that extra propaganda in the bargain. When the men refused, they had to distribute the stationery anyway, and told everyone to write whatever he pleased. They tried a final trick, insisting that the return address be written as, "Chinese Committee for World Peace Against American Aggression." The POW 's refused, and the Reds compromised by leaving out the "Against American Aggression" part. This was the first mail to reach home.

Crazy Week

Crazy Week was part of the spontaneous buffoonery by which the prisoners rattled the enemy and gave their own morale a lift. Bob Wilkins and Herb Marlatt both told me about it. Additional anecdotes were related by other participants. They all agreed on the details.

A particularly obnoxious brainwasher named Wei had the habit of bursting into the camp building long before dawn, switching on the light, and getting everyone up for another agonizing day of mental torture. This was in Camp Two, which was spread over a large area near the Yalu. Wei had come from Peking, where the Reds were conducting courses for inquisitors. They came in relays, a few weeks apart, bubbling over with enthusiasm and venom.

On this particular morning, while it was still dark, just before the brainwasher arrived, all the thirty-five prisoners got up quickly. They grabbed their rags, tins, and miscellaneous junk and dashed outside, hiding in the rear. There they waited, all lights still out.

They heard the confident tread of the brainwasher, coming to start his day's routine. They saw him open the door, and a moment later the light went on in the empty house. They heard a yell and saw him rush out the door and down the pathway, as if pursued.

As soon as he disappeared from view, they picked up all their pitiful belongings and ran back into the dormitory. They arranged everything normally as fast as they could. As they were supposed to be awake by now, most of them sat up wherever they were, chatting or playing with homemade cards.

Sure enough, after a few minutes, they heard a babble of voices, and Wei burst into the room, accompanied by his superiors and other staff men. The prisoners gazed at this delegation as if it were just one more inspection.

"Where were you?" Wei roared.

"Where was who?" someone asked.

"You . . . you know who . . . you," Wei retorted.

"What do you mean?"

The Americans just stared dumbly. The silence could have been cut with a knife. Their eyes took on a puzzled look. Wei's colleagues stared questioning-ly at him, then at the prisoners, unable to make up their minds. The dormitory looked normal and everything was as it should be.

"When I came here a few minutes ago, this room was empty," Wei shouted. "Where was everybody?"

A POW, without budging from his position on the gunny sack, turned his head and replied, "Where were you? Anybody can see where we've been."

Wei's anger increased, which added to the confusion. He tried to explain to his Chinese escorts that there had been nobody in the room. He turned back to the prisoners and shouted, "How dare you say you were here all the time? I came here only a few minutes ago."

"Say, mister, are you sure your eyes are all right?" a POW answered from one side of the room.

"Maybe he needs glasses," another POW commented to a fellow prisoner.

Before Wei could explode again, a sympathetic voice replied, loud enough for all to hear, "Maybe the poor man's blind."

"We've sure been here all the time," somebody else said.

Another exclaimed, "Anybody with eyesight could see that." The act could not have been performed better in Hollywood.

"I'm not blind!" Wei screamed.

At that moment one of the tall Americans, who had been taking everything in quietly, fixed his eyes on Wei, and said in a voice full of hushed amazement, "Man, your job must be a strain! You're going crazy!"

The Americans who joined in this buffoonery swear that he had to be removed from the camp before the week was ended, almost — if not already — a babbling idiot. This was brainwashing in reverse.

Another stunt unnerved one of the indoctrinators so much that he showed the effects for the remainder of his stay. He, too, came into the barracks just before daybreak and turned on the switch. What he saw made him gasp, as if he were in the presence of some eerie congregation of ghosts. Everybody was up and about. Some were playing cards, others were reading propaganda booklets, a few were looking through the quisling-edited *China Monthly Review.* Several were sewing! All was being done in pitch darkness, without a word being spoken. Turning on the light made no difference. The POW 's didn't seem to notice it. The only difference now was that they spoke in hushed tones, which made the atmosphere even more phantom like.

The stimulating effect this had on the POW 's can hardly be exaggerated. This was a time when the communists were exerting every subtle pressure they knew, along with the crudest forms of violence, to gather recruits for petitions and confessions. This was at the height of the germ-warfare campaign, when Peking was insisting that the brainwashers produce material that could be spread around the earth as proof of the charges.

Never before had a hoax been perpetrated on such a mammoth scale. No government before in history had ever lent its name to any accusation so bizarre and patently false. The POW's were called out for "small group" meetings, where germ-warfare articles were read aloud. Everyone was called on to discuss them. Each man was asked if he believed the accusations. Some men said No point-blank. Others hesitated. The Reds were able to choose their potential quislings from those who wavered.

An interval elapsed during which the Reds set the stage for the next act. When ready, with revealing synchronization, the Reds put on exhibitions of purported germ-warfare evidence and played the recordings of extorted confessions.

The walls of one room were plastered with photographs of sick farmers and slogans denouncing the horrors of germ war. A long, narrow table was covered with exhibits, such as bacteriological smears seen through microscopes, glass containers filled with insects, and rodents bottled in alcohol, which the Reds said were germ-laden and had been dropped by the American aviators.

The Reds made sure that every man had to see the exhibition, making it impossible for him not to pass by it. The only passage to the toilet was through this room!

The brainwasher had something tangible to work on when he had provoked a POW into saying, "Sure that's a germ smear. I'm not so dumb as to think it isn't. But you probably made it yourself, just to fool us."

The lecturer then either shifted to a new, softening-up charge, accusing the man of "a hostile attitude," or went into indoctrination, ignoring part of the prisoner's statement and putting all the emphasis on the rest. "Now you're being sensible," he'd say. "You admit this is a germ smear. You see it. That's all we ask. Remember, if anybody asks, you saw this germ smear with your own eyes." Then he would build up from there, bit by bit, until the time came to apply the heat, to produce the final hallucinations during which the sleight of-hand could be performed to extract the desired confession.

Some of the POW's tampered with the photos and slogans, so that the Reds had to post special sentries at the exhibits and keep them on duty day and night during the whole show.

The germ-warfare drive never ceased. Whenever it seemed about to fade out, it would be revived at crescendo pitch. Peking was determined to keep the issue alive, and Moscow was evidently breathing down its neck for material that its diplomats and agents could disseminate through clandestine channels and by whatever overt means were available.

Crazy Week took the sting out of it. The communists appeared baffled by it. A POW would show up outside his barracks, walk to the edge of the path, and go through a series of slow, solemn motions. The guards nearby and any Chinese or Koreans passing would stop and stare. The realization would suddenly come to them that he was riding a bicycle. Only he had no bicycle! The motions and glide were unmistakable. Then, while the Reds were still stunned, not knowing how to react, the fellow would ride his imaginary vehicle past the sentry, out the gate, and down the highway before they woke up to what he was doing. There would be yells and the rider would steer his phantom cycle to the edge of the road, get off, carefully rest it against a bush, and come up and ask if they wanted anything of him. The guard might just order him into the compound, smiling uncertainly, or take a swing at him. Either way, the Reds were not sure what this indicated. Was the fellow beginning to lose his mind? Men did go crazy in camp. How could they tell?

There was the chap, for example, who twice in broad daylight, with the Chinese looking on, tried to escape in a madly futile manner. Was it crazy or real? Another time they found a POW two miles down the road, stopping people and asking the direction to a non-existent post office. He wanted his mail. Was this an act or an obsession? He was escorted back and the Reds decided he was going insane, while harmless.

This was just what the fellow wanted. Insanity was faked on a number of occasions. For a man to get away with it, he had to seize the opportune moment when the Reds were trying to give an impression of sweet reasonableness and not a time when they were resorting to sheer terror.

The Reds never knew what to expect during Crazy Week. Extraordinary scenes confronted them, for which they had no precedent. What would Peking want? Punishment was swift and extreme for errors and mistakes were classified as sabotage. They would gape in embarrassed confusion at a captive walking down a pathway all by himself, yet with a feminine companion to whom he was conversing amiably. If a Chinese passed, he would introduce her. "Meet Jennie, my wife," he might say, or, "This is Susie, my girl." He would take her by the arm that wasn't there and walk on, still talking. The POW's even had petting parties in the moonlight, cuddling closer and talking sweet nonsense to no one.

One day, in an interval between study periods, the Chinese saw everyone run out of the house and arrange themselves in a disciplined but mystifying way over the field. While the camp officials watched, the prisoners began to go through a series of convolutions, uttering strange cries.

Suddenly one of the Chinese military men recognized the scene that takes place on the flight deck of an airplane carrier when planes are coming in and leaving. Men with outstretched arms, like wings, represented the planes. Signalmen brought in the planes or sent them out on their missions. Everything was done with professional exactitude. There even was a helicopter, or rather the man who was the helicopter, who was the star performer. He was a gifted mimic. He hovered about, hobbling like a copter. His grunts sounded exactly like one. He fluttered about as a plane came in, waiting to fly to its rescue if it tumbled into the drink. He had made himself a skullcap, with a small propeller design on top, like a child's play hat.

Once in a while a plane fell into the ocean. Off would go the helicopter on the rescue mission. This was all done so realistically, with each man going through his routine as if it were a real flight deck, that the communists simply were in a welter of indecision. They suspected it was a farce, but at whose expense? They could not imagine a joke except at someone's cost — someone had to lose face. A joke was a very serious matter.

They called in the prisoners one by one and demanded an explanation of these goings-on. They just had to have significance. "What does it mean?" they demanded. None of the replies removed their feeling of unease. If they were told the truth, they were still worried. Their disquiet only stimulated the prisoners the more.

Nobody who witnessed the helicopter change himself into a motorcycle will ever forget it. Chugging so realistically that passers-by jumped out of the way, he drove up and down the pathway. He ran errands for others in camp, solemnly boarding his imaginary motorcycle and tearing away. He did so one day with a swift start — he liked his engine to be quick on the take-off — and ran smack into a brainwasher, sending him sprawling on the ground. The cyclist didn't lose his self-possession, but quickly picked up his imaginary machine and leaned it against the wall.

They killed a rat one day, made a little parachute for it, on which they painted a skull and crossbones, and hung it on a bush. A Chinese noticed it and became very excited. "There's your evidence!" one of the POW's exclaimed. "There's your proof that the Americans are engaging in bacteriological warfare. That's one of the germ-laden beasties dropped from the skies. Don't touch it! You'll fall dead!" The official called a guard to get a stick and lift it gingerly down.

In another hut, a rat was similarly disguised and hung up in the outside latrine. The Chinese indoctrinator who saw it had the Red Army sentry punished. The POW's never knew whether Red anger would strike at them or pick a communist scapegoat.

U.N. planes bombed the vicinity and thousands of tiny, shining bits of tinsel floated down. The POW's knew it was tin foil intended to deflect enemy radar, but the Chinese didn't. They asked the prisoners. "Those are the germs you've been telling us about," one American said with a poker face. "That's how they're dropped."

Whoever made this spontaneous remark never imagined what propaganda use the Reds were going to make out of it. The next morning farmers from far and near, carrying chopsticks and pails, gathered at a central spot. Each wore a hospital mask that covered his mouth and nose, and was made even more grotesque by a coating of some reddish disinfectant painted on his arms up to the elbows. The POW's saw the peasants scatter over the fields and hunt for bits of tin foil. The Americans had a hard time to keep from bursting into laughter as they watched them inspect every inch of ground, every so often thrusting in their chopsticks and picking up a tiny bit of something, which they dropped cautiously into their pails. The scene was like a slow, macabre dance across the horizon.

Some of the Chinese air officers must have known, but kept quiet so as not to be accused of trying to defend germ warfare. Ordinary folk were evidently deceived, and this, of course, was the Red purpose. Everyone went grimly through the motions.

Of a different character was the spontaneous reaction of an American POW whose group had been scoffing at the germ warfare charges. The next day the lecturer brought some of the purported evidence with him, including a container of supposedly infected insects. Before anyone realized what he was doing, the soldier plucked a bug out of the container and swallowed it.

Immediately there was a hullabaloo. The Chinese propagandists went rushing about insisting he was certain to die, doubled up in pain, and rushed him off to a hospital. "Give your hospital bed to someone who needs it; I don't," he protested. He had to go. He was returned after several weeks of "treatment."

His quick thinking and defiance of the foe made this one of the grandest incidents of the war. How could anyone who heard of it give any credence to anything the Reds told them? If they were capable of this deceit, they were capable of anything.

Chapter Six - The Independent Character

Brains

Major David F. MacGhee knew Barnum's axiom, "Never give a sucker an even break," and he soon realized that the communist version in the POW camps was, "Never give a prisoner a break." He countered with his own, "Never give the enemy a break." Dave saw that the moment a man let his guard down, he was knocked for a loop. He learned, from his own experiences, that a soft word by a Red was just as much of a weapon as a slap in the face. He saw that survival depended on opposing one tactic by another and that special weapons of the mind had to be used in brain warfare.

Alan Winnington sidled up to him one day while he was standing outside a barracks, surrounded by camp officials. "Would you like a cigarette?" the quisling asked him. What a question! "I sure could do with one," Dave exclaimed, staring with fascination at the full package which Winnington took out of his pocket. With everyone watching, Winnington tossed it on the ground in front of Dave's feet.

Every face now turned toward him. He noted the glitter in Winnington's eyes, and realized that this was part of the game. Dave didn't bend down to pick up the package. Instead, he moved one heel slowly, so everyone could see it, and ground the cigarettes into the dirt.

He fully expected to be smashed in the jaw by one of the onlookers or whacked with the butt of a rifle. He had calculated, in a split second, that he wouldn't be killed for what he was going to do but would probably be knocked about a bit. He sensed that this humiliation to which he was being subjected was the purpose of the casual sympathy trap into which he had been led. He saw that Winnington was trying to show his Asian comrades how easy it was to humble the white man — an American, too. Dave sensed in that fleeting moment that nothing the Reds would do could be so painful and dishonorable in its consequences as his lot if he bent down in front of them all and abjectly picked up the package of cigarettes.

Dave was able to react swiftly because his views had crystallized long before he went to Korea. "They can be expressed very simply," he told me. "Anything worth having is worth fighting for."

After his release, Dave returned from Korea with the certainty that the development of strong leadership qualities was the main requirement in combatting Red corrosion tactics. This conclusion came out of his own character and the environment in which he had been raised as much as out of his experience in POW camps. As a prisoner, he had merely continued along the road pointed out to him from his boyhood by parents, church, and school.

When only three, he had a habit of wandering away from home in Moorestown, New Jersey, which then had a population of only 4,000. His parents took him to Dr. Robert Brotemarkle, dean of psychology at the University of Pennsylvania, to find out how to break him of it. The professor recommended they let the boy go if he wanted. "Don't worry, he'll always come back home," he told them.

In less than a year, Dave was known everywhere within a twenty-five mile radius. "I went out whenever there was a fire alarm or any excitement," he said. "I wanted to see everything."

His father, whom Dave fondly described as a "self-educated hillbilly from the Great Smoky Mountains area in North Carolina," was an inventor and a chemical engineer. He was without any money sense. His joy came from discovery; he lost interest as soon as he had solved a problem, no matter whether it was for a dishwasher, potato peeler, packaging machine, or dehydrated food. "Dad's creations for the rising five-and-ten-cent store industry made home as exciting as the great outdoors," Dave said. "He produced everything from modeling clay to plant fertilizer."

The stock market crash wiped out the family's capital and Dave had to be transferred from private to public school. His principal become so interested in him that she raised subscriptions for a scholarship so he could go back. He had planned to be a chemical engineer like his father, but she advised against it. "If you go into engineering, you'll never be happy," she said. "You should make people your career." So he switched to political science, which he thought came closer to that objective.

While studying, a forum was arranged at Cornell University to discuss how a democratically minded citizen should react during a war. Dave was picked as one of the delegates. He told me that he wrote a ten-point program which he presented to the forum, which urged a stiff policy against the Chinese Reds, for even then he smelled something fishy in the fiercely publicized line that Mao Tse-tung was only pursuing a program of agrarian democracy. He also recommended wartime controls. Many of the other delegates took verbal shots at him, branding him everything from an irresponsible radical to a blind reactionary.

"This convinced me that leading figures in our country did not realize that there was a fight coming," Dave said, "so I decided to prepare myself for it. I enlisted."

He almost didn't make it. There was a bureaucratic jumble on the alphabetical list of names and, somehow, he edged through as a MacGhee and not a McGhee, which was the original spelling. "I was determined to get into the Air Force and there were no ifs nor ands about it," he said.

The attacks made on him at the forum for his ten-point program influenced him greatly. Did he, a student, have the right to take such a firm stand on matters that his elders seemed to have already decided? He said he thought deeply about this, and came to the conclusion that there was a distinction between confidence and conceit that would have to be his guide. "To have self-confidence was very different from being a conceited ass," he said. "A confident man knows what he can do. He doesn't commit himself to the impractical, but to what is achievable."

He brought this principle with him into the POW camps in Korea and it contributed greatly to his survival, he believes.

He was commissioned a navigator in 1942 and sent to England. At the end of the war he was the only captain in his class at the Command and General Staff School at Ft. Leavenworth, Kansas. He was stationed in the Pentagon from 1946 to 1949, receiving "triple threat training," and then went to the A-bomb and strategic war-plans staff. He volunteered for Korea when that war broke out, reaching Okinawa on September 22, 1950. He was shot down on November 10 while on his tenth mission. He believes his was the first B-29 shot down by a MIG-15.

After his release, he heard that there had been consternation in the Pentagon when he was known to have fallen behind the enemy lines. Dave knew too much. "I was told that thirty Korean agents were dropped in a straight line to bring me out, dead or alive," he said.

The Reds never found out that he had once headed a military-aid program for Chiang Kai-shek, or that he had any knowledge of A-bomb activities, electronics, and the latest long-range warplanes. "The position I maintained throughout," he said, "was that I was a drunken, irresponsible bastard who was being kept by a rich and influential woman. The Air Force, I led them to believe, had tried to get rid of me several times, but my wife had pulled strings to keep me in. Nevertheless, I let them think, they had succeeded in shifting me off to Korea.

" 'I'm not worried about being captured,' I cockily told them, 'My wife's connections will get me out of here.'

"Would they give my story any credence? They did — they knocked me on my backside. I still don't know what hit me, but I expected something. I knew that I was going to have to pay a price to get away with that story."

When I asked how he knew how far he could go, his reply showed how he regulated his life by a set of principles and personal hunches. "I never had any doubt that I would live," he said. "When I went to Korea, I left America with the conviction that I was going to get clobbered. To what degree, I didn't know. On the plane out, I joshed the crew about reserving a lower right forward stretcher bunk for me for the return trip. A little squirt of a nurse couldn't understand me at all. She thought I was a quitter. She was so infuriated that she hauled off and slugged me. I shook my jaw and solemnly told her, 'But I get sick when I ride on the tail.' She just couldn't make me out! I knew the war was going to bang me up, but there never was any question in my mind whether I was going to live. I was sure of it. So I was able to take the right chances. That cock-and-bull story about my wife, who really is a simple, good-hearted girl, was one of them."

He built up the portrait of his character as a man considered by his superiors too much of a security risk to let know hardly anything. "I let a story get to the Reds, that I had made up, how I hadn't been trusted enough even to be allowed to visit some friends of mine who had just bailed out of a B-36 and been rescued."

Canaries threatened his pose on three occasions. One such squealer was an electronics officer who had worked under him. He told the enemy all he knew, then suggested they check it with Dave. "This was at Pyoktong, Camp Five," he told me. "A Chinese officer named General Wang took over my case for personal handling. He brought me into his own house and gave me a terrific build-up, saying he knew how much I could tell them. He gave me a package of cigarettes a day and terrific food, with candy in the evening. I had never been treated so royally before. I even got special snacks of Chinese mooncakes.

"I had what was made to seem like unlimited personal freedom. I could ask for anything I wanted. They treated me as one of themselves, only better. It was September, 1951.

"I knew I was in a trap, and that I would have to make use of this respite to figure out a plan to get out of it without being shot. They didn't ask me any questions the first week. They only told me what they knew themselves. They gave me interpreters who spoke flawless English, three from Peking and one from Tientsin. During this period, I built up the impression that I hadn't known about the material they showed me, nor the man who had given it to them. I told them that while stationed at Okinawa, I was being taught to use radar for navigation, and that if I hadn't been shot down, I would have

111

learned how to use it in bombing. I changed my role from instructor to dumb student. Actually, I had been an instructor in advanced bombing radar.

"I assured them that I would do everything I could to help them within my limited knowledge, and that when I didn't know something, I would make the best guess I could at it if that was what they wanted from me.

"General Wang was a Chinese Air Force man, young and quite brilliant. The Korean house he had taken over was much better than the average.

"In the second week, I was requested to write everything I knew about electronics, and particularly to draw diagrams of equipment, indicating its characteristics and how it was used. They asked me for everything I knew on the theory of search radar or any other kind. I was given a good typewriter and plenty of paper and drawing tools. I was left to my own initiative, under the general supervision of one of the interpreters. All he did was pile up what I had written each day.

"I had to work prescribed periods of time, and I used up as much of it as I could reading books. I made meticulous drawings of a radar APQ-13 that everyone knew about. I denied the existence of newer models, saying this was one of the latest. On each of the drawings I misnamed and mislocated the controls. They had the equipment itself from a B-29. I had given myself an objective and I fixed my mind on it. That was to give them the idea that my drawing was the improved version, when actually it was the original and almost totally out of use.

"Wang had to leave two days before I finished my work. In a good-by visit, he came and thanked me and said that he had made sure that as soon as I finished, my material would be forwarded to him.

"I worked in an apparently thorough manner for three weeks, completing a forty-two-page document in duplicate. I ate and lived well all that time. After handing all this in, I sat back comfortably waiting for the blast I knew was coming.

"It came in three days. Wang returned in a rage. He charged me with trying to cheat the 'peace-loving people.' I went at once into an histrionic routine that I had planned in advance. I did my best to look like a child caught with jam smeared all over his face. With a final roar about me having wasted the people's paper, he stalked off, leaving the interpreter to continue the threats and expound on the horrors of my future punishment. 'You'll never see your family again,' he told me. 'You're going to be shot. Wang is getting the approval of headquarters. The only place for people like you is in a dungeon. People who try to cheat peace-loving people don't deserve to live. You only think you're sly and cunning. You're really not very clever.'

"That night, at eleven p.m., I got up and turned on the light. I let my blackout curtain drop and opened my door, so everyone could see me. I took paper I had saved for this occasion, and sat down and started writing. Within a few minutes, several interpreters came and demanded to know what I was doing. I told them I was writing a self-criticism. They hadn't anticipated that!

They looked surprised but said this was very commendable and that as soon as I finished, I should bring it to them.

"I wrote a three-page self-criticism in which I pointed out the innumerable times I had insisted that I knew nothing about electronics. I enumerated, step by step, the many things General Wang had done to build up my ego. I elaborated on how I had to give him something that appeared impressive, to save face. So I lumped together the little I knew and had heard during my years in the Air Force, and what I had read in our magazines, and tried to produce as impressive a paper as I could. I said humbly how I realized that I had been very deceitful in writing that paper, and how I had wasted their time and their scarce materials. I recalled that I had insisted time and again that I didn't know anything, but my admiration for General Wang required that I present him with some sort of a paper, doing my utmost to match the superior qualities he attributed to me. I had gambled on his ignorance and lost, and hoped he would not think unkindly of me, but that really I was only a stupid person and a ready victim of flattery. In the future, I promised to control myself so as not to waste the time and efforts of the leaders of the peace-loving peoples.

"I finished this about two a.m., and then asked for more paper so I could copy it out, as my emotions had made it illegible. Instead, they took it straight to General Wang. At three-thirty a.m., he summoned me to his office, receiving me like a long-lost brother. He kept me almost to dawn, subjecting me to every form of communist ideological argument. The company commander and all the interrogators were present. They cooked pork, chicken, rice, and fried eggplant, treating me like a prodigal son. Then they told me to go back to my room and, after getting some sleep, to study harder. Wang shook hands with me and said he hoped to see me again soon.

"And that was that! The fellow who had got me into this jam died after Wang went to work on him for lying. He had to pay the price for Wang's humiliation. I am positive that a guilty conscience helped kill him. He did not die because of what the Chinese did to him, but of a broken heart.

"The reason he had broken was because he couldn't stand solitary confinement. He had been separated from all the other white men. He had two Asians — his interpreter and guard — with him all the time, yet he felt completely alone!"

Guts

Dave had two other crises when canaries were almost his undoing. "An officer, desiring to take the heat off his own back, informed the Reds in writing that every statement I had given them was a lie," Dave said. "This fellow advised another U.S. air officer not to follow my example because it would only lead to trouble. The Commies landed on me like a ton of bricks and I knew this was going to be a bad time."

113

Dave had built up a fanciful story about himself so they could discount his reliability and had given them fabricated data to put them off the trail of where his real knowledge lay. He had worked at its construction brick by brick. He knew well enough that nothing infuriated the Reds more than to discover they had been made game of. Horrible tortures had been meted out to many men for "cheating the people," as they called this. A quick execution was preferable to the alternative of a slow death by cunning tortures. In cases such as his, he realized that it would be one or the other.

The shock of this betrayal came suddenly, too. Everything that he had planned with such infinite care was now at stake. How was he going to get out of this fix? He wrestled all night with the problem. The next morning, as soon as his Chinese interpreter saw him, he exclaimed, "Comrade MacGhee, you have changed!"

"I was feeling so tense that I can still see the entire scene," MacGhee told me. "I can see the water dripping from the roof into a puddle outside. *Plop,* and a drop fell, spreading circles on the surface. I can see it just as clearly as then.

" *No, I haven't changed,' I said, wondering what he meant.

" 'MacGhee, have you seen yourself?' he replied.

"I tried to laugh. 'How in heck can I see myself?' I asked. He took a small round mirror from his pocket and held it in front of me.

"One look and I knew that I was headed for even more serious trouble. My hair had turned gray overnight! Sheer strain had done it. Worry did it, worry because I knew that I was only one fellow, and the fraction of an error could destroy everything I had built up. The canary had them breathing down my back for what I knew, furious over having been fooled.

"During the next seven months, from February to August, during constant interviewing, re-interrogation, and ideological indoctrination, I succeeded in re-establishing my integrity as irrefutable, to use their own word for it. I was able to explain the change in my appearance by the strain of waiting for the camp commander to sentence me on a charge they had already made against me. They had accused me of what they called 'hostile and subversive organized activity within the camp.' Actually, this was no worry to me at all compared to the other problem.

"My main tactic in beating them this time was to remember every single word I had said or written for them, and writing it all over again, with convenient allowances for forgetting! I wrote 480 pages! The only mistake they were able to find was where I had reversed two phony names in a phony organizational chart. All this time, I was kept in solitary in a room in a Korean house.

"I had no sense of loneliness and even relished being alone. My gray hairs gradually went away. I kept myself busy. I relaxed by focusing on anything that could take my mind off the Reds. I observed everything possible. I made a study of how a fly lands on the ceiling. Does he do a loop or does he fly up, roll over, and hook on with his first two feet and then swing his body up? I examined what spiders do when nonedible matter entered their webs. When a chicken jumps off the roof, what lands first, his fanny or his feet? When a hen is laying an egg, does she go to sleep? I saw some hornets drill a hole in the wall, so I rolled up a small piece of paper, finally finding a place where it fooled one of them. Two weeks later I took the paper down to see what the hornet had been doing. He had done a plaster job."

MacGhee pointed out the importance of keeping busy. He found that when a man gives himself an objective and concentrates on it, he keeps busy. "Escape can become such an objective," he said. "This becomes a passion to live by. You think about it always. When caught, you observe local conditions and whatever else might help you get away. When called for an interrogation, you don't worry over it because you don't think of it as an interrogation. You're busy thinking about the maps you might get a chance to see and what you can steal.

"I also took every opportunity to make friends with the guard," he went on, "so as to learn and practice some Chinese. Guards and others sometimes would teach me Chinese if I taught them a bit of English. I taught pronunciation to the interpreters and once I gave lessons to a medical corpsman on the names of medicines in English. In turn he taught me the phonetics of characters I had copied down.

"A Korean family still occupied part of the house. I grabbed every opportunity to help the old couple, even when the guard got angry about it. Then I'd say to him, in the properly pained intonation, 'Nee dee boo how' — ^you're not being good. When addressing the Koreans, I always used the few words I had picked up in their own language. I wouldn't have used any Japanese in talking to them for anything in the world. I wouldn't hurt their feelings that way. The result was that they smuggled food, matches, and tobacco to me. I called this Operation Wedge, and it gave me a sense of accomplishment.

"I tried to earn their respect in a thousand ways. One of their relatives died, and the family had a weeping ceremony that lasted six weeks, with gnashing and wailing. Whenever one of those scenes took place, I'd go into my room and close the door. When the wailing was over for the day, I'd open my door a little, and the old woman would nod that it was all right for me to come out. No, I was given no chance to be bored during my isolation."

Yet this so-called isolation was one of the pressures that led Colonel Schwable to confess to germ warfare. He became desperate in his desire to get back among his fellow POW's. He couldn't stand "loneliness."

The result of Dave's Operation Wedge, too, was that the guard finally let him grind corn for the old lady. "I made a point of doing it in the worst weather," he said. Although this was a tiny operation, he saw it widen the gap between her as a Korean and the Chinese communist. She had friends, too, to whom she must have spoken about this helpful American. Such small things all helped keep his mind busy and boosted his morale.

He needed all the stamina he had gathered, too, for his final canary crisis as a POW An observer in the electronics field caused it, Dave said. "He had a V.I.P. complex. He wasn't important to us, and had to be to someone and only the Reds were left. The only way he could be important to them was to give them something they didn't have. He was an intelligent man but he spilled his guts. They needed someone to verify the truth of what he had told them, especially about designing computers. They brought me his completed work, telling me he had said I was an expert at it.

*'By that time I had been a POW for two years and had successfully established the integrity of my position. I examined the documents thoroughly and then asked my interpreter, who had been interrogating B-29 personnel for a long time, 'How can you be sucked in by such a stupid piece of work? You surely should be able to detect such baloney.' I told him that even to have it was risking his life if his superiors ever found out how he had been fooled. We talked this over for two hours and I convinced him. He asked plaintively what I thought he should do. 'Really, it's none of my business, as I'm an officer in the Air Force,' I replied. 'As a matter of fact, the smart thing for me to do' — I said this as if it were an offside remark — 'would be to hint to your superiors that you have such a document, and that they should get a look at it. But you've been good to us, and you've even got some of our sick men into a hospital. So my honest advice is that you dig a hole, burn this document in it, and cover it up. Do it during chow period. It's almost a mile to where we eat and the Korean family will still be out in the fields, so nobody will see. As you're my friend, you can be sure I won't tell.' He burned it up.

"The fellow who welched was returned to the POW compound the next day and was never interrogated again. He was miserable because we let him know we had no use for him any more. He was isolated by the boys."

They came to Dave about germ warfare one day and demanded he write something about it. He did. He wrote that it was contrary to the principles of the U.S. He added that he himself saw no reason why America shouldn't use it, that he wouldn't hesitate using it himself, but that he was sure the U.S. hadn't done so. He was serving a three-month jail sentence at the time, and they doubled it to six months for this frank opinion.

Agony

When it came to giving a true picture of the mental convolutions and the circuitous thinking that the communists set in motion to break down minds, I came up against the same hurdle with Dave as with the others I had interviewed. You soon lost yourself in circles. When you tried to straighten out the crazy logic, to make it intelligible, you no longer presented an accurate account. The upside-down talk and the twisted thinking was what did the trick for the Reds. Making it plain was like trying to show someone the jitterbug by dancing the waltz and saying this was it, only hopped up.

Efforts to simplify Red argument or change the semantics into plain English defeated your purpose. Unless a reader is willing to plow through the jungle of Red verbiage, he cannot get a picture of what it really is.

The most critical stress that Dave went under was this tricky and subtle mental subversion. His case was typical. He went through actual physical agony over it.

The Reds had found that the easiest way to subdue any group of people was to give its members a guilt complex and then to lead them on from self-denunciation to self-betrayal. All that was required to put this across was a sufficiently heartless exploitation of the essential goodness in people, so that they would seek self-sacrifice to compensate for their feelings of guilt. The self-sacrifice obviously made available to them in this inside-out environment is some form of treason.

Dave obtained some very shaking examples of this and needed every bit of his mental agility to keep his balance. Not the least of the difficulty was that every negative, dirty demand was camouflaged in a thick sugar-coating of pious and patriotic expression. How were men, still mostly in their teens, at most in their thirties, who had made plain talk second nature, to see through such artifices? Of course, when a man knows what to expect, the entire situation changes.

Dave found simple incidents the most threatening to one's equilibrium. He tore his padded coat and asked his guard for needle and thread. Sewing the hole, he noticed a tear on the guard's trouser leg and offered to sew it at the same time. The guard refused, saying simply, "We're allowed to do things for you, but we're not permitted to let you do anything for us."

Dave insisted, saying, "Don't worry, nobody will see me do it." The guard finally gave in, but when Dave was halfway finished, ran to the door to see if anyone was coming.

A few days later he didn't show up and was replaced by another. "Where's the other fellow?" Dave asked.

The reply stunned him. "He confessed at the self-criticism meeting on Sunday to letting one of the prisoners sew his uniform," the replacement said. "He's been broken from headquarters squad to rifleman."

Such examples, repeated infinitely, were more effective for the Red propagandists than all their political haranguing. This peasant sincerity was being callously exploited by a political faith — communism — that had adopted all the overtones of religion and ethics. This, too, was bait to trap the POW's. Dave gave me other examples. "You would see a detachment coming in dead tired after training all day. They would see the old farmer and his wife still working on the hillside. 'Let's go up and help her,' someone would say, and up they all would go. Things like that do something to you."

Of course it wasn't noticed that political commissars in the ranks directed these activities. The fact that everyone was being worn out mercilessly in a grind like a rat race was concealed by the complexion of self-help and mutual help.

A typical instance of the unprincipled exploitation of even tender emotions was provided by one of the guards who had been shanghaied into the Communist Eighth Route Army when only twelve. He had never known anything except a Red environment and was convinced by constant indoctrination that, like a parent who sometimes is kind and sometimes punishes, everything the Reds did to him was for his own good. Dave happened to be at the guardhouse one day when a political functionary came up with a flourish and handed this man the first letter he had received from his family in several years. He hadn't known whether they were still even alive.

Immediately there was a terrific celebration by the little group. Everyone congratulated him. Grateful praise was voiced to the People's Liberation Army and to Mao Tse-tung for giving him the letter. Nobody mentioned that instead of being thanked, they should have been denounced for cutting off simple family communications this way. The guard admitted he had often written and the letter mentioned efforts to write to him! The communists have created a very renumerative tactic out of depriving a man heartlessly of his just dues and then, with a great show of generosity, giving him back a wee bit of what was coming to him all along.

Dave had to keep his wits about him every second. He saw fellow POW's get into serious trouble when they had only been trying to be polite. A man would say, "You're a fine fellow," and be accused of being insulting because he pointed when he said it. This was called showing a "hostile attitude."

"The Reds were constantly on watch for some excuse to charge you with having a hostile attitude, and when they got the slightest chance, squeezed every bit of advantage they could get out of it," Dave said. "When anyone would say something to them with conviction and they couldn't refute it otherwise, they were quick to retort, 'You have a hostile attitude.' This took them off the hook and put you on it.

"Another opening the Reds eagerly waited for was loss of temper. This was a major crime in their book. Once when they started on the germ-warfare charges I became angry and shouted that they were a pack of lies. I was reported to my interpreter, who ignored what I had said about their lying but only accused me of losing my temper. They gave me a rough time for it, letting me know I could receive up to a two-year prison sentence."

I asked Dave to be more specific about the mental agony the men suffered. What brought it about, he said, was not worry over one's own motivation, but a feeling of futility and frustration in attempting to combat the communists' upside-down logic. Deprived of background material, a man was at a tremendous disadvantage. They would mention specific cases, and the data they offered as a proof usually sounded slanted or faked, but how was a person to prove it? The Reds determined, through their controlled environment, just what facts — ^and what lies — would be given the POW's.

Dave said one argument was critical for him. "I had made the point," he recalled, "that the communist leaders promised one thing and did another, that they cheated the people and generally were no good. Instead of answering these charges, they ignored them completely and switched the whole discussion to another level entirely. Whenever you were trapped in this way, you were in for difficulty."

The indoctrinator told Dave: "Under our educational system, we are training people to accept the concept of the 'new socialist man.' When we have created this new socialist man, he will know and value only the principles that represent the best that communism advocates. Our present leaders may not be acting in accord with those principles. But when 500,000,000 people know only those principles, our leaders will be forced to act according to them because no force on earth can keep 500,000,000 people in submission."

Since then, the official Chinese communist census has claimed a population of more than 600,000,000 and steadily growing!

"This is like a circle," the indoctrinator said. "We use a bad man to teach people good ideas. Once the people learn those good ideas, they will demand that their bad leaders live by their principles. They will rid themselves of their evil leadership and establish a control that will abide by the good ideas."

The cleverness in this argument, too, was that it presented a mirage to their own people who were dissatisfied with Red leadership, persuading them to be patient and they would soon reach this oasis when they would be able to change things for the better. This was a safe outlet for subversive tendencies.

The statement was packed, of course, with double-talk and doublethink. The essential points were just left out entirely. Inferentially, this set the sights at half a billion "new Soviet men." How were Dave and his fellow prisoners to know anything about the Pavlovian theory, with its bestial, clinical basis for this human being who is to be given a changed nature? Unless they knew about it, how could they offer any judgment or make up their minds intelligently?

**My knowledge was too limited to reply properly," Dave frankly admitted. "When you had no facts to go on, their argument appeared logical and was hard to counter. Yet we had to answer at once. This was part of the rules. We were supposed to make up our minds without knowing the facts. You couldn't avoid this situation.

"I kept asking myself what the loophole was in this argument. This built up into a terrific mental problem for me. I had concluded that I was bound only by allegiance to my own mind. This, I was confident, would be a sure enough guide under those pressures. All other loyalties, I felt, necessarily emanated from that source. I was in real agony."

119

He had been lured into a position that exposed him to the enemy while depriving him of any support by his own side. "The Commies were playing for big stakes," Dave said. "I had in my safe-keeping important pieces of knowledge regarding nuclear weapons, electronics, advanced heavy bombers, and strategic war plans. I felt that I was responsible to my own conscience that I throw my weight the right way. This was a critical ideological problem that I struggled through all alone."

Actually, he did not have to do so, because it was a trap and he was under no compulsion to go into it, any more than a man is required to go on playing dice if he knows they've been loaded. But how was he and others in his position to appreciate this? They were babes in the psychological woods. They had been taught everything except what this was all about. Instead, they went back for guidance to their liberal teachings of American educational life. This had taught them only that one must always listen to the other fellow's argument and always be on the side of the underdog. Of course, the assumption was that the other fellow, too, wanted to exchange ideas and that the underdog was only a man in a less fortunate situation, holding the same ideals as oneself. Dave was up against a strategy deliberately devised to make one point of view rigid at all costs, which considered it to be "sentimentalism" and therefore criminal not to take advantage of weakness.

"Beria was liquidated about that time," Dave recalled. "I brought this up in a little group of Chinese guards. They came right back at me, presenting Beria's execution as part of a pattern for the development of this 'new Soviet man.' This conception seemed to fit any of their awkward positions! I had no idea of the dirty intrigues that surrounded the case. We were only told that it was a glorious example of how communism expelled its cheating leaders. That got me into a state of mind when I asked myself whether this was a law of society or whether it could be made into a law of society.

"Mind you, those who argued this way with me were not the indoctrinators but kids eighteen to twenty maybe. They were parroting propaganda they had been fed, but coming from their mouths, it was a most effective form of persuasion. The plain people, once taken in, were the strongest apostles of communist ideology. They were much more convincing than the regular lecturers."

The tussle for his mind revolved more and more around one philosophical point. Could *A* sometimes be *B*, if only for a moment? If he could be made to admit this, the Reds were confident the rest would follow. But Dave insisted at all times that *A* was *A*, and when it was *B*, it was no longer *A*.

His ability to stick to that principle saved him from collapse in spite of the manner in which he had been trapped into agonizing discussion with the information and power all on one side, the enemy's.

The Reds used not only verbal arguments, but physical ones, too, and at the same time! They put Dave into a bathhouse where they tried to freeze him into submission. The bathhouse had been built by the Japanese when they ran Korea as a colony. An indoctrinator whom Dave knew as General Ding Chan used both these forms of persuasion on him.

"One night they suddenly woke me up in this freezing bathhouse to give me the first letter I had received from my wife since my captivity. They made a lot of fanfare about it, bringing me a flashlight so I could read in the dark. They brought me hot water to drink. The big brass and all the English-language interpreters showed up to congratulate me. This was the first letter they had let me have in two years!

"Then they all left, only to return and wake me up once more at three a.m., when I was fast asleep. An interpreter came with the message that General Ding wanted to know what I was thinking. He wanted a reply immediately. What was in my mind just then? Imagine, at three a.m., after I had been given my first letter at eleven p.m., in what was in effect a cell crowded with cakes of ice! I took a split second to think, then, using the envelope from my wife's letter, I wrote:

"Black is black and white is white. Neither torture, maltreatment nor intimidation can change a fact. To argue the point with me who is color blind serves no useful point.

January 19, 1953.

"The words came to me in a flash, just as I am telling them to you now. The whole incident lasted only a couple of minutes. After they left, I didn't go right back to sleep, but wrote it over again on the wall, using a piece of carbon out of a broken-down flashlight battery. I did it in the dark, worrying whether I was missing a line or writing over the same words. I spread my fingers out on the wall to space the letters. When I looked next morning, I saw it clear and legible. I couldn't have done better in the daylight."

"What was this bathhouse?" I asked him. He said it was a room five or six feet by seven, with a layer of eight inches of ice on the ground. "A man could barely stretch out on it," he said. "Two cakes of ice also were in the room, that I figured were the equivalent of ninety gallons of water. One of the blocks of ice was in a huge cauldron and the other filled the tub.

"The place was so cold that the guards were relieved hourly. They sat huddled in a corner with a charcoal brazier at their feet, yet they were covered with hoarfrost by the time they were relieved.

"When I was put in, I knew I had to beat the situation somehow, and simply had to think out a way. They had allowed me to bring a comforter with me. I noticed that the moisture from my body filtered through it, appearing on the outside as a coating of ice. I figured that if I could get enough moisture into that comforter, I would get the same effect out of it as an Eskimo does with his igloo.

"The comforter became one solid piece of ice. From then on, it served as a little house for me. I stayed in it as warm as I needed. I had a cotton-padded coat which I used as a protection from the ice under me."

121

One day the Reds came and asked Dave how he felt. He replied, "Eighty-eight days to the first day of spring; one hundred and sixty-eight days to the first day of summer." He was put into that torture chamber on January 12; when the snow was crisp outside, and when he came out it was January 28.

About a month later, he met another American who had been put into the bathhouse after he had left, whom the Reds were trying to intimidate in the same fashion. He told Dave that one thing that kept him going was a paragraph that someone had written on the wall. He quoted it verbatim. He hadn't known that Dave had written it.

Five other POW's memorized it in the next three months and didn't give in to their tormentors. The Red examiners hadn't seen it: the bathhouse had been too cold for them to enter.

Combat

Dave got the full indoctrination treatment. He was given fourteen hours daily study and classwork. His textbooks ranged from the fictional-style writings of Howard Fast to Stalin's super-work. *The History of the Communist Party, Short Course.*

"They gave you a tremendous volume of material that presented only their own side," Dave said. "You read it out of sheer boredom. The average intelligent man just had to read something to keep from going crazy. They had plenty of novels for your entertainment, but they all had a Red slant. Then they let their serious works trap you by sheer repetition. They forced you to dig your own mental rut, and then to deepen it yourself by dragging a hair across the same path a million times."

Dave thought up a combat tactic for this. He made a point of thoroughly reading all these works he could lay his hands on. "I hunted for material with which I could fight them back, using their own arguments. I found enough quotations to wreck them. They stopped bothering me about indiscriminate bombing after I quoted Stalin's general order that both the front and the rear were fields of war and that one could not be defeated without overcoming the other.

"They put a great stress on co-existence. I replied with what their own literature said on the strategic use of this to bring about the dictatorship of the proletariat. I made a big point out of the Brest-Litovsk Treaty and their own admission that they had never intended keeping it."

Dave frequently referred to the page and paragraph from which some quotation came. "How can you remember it all?" I asked. He laughed. "I studied those books like the Bible, and could often tell them the exact line on a page where something was to be found. Those books gave me my best ammunition and I had to be exact, for the Commies blandly denied anything you couldn't pin down. By throwing chapter and verse back at them, I put them on the spot. The lecturer often had to go to his superiors to have the point cleared up. Frequently, his superiors had to go even higher. They had to go through with the whole rigmarole because they had built up a mysticism that they couldn't let go of without crippling themselves."

He patiently wrote long papers, taking his time at it, assembling his arguments calmly. He made a point of finding the many times they could be quoted on both sides of an argument. He found this was the principal Red vulnerability available to him in the closed environment of the POW camp. He focused on it, filling notebooks with such destructive evidence. This kept him busy and was like a game. The time came when he had a contrary argument out of their own ideology for every one of their claims. His quotations always came from the source. They could neither be denied nor refuted; the best the Reds could do was to interpret them, which usually took more background than the indoctrinators possessed. "That was my ammunition," Dave said. **We were now on even terms. So long as they didn't dispose of me once and for all by killing me, I felt perfectly safe.

"I used those Red quotations for every conceivable purpose. I got the heat off my back one time by getting them to lecture me about Kalenin's thesis that what is black today can be white tomorrow and orange the next day. I said this was impossible and that black was always black. I had been worn out when this came up and was very pleased over how they spent the next half-hour lecturing me about it. It gave me a rest I badly needed.

"I sat back relaxed, listening. As I had my own purpose, I wasn't worrying. I remembered what they said. They told me that a steel ax is the color of silver when new. If not used it quickly turns black, and after prolonged idleness, turns red with rust.

"The Reds noticed my exhaustive reading and the notebooks I kept filling. They finally were fed up with my tactics. I hadn't been able to conceal the use I made of my textbooks, so one day they confiscated the batch of them."

The men in Dave's camp were broken up for indoctrination classes into companies, platoons, and squads, with monitors to record the ideological consciousness of the men.

One senior instructor, twenty-seven or twenty-eight, known as Lee, said he had been educated at Stanford University and knew American slang. He was very thin, with harsh, vulturelike features. "When he lowered the boom, he really lowered it," Dave said.

"You'll finish your lectures in whatever time it takes you to learn the truth, whether ten, twenty, thirty, or forty years, and if you die in the meantime, you'll be buried in a very deep hole where you won't stink," he told the men one day.

From the back of the auditorium, a clear voice replied, "I hope they drop an A-bomb on Moscow! That's the only cure for this."

"I'm sorry to hear you say that, comrade," Lee replied. This remark was at once incorporated into the camp language, and helped the men keep their feelings from dangerously boiling over. Henceforth, whenever anyone made a strong, positive statement, wildly exaggerated, a dozen voices would chime in, "I'm sorry to hear you say that, comrade."

At the start, the Chinese picked their own representatives among the POW's for what they called a Daily Life Committee. They set up committees for recreation, sanitation, food, and study. "I infiltrated the study committee by putting on a very sincere attitude," Dave said.

" 'I want to learn everything you got, comrade,' I'd say. 'Bring it on. If you convince me, I'll buy it.' We had to fight fire with fire. I knew that before you can administer an antidote, you have to know the poison.

"The men strongly objected to forced study. They resented having the stuff rammed down their throats. The insults against our country and its leaders infuriated but didn't rattle us as the Reds had expected. Instead of losing our heads, we set to work to upset their program.

"The Commies put a lot of hope in me because I was educated. 'If we convince you, MacGhee, we don't have to convince the others; you'll do it,' they told me. They got rid of the chairman they had and made me head of the study committee. This put me in a strong position.

"We used all sorts of tricks to root out the canaries and progressives. They squealed on us several times, but we kept them from damaging us by destroying communist faith in them. 'They're just trying to ride the cigarette gravy train,' we'd say. 'They're only being spiteful.' We reactionaries told the Reds: 'We're sincere students, comrade. Those fellows want to get all the loot they can out of you, but we don't want loot.' When we got rid of a progressive, we'd bring in someone who thought as we. Although it took a lot of patience, we finally got the stool pigeons out of the monitoring jobs, anyway.

"We worked, too, to stop the Chinese supervisors from coming into class, using ridicule and fast reading as our tactics. I can read at a tremendous speed. As a result, we finished the required reading quickly and had the rest of the time for whatever we could get away with.

"We succeeded in cutting down greatly the time the supervisors spent in class. When they came, some such scene as this often took place. The examiner would listen a while, then stop me in the middle of a page and ask the men questions, to see if they understood. They did. He'd then ask me why I read so fast. My stock reply that stumped them was, 'I know Americans and you don't.' Then I'd say, 'You asked me to run this study program. I can't if you don't let me. Go ahead and take it over yourself if you want.' They never did, of course. I was careful to pick four or five basic questions and give the boys the answers in case the Reds asked afterwards.

"Sometimes, while reading a piece of Marxist learning very fast — they call Red propaganda 'learning' — I would insert, in as ridiculous a spot as possible, some such line as, 'But there is no joy in Mudville,' or, 'An' I learned about women from 'er.' The boys would burst out laughing, and if one of the Chinese was about, he'd grab a copy of the book and try to find out what was so funny in it. He'd be bewildered. No, we had no trouble about attendance at our meetings and no catcalls, either, as the others had. So he was generally quite satisfied, and we sure were.

"We grabbed at anything that would have the desired effect, such as puns or a play on words. A paragraph might say that automatic farm machinery in the U.S. was much inferior to that of the Soviet Union, and end up with the sentence, 'These are irrefutable facts of decadent capitalism in the U.S.' Whoever read it would modify it into something such as, 'These are easily refutable facts.' The examiners missed this sort of thing, and would only sense something was wrong when the fellows couldn't help laughing.

"Emboldened by our success in class work, we branched out into two new fields, resistance to propaganda and frustration of military interrogation. The mixed background of the POW's helped us sabotage the propaganda. Almost every profession and branch of knowledge was represented among the prisoners. So when the Reds came up with some statistics about steel, for instance, we first told them to the class as the Reds gave them to us, and then chose somebody to analyze the communist claim who understood the industry. When they gave details about textiles or anything else, we always had someone who could pick holes in what they said.

"In military intelligence, we got the interrogators all keyed up, for example, over what we called 'Philip's famous precision bridge.' We spread rumors that it solved all the requirements of warfare. As soon as some canary told them about it, they asked for a paper. We dillydallied until they finally picked someone specific and ordered him to write it up. We briefed him on what to say. He wrote twenty to twenty-five pages, which pleased the examiner until he read them. Then he was furious. 'What are you so mad about?' our chap asked him. 'You told me to do it.'

"We built up whispering campaigns in this sort of thing. We talked about a B-108 super-bomber and let the canaries eavesdrop. Then we sat and waited for it to come back from the interrogator. It did, and as usual one of our men was instructed to write it up. We planned exactly what he would say. 'Tell me all you already know about the B-108 so I won't waste time,' he said to them. 'Then I'll tell you all I know.' He wrote a paper containing all the information the Chinese had collected from canaries and added only this statement at the end: 'You already have almost all the information there is about the B-108. The only additional point of importance I know is that the B-108 is so big it lands only once every three years to enable the crew to re-enlist.'

"We never heard another word about the B-108. But it helped our constant fight to discredit the progressives who carried those rumors. Then they became reactionaries, too. We didn't fully accept them into our ranks, but gave them nasty jobs that came up. A squad of such ex-progressives once gave a particularly obnoxious examiner a terrific beating."

The problem of how far a person was justified to go in "dirty war" in camp caused endless hours of worry. Dave had a code for this. He firmly believed

125

that a man in such a situation had to draw a moral line somewhere, beyond which he would not cross. "Deceit is part of war and can properly be used to advance a military purpose, but not to gain a mere personal advantage," he said. "I tried to live up to that rule. This was a matter of my integrity and included even such vital issues as one's own safety and repatriation. On matters of personal advantage, I would not lie."

One test of his loyalty to this code came when repatriation approached. The Reds distributed five forms to be filled out by each man. Their purpose was to get together a small group of men who would promise to present the Red side in exchange for prompt release. They expressed it in double-talk, but everyone knew what was meant. Dave's indoctrinator took him for a long walk one day. This was unheard of!

"I know you are having trouble with that fifth form, so I'll help you make it out," the brainwasher said, taking one from his pocket. He led Dave to a pleasant spot on the hillside, where they sat down to "discuss." All he wanted, he told Dave, was his promise to tell the truth about the Korean War when he got home. The word *truth,* like people and learning, had a special Red meaning, and everybody in camp understood it. *Truth* meant what helped the communist side.

Dave flatly refused to use language that could be interpreted two ways. "I'm not for sale to the highest bidder," he declared. They walked slowly back, the indoctrinator glum. Before they parted, the indoctrinator told him, "You've made a mistake that the peace-loving people can hardly forgive."

Peace-loving people was another well-understood Red cliché.

When Dave finally was put across the lines, he was at peace with himself.

Chapter Seven - The British in Korea

Subtlety and Horseplay

The idea for Crazy Week that the Americans organized and made into a spectacular extravaganza came from the combined horseplay and subtlety with which the British POW's maintained their morale.

"How did it start?" I asked some of the Americans. They weren't sure, but several remembered seeing British prisoners pull off crazy stunts. These were individual cases, but the potentiality in them struck the Americans. More accustomed to organizing things in a big way, they couldn't let this opportunity pass.

Bob Wilkins, in Detroit, mentioned Jack Hobbs, a British regimental sergeant-major, whom he said was his best friend in camp. Hobbs, nearly thirty years a soldier, had seen crazy stunts pulled off in the German POW camps in

World War n, where he also was a prisoner. I was given more details by a lean comrade of his, one of the stanch "reactionaries" of the war, named William Westwood. Hobbs and Westwood belonged to the 1st Battalion of the Gloucestershire Regiment which was awarded the U.S. Presidential Citation for its sacrificial stand in 1951 that contributed so vitally to saving Seoul.

Westwood, who has a droll type of British humor, with a subtlety that is almost Chinese, must have got deeply under Red skins. They finally brushed him off as "a. bit loco," which was just what he wanted.

He enjoyed playing cards in camp. This took the boys' minds off the Reds. He played a new type of game not found in Hoyle. This game had the advantage that it outwitted kibitzers, although there were some, anyway, who kept looking over his shoulder and telling him just what to lay down.

This was strange, because they were playing without cards.

The Reds didn't like it because they felt sure it was mocking them. They'd stare goggle-eyed. There was no doubt of it; the men were playing cards. The POW's would look over their hand and one would lay down a card, exclaiming, "Here's a three of clubs," and whoever won the hand would brush in the non-existent cards. The Chinese are no mean gamblers themselves, but they never played a hand like that.

Bill also enjoyed riding his imaginary motorcycle, especially when he had somebody on the back seat. One of his greatest sports was billiards. The fact that they hadn't a billiard table or billiard balls, or anything else ordinarily necessary in the game, didn't stop the men from playing it. Bill and a fellow POW had a competition. They had spectators too, betting on the results.

A brainwasher walked in when one of these games was being played. He almost walked smack into the table. A POW dashed over in the nick of time, calling out, "Mind that table, you're knocking right into it!"

He carefully escorted him around it, while another POW remarked, "He must be blind." The Red heard him and felt sure there was something subversive about it; he tried feebly to stop it, but there was nothing tangible to forbid.

This British group stymied the Red indoctrinators on the germ-warfare charges by listening to the accusations for a while and then popping such questions as, "Tell us, how did those infected flies live at a temperature of 40 degrees below zero? Did the efficient Americans design special little overcoats for them?"

British sense of humor went from this to roughhousing. A POW, wanting some cigarette tobacco, would ask, "Anybody got a roll?"

Someone would reply, "He wants a roll, fellows," and they'd all pounce on him and roll him along the floor. Then they'd politely help him to his feet and give him what he first asked for — if they had it — in a poker-faced, most dignified manner.

The Reds didn't get this, either, but couldn't think of a way to ban it.

The men had to feel just how far they could go. One trick was to sing or talk fast, so the enemy would suspect something, but be unable to pin it down. They had their own poesy for this, which they rattled off to their utmost satisfaction:

"They seek him here,
They seek him there.
They seek old Mousey everywhere.
Will he be shot.
Or will he be hung.
That darned, elusive Mousey Dung?"

A British sergeant named Arthur Bertram Sykes first recited this on a makeshift stage when the Reds were trying to edge the boys into propaganda shows. The English pronunciation of Mao Tse-tung is elusive enough, and when translated into "Mousey Dung" and then blurred, even indoctrinators who spoke fair English couldn't get it. But the enthusiasm with which the verse was greeted aroused their suspicion and they called the speaker off the stage and asked him to explain. They said they knew it was supposed to be funny, but not that funny; they didn't understand it and didn't want it repeated.

So he went back to the stage and told a joke instead. He told about an American, Englishman, and Chinese who died and went to heaven together and knocked at the pearly gates. St. Peter opened, looked them over, and asked the Englishman what he wanted to eat.

"Oh, ham and eggs will suit me fine," he replied.

St. Peter let him in. Then he asked the American the same question.

"Ham and eggs will do for me, too," the Yank said.

Then St. Peter glanced over at the Chinese and asked him what he wanted to eat.

"I want some rice," the Chinese replied.

"Sorry, but we can't cook rice for one," St. Peter said, and slammed the door.

The roar of laughter that greeted this was too much for the communist overseer. He ordered the sergeant taken to the hole at once and the next act to come on.

As a man, the audience stood up smartly and marched out, refusing to go on with the play. The British remember that one of the pleased spectators, who had been brought in to photograph this happy POW family, was Frank Noel, who stood in a corner grinning from ear to ear.

The Reds were right in their suspicion that this joke had significance and was a weapon. It was one of many that counteracted the communist efforts to split the Americans and British. The main emphasis of the Reds in dealing with the British prisoners was on this hate-America line. The communists showed the priority they gave it by hammering at it at every opportunity.

Burchett, who tried so hard to put on a palsy-walsy act with the Americans, was the eager beaver in this. When Winston Churchill sent Field Marshal Alexander, then Minister of Defence, to Korea for a quick look-see, Burchett burst into the camp waving a long sheet of paper.

"The British POW 's have started a petition to demand an equal voice with the Americans at the Panmunjom talks," he said. A quick glance showed the signatures were those of known collaborators. There was no mystery over who had started it. Sowing seeds of hate was the Burchett-Winnington specialty.

They were met in the British camps by men who stood about with cords tied like hangnooses dangling from their hands. At one time, as Burchett entered, the POW's started singing, "You'll hang . . . you'll hang," and spontaneously followed with the words of the song, "Land of Hope and Glory." Little hangnooses dangled from their hands that time, too.

One of the reasons the Reds divided the POW's into racial and nationality divisions, after first mixing them all up, was that they got on too well together instead of getting into fights as the communists had hoped. When the Americans and Britons remained friendly even while separated, the Reds exposed their hand by trying to forbid them to meet, even ordering the POW's to stop calling across the roadway from one company to the other. Men went into the hole for breaking this regulation.

"Why can't we talk to each other any more?" the British asked their indoctrinators.

"We don't want any outbreaks," they said. "The Americans have been threatening to come across and beat you up."

The British sent some of their boys to sneak into the American side. They found out that the Reds had said the same thing over there, only making it the British who were threatening to go over and fight the Yanks.

"The Americans have occupied your country," they kept telling the British. "Your girl friends back home are all going out with the Americans," they'd say with a sneer.

That they did not have some success with their line would be fooling ourselves. A big factor in it was the *Daily Worker* of London. This Red sheet had made a cunning technique out of playing up sports. Its propaganda-wise editors made sure to give good coverage to the games in which the Britons were interested and the Reds made certain that the paper came regularly into camp.

The information-starved POW's would grab the rag and turn quickly over to the sports page. They enjoyed it thoroughly, and the Commies didn't interfere. Then, because there wasn't anything else to read, the POW's looked at the rest of the paper. Cartoons smearing the U.S. and articles dripping hate and lies about America filled a large part of the pages. The receptive mood into which the sports page had put the men paid off for the Reds.

While the indoctrinators, in dealing with the Americans, harped constantly on Wall Street, saying the communists were really the friends of the American people, they had a different slant in talking to the British. They grouped all Americans together then, Wall Street or not, as warmongers and fascist enemies.

"We're not fighting the British people," they would say. "We're fighting the Americans. They're your enemies, too. We're really on the same side."

The eternal search for a scapegoat was slyly exploited. The communists did all they possibly could to divert attention from the Americans to the British and from the British to the Americans whenever a psychological need arose in a man to pin his troubles somewhere.

The real feeling of the communists was demonstrated when an English POW died two days after receiving his first letter from his wife. His "muckers" got their heads together — muckers is a favorite British Army word for chum or comrade, and comes from men fighting together in the muck and mire — and decided to write the widow and tell her how her husband's end was made peaceful by her timely letter. They asked their indoctrinators for permission.

"Of course, if you put in the letter that he died of a guilty conscience because of the atrocities he committed," was the answer they received.

A number of the American POW 's told me about British pluck and comradeliness. "They managed to have their tea at ten and four," Wilkins told me. "They rarely had any tea, of course, and were lucky when they managed hot water. But they had plenty of ceremony and went about it with the utmost composure and seemed not to have the least worry in the world. They might have been worrying themselves sick a minute before and would start right afterwards, but not during teatime.

"They simply didn't notice that they weren't drinking tea. The only mention of tea was the call, 'Tea's up!' Then nobody referred to there not being any; any more than they would have complained about the lack of it if they had been guests somewhere. They were very English about it. This break did a lot to keep up morale."

While they still were able to get together, British and American POW's who hadn't seen a square meal for a long time would engage in animated descriptions of each other's choice dishes. Some fellows filled notebooks with such recipes when they were supposed to be writing Marxist ideology.

The Coronation

The Anglo-American hate line came a real cropper at the time of the Queen's Coronation, when the Americans acted as guards for the British to conduct their own Coronation ceremony in peace — and face the music later on. This was at Song-ni.

Of all the services held that day, in London and around the world, none could possibly have exceeded this in solemnity and depth of meaning. This was surely Elizabeth's greatest tribute on that momentous day in her life.

The Reds tried to block any information on the subject from slipping into the camps. Anyone who became excited over the Coronation was in no shape to absorb dialectical materialism. But unless the Reds clipped references to it out of such Communist Party publications as the *Daily Worker,* which would have given their game away too obviously, they had to let some details through. These were sufficient for the British to figure out the time of the Coronation to the hour and minute.

When they determined to hold their own formal ceremony, the Americans said they'd like to participate. So each side set about making a flag. This meant sacrificing a couple of shirts, some red antiseptic stolen from the doctor's office, and blue ink. Bill Westwood and Marine Commando Corporal Rickey Beadle made the British flag. Bill recalls that the American flag was made by Corporal "Chip" Wood and a chum of his. The Americans had difficulty with the forty-eight stars, so Bill helped with these, too.

Rats tipped off the Reds, who reacted swiftly. They sent orders strictly forbidding any activity in connection with the Coronation, threatening dire punishment if any attempt were made to violate this injunction. The British decided that a service would be held, come hell or high water.

When Coronation Day came, the British wore rosettes! They had been secretly made ahead of time by John Varney, a Londoner, out of bits of blue prison jacket and shreds of a white shirt, colored the same way as the flags.

Everyone, in accordance with daily routine, had to appear for roll call in the morning. This always included whoever occupied the hole — they had to climb out for those few minutes. Six Britons were in the pit that day. They stood up with rosettes on their jackets. These had been smuggled to them the day before with their gruel, along with some tobacco for special celebration.

The Reds stared in amazement, particularly at those who had come out of the hole. They became very angry and demanded that the rosettes be taken off and handed over to them.

The POW's stood stiffly, not making a sound. The Reds picked on a corporal up from the pit, Frank Upjohn, and insisted he give up his. He took it off and gripped it tightly in his clenched fist, a determined gleam in his eyes. The Commies grabbed him and tried to open his fist. They failed. They called a guard to bring a crowbar. It took that and three men to open Upjohn's hand and get the rosette out of it.

The others, standing in line, hastily took their rosettes off and pinned them under their jackets. After the experience with the corporal, the Chinese just stalked off. The one rosette they had seized was a face-saver. The Britons wore their rosettes all day, even Upjohn's comrades in the hole.

At the time they figured the Coronation was starting, about twenty-five Britons — all in that particular company — gathered in a squad room while a dozen Americans stationed themselves at strategic points on guard rounda-bout. A church service was conducted by Charles Bailey, a corporal, although this was against the rules. At the exact moment they calculated the crown was being placed on their lady sovereign's head, they sang "God Save the Queen." They let go at this moment, singing at the top of their voices.

The Chinese rushed in, but were too late to do anything about it. The Brit-ish POW's had had their Coronation service and the Americans had had a hand in it. The Reds grabbed two of the Britons and took them away, de-manding an explanation. Then they sent them back to say that they were hostages for their fellow POW's, and would be severely punished if any fur-ther effort was made to disobey instructions to ignore the Coronation.

At 8 P.M., the Britons gathered in a corner room with the Americans again acting as sentries. The two men designated as hostages went in, too, but were not visible from the door. Then they began a loud sing-song. Their voices soared. The Americans came in and they all sang together. They could be heard over the entire valley.

The hut of one of the main indoctrinators was near by. What were the Reds going to do about this? They did nothing. The issue was too explosive, and at this stage any action would have had to be very drastic and could have lost them the propaganda gains they had already won with some of the POW's.

Another instance of comradely Anglo-American feeling, in spite of the cal-culated hate campaign, was on New Year's Eve of 1953. At midnight, the Brit-ish sang the American national anthem and the Americans sang Britain's.

The British change of pace from droll subtlety to horseplay stood them in good stead. The Reds never knew what to expect. They found out that one of the Britons had served in the Navy. They had only a few prisoners with naval experience, and so eagerly got to work on him. "We'll make a fair deal with you," they said. "We'll not bother you any more if you tell us just one of the secret weapons in your fleet."

The fellow thought for a few moments, and then said, "It's a deal."

He said he'd tell them of a secret device he learned about on a destroyer. When an enemy submarine was about, the destroyer spread green paint over the surface of the water where the undersea craft would have to poke up its periscope to see the target.

"Because of the paint, the submarine commander would not realize that he had already surfaced and would keep coming up. When he reached an alti-tude of about 1,000 feet, the destroyer would shoot him down with its anti-aircraft guns."

The interrogator had been listening intently, taking notes, so it took him a minute to catch on — and explode!

Bill Westwood learned to draw in camp. "I couldn't draw two straight lines before I was captured," he said. His pen and ink and pencil sketches possess a gripping quality of depth and simplicity that the grim realism of camp life taught him. One POW did a small caricature of a man hanging, entitling it, "Squealer Getting his Just Dues." He pasted it on an outside wall. The Reds found out who had done it and put him into the hole. At once a number of POW's started drawing sketches against canaries and posting them up wherever they could. They got a kick out of hearing Chinese go about at night with a searchlight, hunting for them to tear down.

"I wanted to do something constructive, too," Bill said. *Tm one of those blokes who believes that a man can do anything if he sticks his mind to it. So I started drawing. I got to enjoy it, and found that this was what I was after to keep my mind busy and off the Reds. From then on, every chance I got, I'd draw."

He took his life around him as his subject. "What I saw engraved itself so strongly on my mind that I had no particular difficulty transferring it to paper," he said. Unfortunately, he was not allowed to take any sketches out with him. "But I remembered every line in them," he said, "and I've reproduced a number."

He showed me some. One, a scene among Americans at the entrance to the "death house," is unforgettable. This was a room or hut each camp set aside for patients on whom the Reds decided any treatment would be wasted because they were going to die anyway. A lanky American lad is seen sitting outside, naked to the waist, his ribs protruding, his head held up by two skinny arms. "I can still see him sitting there," Bill said. "He was starving, and was sent to wait his turn at the death house. The space was all taken up."

A couple of American stretcher bearers, followed by a Chinese soldier, are shown in the foreground, against the Korean mountains. An almost naked body, nearly a skeleton, is on the stretcher, its head hanging over one end, staring into the sky, its hair flopping below the canvas. One arm, as thin as a rail, hangs limply over the side.

"That's exactly as I saw it," Bill said. "The fellow in front, carrying the shovel, had to come back alone because his buddy in back, with the pick, succumbed to malnutrition and general debility before they finished digging the grave. He fell dead, and was buried in it, too."

A Red soldier is seen bringing up the rear, carrying his bayoneted rifle, striding forward in the peculiar gait of the Chinese troops.

Many of Bill's sketches were of hungry men. He saw plenty of them. A remark he made about malnutrition was unlike anything I had ever heard before. "You mention hunger in a strange way," I said. "What actually is hunger? I mean the sort of hunger the POWs experienced at camp. Can you describe it?"

He hesitated a few moments and then, in a very low voice said, "Yes, I think I can." He spoke in a meditative sort of way. "When you're starving," he said, "you're so weak that if you stand up, you black out. You just can't stand up. You have to grab onto something, and if you let go, you fall down.

"I have seen men fall down this way and never get up again. They'd be walking one minute and fall dead the next. You can't always tell from looking. Starvation doesn't mean being thin. You don't have to be thin to be starving to death.

"When you're starving, you feel just tired. You just want to go to sleep. You feel fatigue every moment. You feel it with every motion you make, and it hurts, and so you try to keep as still as possible and to go to sleep. The moment you rest, you want to go right off to sleep.

"When you're really starving, you don't feel hungry any more. You feel completely listless.

"Eating, when at last you get the chance, is terribly difficult. When you're on a starvation diet, it's the same as when you go entirely without food for many days. You're just not hungry any more.

"The first few bites you get to eat make you want to retch. You have to force them down your throat.

"That's the stage when a man either lives or dies. If he can force those few bites past his gullet, he'll probably live. The trouble is that he doesn't have the will power. That's what he has to force, too.

"Just to lift a bite of food from a table to your mouth hurts — here — and here."

He lifted his arm and looked at it, and pointed to a spot in the muscle above the elbow, and on the tendon below it. The way he pointed was so precise, although he did it with the utmost simplicity, that I stopped him.

"How do you know all this so exactly?" I asked. "Did you . . . ?"

He nodded. "Yes," he said. He was three full days without a bite of food during the Imjin River battle, and for the next two days he wasn't given a morsel.

"A time comes when a man hasn't the will power any more," he went on. "We weren't pushed quite that far. The Americans got it worse than we did at that stage, during the winter of 1950-1951, and it knocked the will power out of a lot of them."

"Are you sure it's will power that prevents a man from swallowing, or is it something that happens to his throat muscles when he's famished that makes him gag?" I asked.

"I don't know — a doctor might be able to answer that," he replied. "I just know the feeling."

"What is the feeling?"

"As if something at the top of your throat is repelling the food. A revulsion for the type of food you're given may come over you. If we had been given better than the bit of slops we got, maybe it wouldn't have been so difficult.

"If I could have had one egg. Just one egg. . . .

"That's where the danger lies. Even if a mucker tries to help you get it down, there's nothing he can do except encourage you. You've got to have the will power."

134

Bill came down with pneumonia at one time, which on top of scurvy and malnutrition nearly finished him off. The Reds waited until he was almost dead.

"I must have been in a coma, for the next thing I remember," he told me, "was seeing a blurred figure in front of my face. He was so close he could nearly touch my nose with his. I was beyond sensation. I just remember the face — how could I forget it? His words still ring through me. 'Listen to me,' he was saying. 'Listen to me very carefully. I am going to save your life. We are going to save your life. I am going to give you an injection. We are going to save your life, remember that. Remember that we are saving your life. We are saving your life for you. . . .' "

The words droned off. Bill must have become unconscious again. This sort of thing happened too frequently for it not to be a deliberate tactic.

Chapter Eight - What Brainwashing Is

Two Processes; Many Elements

The original disclosures about brainwashing came out of the agony of the people who went through it and had the will and courage to describe it. Information came, too, from the writings and statements of the communists themselves, in their overt and covert literature and documents, ranging from secret instruction sheets for teachers in Red schools to diaries and texts of speeches and orders.

No matter whether I was speaking to Robert A. Vogeler, the American engineer who was arrested and sentenced to ten years in prison by a brainwashing court in Budapest, or the Chinese student, Chi Sze-chen, from the North China People's Revolutionary University outside Peking, the essential details given me were identical, varying only in the intensity of the different pressures used.

Brainwashing was revealed as a political strategy for expansion and control made up of two processes. One is the conditioning, or softening-up, process primarily for control purposes. The other is an indoctrination or persuasion process for conversion purposes. Both can be conducted simultaneously, or either of them can precede the other. The communists are coldly practical about it, adjusting their methods to their objective. Only the result counts for them.

If what they seek is only propaganda or a sworn statement for some immediate objective, as a radio talk or court evidence, so long as the first process — softening up — can get it for them, they do not waste their time and energy going on to indoctrination. They operate strictly within the "practical" framework of dialectical materialism, which recognizes only power. The sole reason that the Red hierarchy concerns itself at all any longer with indoctrination is for Party discipline, their only protection. They want to make sure, so far as they can, that their followers will not grab the first opportunity to turn against them. That is their eternal nightmare, the dilemma they have been unable to solve and never can — short of creating a "new Soviet man" with the instinctive obedience of the termite instead of a free will which is subject to reasoning faculties and is therefore never "reliable."

William N. Oatis, the American correspondent seized in Prague, was given only the softening-up treatment, not the indoctrination. When he asked for Stalinist literature to read, thinking this might influence his persecutors, to his amazement they turned him down! They weren't interested in his conversion. He was what the Red ideologists refer to in horror as a "cosmopolitan," a weak link. They could never have been sure of him. The Reds wanted Oatis for a very specific purpose, to provide confessions that could be employed in an anti-Semitic frame-up within the Communist Party known as the Slansky case.

When this was achieved, the communists had no further use for him. Except for the fact that he was an American citizen whose case was being vigorously followed up by the press, they would have cast him into a slave-labor camp to get whatever additional profit they could squeeze out of his bones before his death. Their treatment had already started him on the road to tuberculosis.

The Reds always trim their sails in brainwashing to what they are seeking to accomplish. Their strategy almost invariably has a major and a lesser objective. This dualism is one of their tactics. Then, if the big objective fails or is long delayed, they hope to achieve the other. They stand to profit either way. By aiming at two targets, too, they gain flexibility and keep their enemies baffled by a sort of "now you see it and now you don't" act.

The long-range objective of brainwashing is to win converts who can be depended on to react as desired at any time anywhere. This is the inside-out meaning they give the word *voluntary* and is why they condemn free will with such ferocity, for its existence is basically inconsistent with communism.

Even when he stands by himself, the truly indoctrinated communist must be part of the collectivity. He must be incapable of hearing opposing ideas and facts, no matter how convincing or how forcibly they bombard his senses. A trustworthy communist must react in an automatic manner without any force being applied. Only then is he the "new Soviet man" that Lenin foresaw. The only real guarantee for this, he believed, was to grab a baby from its cradle and then to keep it all its life from the slightest contact with outside ideas or places, so a subversive word can never enter its ego. This is patently impossible so long as a tiny isle exists anywhere outside the Red orbit. That is why the iron curtain is vital to a totalitarian state.

So long as this iron curtain is impenetrable, actual conversion to communism is not always necessary. So long as the individual does what the Party wants, it is usually sufficient. The achievement of this submission is the immediate shortrange objective of brainwashing. The man does not have to be a true believer so long as he is convinced that he has no alternative to following Red instructions. Hope — the prospect of any alternative in life, no matter how slim — must be wiped out of his mind entirely before communism can feel safe with him.

Communism, as practiced in real life — and brainwashing amply proves this — has nothing whatsoever to do with the word as defined by the dictionary. The Party's own name is one of its most striking examples of doubletalk. Communism is a sheer power system, gang rule with modern appliances. So long as the individual submits unquestioningly, he is what is referred to as a "disciplined Party member."

Brainwashing is a very intricate manipulation, more like a treatment than a formula. Each of the two processes that make it up are themselves composed of a number of different elements. They are found in every case of brainwashing, although the proportions differ according to the patient's resistance and the purpose for which the Reds are treating him, and range from a very mild and disarmingly subtle application to crude force polished over with Marxist lingo. These can be easily catalogued.

They are hunger, fatigue, tenseness, threats, violence, and in more intense cases where the Reds have specialists available on their brainwashing panels, drugs and hypnotism. They are applied in two broad ways, one by what is called "learning" and the other through the confession phenomenon. "Learning" and confession are inseparable from brainwashing. Everyone has to participate in them, whether a party member or not. *Learning* in this sense means only political teaching from the communist standpoint. Confession is an integral part of the rites. In China there are no exceptions from it for anyone, any more than for attendance at "learning" classes. Everyone within reach of Party cadres, security police, and soldiers has to attend, even if a hermit in a cave. The retention of his own individuality by a single person is recognized as a deadly menace by the whole monolithic structure.

"Learning" begins with the study of communist literature, but soon embraces what is called criticism, self-criticism, examination, re-examination, thought conclusions, and "learning by doing." These are obligatory in schools, factories, government bureaus, army battalions, and prisons.

The methods used to make "learning" and confession palatable and workable are borrowed freely from three sources. These are evangelism, psychiatry and science. The language and ideals of each of these fields were taken over and given new meanings and new interpretations in accordance with communist needs. Brainwashing is a combination of this fake evangelism and quack psychiatry in a setting of false science.

The entire mechanism of brainwashing, so as to condition the patient and to indoctrinate him, particularly to accomplish the latter, is geared to putting his mind into a fog. That is the purpose of all the sly and harrowing pressures used. If it were not for the need to deeply confuse the man, there would be no necessity to deprive him of a balanced diet, of a recuperative sleep, of a mind free from horrible fears. Brainwashing is a system of befogging the brain so a person can be seduced into acceptance of what otherwise would be abhorrent to him. In brainwashing, a fog settles over the patient's mind until he loses touch with reality. Facts and fancy whirl round and change places, like a phantasmagoria. Shadow takes form and form becomes shadow, inducing hallucination. However, in order to prevent people from recognizing the inherent evils in brainwashing, the Reds pretend that it is only another name for something already very familiar and of unquestioned respect, such as education or reform, or, at worst, a synonym for old-fashioned atrocities. Further, the Reds bring forth the argument that it isn't anything new, but what has been happening all down history, nothing more than the Spanish Inquisition, the atrocities committed by conquistadors, or the excesses of colonialism.

The concealment and subterfuge are intended to distract attention from the glaring fact that brainwashing is something new which is contrary to human nature and inseparable from communism. Brainwashing is no more just indoctrination than a pumpkin pie is any longer a pumpkin; something more has been added and a fundamental change made by a cooking process. That is exactly what happens in brainwashing to innocent factors such as persuasion and discussion. They are chopped up and parboiled. Neither is brainwashing just atrocities or even a revival of the Inquisition. The Inquisition had no Pavlov and was not thought up in a physician's laboratory. Science was not enlisted to put it across.

Each of the elements that goes into brainwashing and the methods used in their application requires detailed explanation before the system can be properly understood.

Some of the Elements

Hunger is ever-present in brainwashing cases and ranges from outright starvation, which anyone can see, to a planned malnutrition. Diet deficiencies were cunningly thought up by diet specialists whose job, unlike elsewhere, was to keep meals scientifically unbalanced instead of balanced.

Hunger has many forms, some unknown to those suffering from it. I remember the shock I got as a boy when I read about the small son of a rich family who had to go to a hospital to be treated for malnutrition. How could wealthy parents lack food to give their child? I could not understand how a boy could live in the midst of plenty and still be hungry. The explanation, of course, was that a lopsided diet can deprive the body of necessary nutriments just as easily as insufficiency, and it makes no difference whether the cause is lack of money or an improper choice of foodstuffs. The effect is the same.

I recall, too, my surprise when I first traveled in a faminestricken area in China and saw so many pouchy stomachs. People looked well fed, yet they would collapse in their tracks and perish of hunger. An uninformed observer would mistake their bellies for the corporations of the well fed. That is because the starving fill themselves with anything that has bulk, even the bark of trees, no matter how injurious to the system.

The usual communist tactic was to provide just enough food for survival but not enough for a person's brain to function adequately. The common plaint of people who have come out from brainwashing is, "I was always hungry." That was their chronic state.

This tactic is used against entire populations inside the communist-dominated countries. The masses are less likely to make trouble that way. In their befogged mental state, they react uncritically to propaganda pressures. Hunger is the weapon which Soviet efficiency experts have discovered will make a man work himself to death "voluntarily." Hunger, too, will goad a person into horribly heartless and unfair competition with his fellows, to which the Reds have given deceitfully progressive names in a speed-up system unparalleled by the worst labor exploitations of the first days of the industrial age. Indoctrination is a means toward increased production of that sort and is employed this way throughout Red industry.

A new and topsy-turvy role is entrusted to the dietician. That profession was developed by the Free World to give people a balanced diet. Under communism it adjusts the food quota to the purposes of political pressure. The POW camp in Korea, set up in hideous caves north of Pyongyang, which the prisoners with grim humor nicknamed Pak's Palace after the sadist who set it up, was under such rigid mind-enfeebling dietary rules. That was a specialized institution. Prisoners had to go through a special screening to be admitted. They had to possess some particularly important contribution that the Reds felt they could make to the communist cause. The purpose of Pak's Palace was to get it out of them. Soviet Russians were attached to it. The prisoners always knew when questions came from them, for they were written in a terse, professional manner. POW's saw them in Russian Army uniforms. Pak's Palace worked closely with brainwashing establishments directly under Soviet Russian inquisitors in Manchuria, to which some of the prisoners were transferred for advanced treatment. In Pak's Palace, the minimum amount of rice that a man could eat and still survive was carefully tabulated and then cut by one-third. While the portions were being distributed, a knife would be passed over the top of the cup to make sure that not an additional grain slipped in. The mortality rate can be imagined.

Looking back over their experiences, the ex-prisoners were able to see how cunningly the hunger motive was used. The amounts of food ladled out were adjusted to the effect desired, like a treatment, without any relation to available supplies. Food was apportioned according to a man's resistance qualities. This was even done openly. Every POW in Korea knew that the boys who collaborated got extras. An additional spoonful of cabbage in a bowl of rice can become the most important thing in the world to a man, inciting any sacrifice. Unless he kept his balance, the invisible line between self-sacrifice and sacrificing one's buddies and country became lost in the pangs of hunger. Treason slipped in when such a person let his guard down for a moment. The "gravy train" was a common expression and each man knew what it meant. What it meant was not gravy, but perhaps an ounce more of the native grain *kaoliang* or a single cigarette. In the same camp, some ate better and others starved. Without a word being said, this constituted a powerful argument and a not so-subtle pressure.

Fatigue is another of the chronic conditions under brainwashing. No more insidious poison exists than fatigue and no worse torture than prolonged fatigue. Its wearying, debilitating effects are maddening. Most people at some time or another have gone for twenty-four hours without sleep. Many have survived several days in a row with very little sleep. But kept up, this cracks the finest mind and drives the strongest person insane. Suicide is a welcome relief to prolonged sleeplessness. "I can't sleep" is one of the most common complaints of people removed to a mental asylum to keep them from killing themselves. When a vigilant armed guard is put over a man day and night, watching him even when he attends a call of nature so that he cannot escape by suicide, submission to any communist demand can be a welcome relief, a boon accepted with real gratitude.

Like hunger, fatigue was scientifically calculated and subtly applied. Did the student of the "learning" class like basketball? Let him play it hours at a time, daily. Then let him attend hours of discussion meeting each day and night, too. Compulsory! Let him, on top of this, do his full day's study, with such overtime in the form of "social work" as was called for by the various "patriotic campaigns" always underway. The routine was the same from factory to prison.

Does a man have an inquiring mind, and did he bring up some taboo subject at a "discussion meeting"? Then let him become a "model worker," without being released from his "studies," and give him plenty of opportunity to join in "democratic discussion." Give him so much politics of a routine nature that he'll have no time for any unorthodox form of it.

Dr. Henry P. Laughlin, of the medical school of George Washington University in Washington, in discussing a clinical study that had been made of prolonged wakefulness, referred to the "more or less abnormal state" created in all such cases, "characterized by loss of the sense of reality and the clouding of mental faculties. The individual becomes increasingly dreamlike and out of contact. . . . The individual who has suffered sleep deprivation is more amenable to suggestion. He is more apt to carry out demands of those who would have him undertake certain specified behavior and he is less likely to put up resistance to the demands of someone in authority."

Sly, depraved minds find almost limitless possibilities in the exploitation of fatigue. Interrogators create an environment in which sleep becomes almost impossible. When the plagued subject finally dozes off, it is into a restless, unsatisfactory sleep, or into a deadening stupor. If the former, he is awakened at any unusual hour. If the latter, he is forced up again after maybe only an hour of rest. The trick is to let him fall into a deathlike slumber, every pore of his body in agony for sleep. After giving him just enough time to reach this state of complete slumber, he is roughly awakened and brought back for a new session of interrogation. He is kept up half a day, a whole day, or sometimes even longer, while relays of examiners, who have had plenty of rest, take turns at harassing him.

This tactic, like hunger, is manipulated in its comparatively mild form against entire populations inside the curtain countries. Observers of communist affairs have often been amused or bewildered by what looked from the surface like the grossest form of inefficiency. Moscow and Peking constantly stress the critical need for increasing production. Every possible means of improving output is scientifically thought up. More overtime work is constantly demanded. The "model worker" and the "labor hero" are given all the glory that the co-ordinated communications system of the communists can work up. Yet these same workers are required to give hours and hours of the little leisure time that remains to them to "social activities" and "discussion" that drag on drearily hour by hour. The observer cannot understand why the Stakhanovite specialists have not done away with most of these obvious handicaps to production, for there could be no doubt that they were dangerously lessening the stamina of the peasant and the working man.

The analyst from the Free World who thinks the communist rulers were merely being silly about this reveals his own ignorance of their methods. The communist hierarchy is not so foolish as to miss noting the corrosive effect of all these extracurricular hours on the minds and bodies of their people, already strained to the utmost in endurance. If they keep these pressures going, it simply means that they want to do so and that they have a purpose in doing so.

The Forbidden City-Kremlin Axis has well calculated the sacrifice that it must pay to stay in power. The Red chiefs, who have made greater production instead of improved working conditions the objective of trade unionism, well understand how ridiculous it is to expect more efficiency from an already tired worker if he has to participate in these grueling "study sessions" instead of being allowed to go home and relax. He cannot be permitted this relaxation, for during this uncontrolled leisure time he will surely become dissatisfied over his exploited, unhappy condition, and think up ways of freeing himself. These interminable "discussions" and "study" are intended to help create the fatigue that is part of brainwashing.

Tenseness is another chronic state artificially aroused. Every prisoner worries about how long he will be kept and what will be done to him. "What do they actually want from me?" The Reds don't tell him. Accusations, when made, are vague generalizations. They set up a quarantine against outside information coming to him. Nobody will tell him anything, even the most innocuous detail. Ignorance over why he is being held or what is wanted from him becomes an agony that feeds on his own doubts and fears. Readers were amused in August, 1953, to hear that Edgar Sanders, the British businessman held for four years in an Hungarian prison, did not know that Stalin was dead or Elizabeth was his Queen. That is no joke to those kept in such an unworldly atmosphere.

I remember the peculiar feeling I got one day after sitting a number of hours in a modern broadcasting studio in New York. I had asked someone how it was outside and he had told me about the rain. "When did it start?" I asked, and he gave me details. This made me change my plans. Then, when I stepped out into the street, I found out it was sunny and pleasant and there had been no rain at all. My friend laughed. He had been kidding me, taking advantage of the windowless walls of the air-conditioned studio. He had caught me unawares on a matter of almost no importance. What if I had been kept in such a conditioned environment for a year, two years — several years — on what political facts might I have been caught unawares? The thought wasn't pleasant.

The prisoner of the Reds is thrust into an iron-curtained compartment inside an iron-bamboo curtain, the prey to petty and fearsome hints and warnings, with no means of checking up on any detail. Every human being craves someone he can trust. The Reds develop their Winningtons for such occasions. The usual Red tactic is to leave a prisoner alone for an extended period, without any charges being made against him, without him being given any news of his family or the outside world — indeed, without his family being given any hint about his whereabouts or condition.

Is it true that his loved ones are being penalized along with him and their only hope is in his confessing? His best friends won't dare ask his whereabouts or indicate they have known him, otherwise they court arrest, too, and may be asked why they are so worried, or in what crimes they have been co-conspirators along with him. Relatives will eventually tire of asking or else will be given the pointed hint that it would be much safer for them just to go home and await developmerits. Just wait . . . wait . . . wait. That, too, is pressure.

The secret police may have knocked at 3 a.m. and taken their man away, or may have politely made an appointment with him to visit their headquarters at some convenient hour, and then have detained him.

The usual Red tactic then is to leave the prisoner alone. The Russian communists usually do it for a few weeks or some months, allowing the tenseness to draw tight, like a noose, before they begin their questioning or give him any idea what it is all about. The Chinese are more patient. They leave the prisoner this way for many months, even a year or two, without providing a clue as to why he is being held.

The agonized victim tortures himself thinking up every possible blunder he might have made, even by omission, every possible act of his that might be considered a crime under far-fetched communist law and its all-embracing theory of responsibility. Whom did he know; whom had he met? So, without a word being said, long before his first formal interrogation, each man desperately probes his mind and soul for personal guilt. Soon he stops figuring about whether he will confess, but concentrates on figuring out what to confess that will satisfy the authorities and be the guilt they seek so he can escape from bondage. The self-criticisms that every man has to write, in or out of prison, enable him to feel out the authorities on this. When officials express approval of his self-criticism, the confession they want will have been indicated in it. The game is like searching for a concealed toy and being told you're hot, cold, warm . . . warmer . . . until you locate it. Until the officials say his self-criticism is getting warm, he is told that he is not being frank and to do it all over again. If he doesn't remember each detail exactly, and contradicts himself on any point, he will have baited his own trap. He is given ample time to build up his own case against himself, to be his own prosecutor and to convict himself.

When he asks what he's done wrong, he's only told, "You know what you've done; you know your own misdeeds — confess!" What guilt? No man is perfect. Any normal human being can conjure up many possible transgressions which he may have committed, unwittingly perhaps.

Everyone has heard of false accusations made against others, built up out of nothing, interpreted out of doubletalk. These add to the man's worries. "Are they trying to frame me?"

Meanwhile, continually dinned into his ears is the refrain, "Mao Tse-tung is merciful to those who confess." Confess to what? A man cannot be freed until he confesses. This, too, is part of the ritual.

When the Reds have designs on someone for important political use in the future, either for a propaganda appearance or as a prosecution witness in someone else's trial, they first arrest and hold him. They have plenty of time to think up some accusation. They usually wait for him to think up the evidence they want all by himself, through the trial-and-error method of self-criticism.

Then one day the questioning suddenly begins, blowing hot and cold, raising the man's spirits one moment, dashing them to the cold floor the next. The prisoner will likely have sufficiently broken himself by worry to have thought up plenty of confession material and be in a beaten, contrite mood.

He will be so weakened by this prolonged agony and the accompanying physical pressures that he can no longer remember exactly. He becomes more than absent-minded. Big gaps come into his mind. He isn't sure of anything. Any suggestion forcibly or subtly presented is likely to sink into his mind with slight if any resistance. What is real and what unreal in such an environment? He no longer is sure of anything, much less what happened or didn't happen in the faraway past.

Tricks that would be normally seen through in a moment have great shock effect. I heard of cases in which a prisoner, held for an indefinite period, was called out after lingering almost a year in his cell. The examiner greeted him cordially, shaking his hand as if they were old friends. He gave him a chair to sit on, cigarettes to smoke, called out loudly for someone to come and pour tea for him, and acted as if he were an important visitor, not the wreck of a man just out of a filthy cell.

"I just don't know how it happened," the brainwasher said. "We were going to start your questioning right away, after a few weeks at most. You've been held nearly a year. That's horrible. We're terribly sorry that happened. Your name somehow got mixed up in the lists. I only found out about it yesterday."

Any human being, unacquainted with such deviltry, will feel a surge of hope going through him. His guard will be down. Actually, this will be just the beginning of his prolonged persecution.

Tenseness has many forms and the Reds take advantage of them all. They range from uncertainty and frustration to hopelessness and inevitability. They include a dualist sense of betrayal — of betraying and being betrayed. The Reds do everything they can to persuade a man that his country doesn't give a hoot about him any more, that his loved ones won't raise a finger on his behalf, and that his friends have let him down. Every bit of evidence that can be twisted out of shape to give this impression is presented to him and elaborated upon. Where there is some support for this evidence, they squeeze every drop of effect from it. The captive is skillfully led up this dismal trail until he feels completely abandoned. During this stage, the examiners are usually very harsh on him. They give him the works.

No matter whether the men I interviewed came from a satellite country in Europe or from Red China, his brainwashers had told him he had been deserted and betrayed by country, church, and friends, so that he now stood all alone. This was impressed on Robert Vogeler in Budapest until he tried unsuccessfully to climb over a railing and hurl himself to death to escape from this awful loneliness. This, too, was told to Robert T. Bryan, Jr., the China-born American lawyer in Shanghai. The prisoners of war in Korea were told the same.

Tenseness is aroused by conveying a semblance of omniscience, of knowing everything. A prisoner from Korea told me how stunned he was when his interrogator casually asked him, "How's that farmer brother of yours getting

144

on?" He had only told them about the brother who was a mechanic. The effect can hardly be overestimated. "I couldn't get it out of my mind," this man said to me.

Another said he was "knocked for a loop" when his questioner mentioned his full name, with a middle initial that he had not used since a schoolboy. "If they can find out even such small details, they must know everything, I thought."

What they really do know is exaggerated out of all proportion. As a consequence, their victim feels trapped by his friends and begins to distrust them, suspecting that his bosom chum back home must have been an enemy agent all the time. He retires fearfully into his shell, bringing success to the Red effort to make him feel all alone, desperately all alone, even when among his pals. They lure him into closing his mind against his own people.

When this is accomplished, the Red attitude changes precipitously. Nowhere to go? Why he has a new and wonderful home waiting for him, a paradise, a virtual rebirth. Communism is waiting for him. He has somewhere to go, into their embrace, where he will be coddled and protected. The Reds put on an act of tender understanding. They stand with waiting arms. That is his safe haven, the alternative they offer him, after ridding him of all other supports.

"You are all alone!" is the forceful, first part of this pressure line. "There is nowhere else for you to go," is its companion expression. Another form this takes is driving hope out of the mind of their victims and replacing it with the feeling that Red victory is inevitable. All add up to, "You have nowhere to turn but to us."

The hopelessness-inevitability line permeates communist strategy everywhere the Reds go, no matter whether in an international conference as at Geneva in 1954 or in a torture chamber in a grim Leningrad prison. Communist strategy, often so incomprehensible otherwise, makes sense when analyzed from the standpoint of hopelessness-inevitability.

Confess your guilt, cleanse yourself, and you will be accepted into our paradise, is what they seem to say. They funnel right down to a man's subconscious and offer him a new life, rebirth.

We make a joke out of the "*nyet* complex" of the Russian mind and say that this persistent negative attitude is just stubbornness, making a mountain out of a molehill. No, the Russian is not being funny, nor is it a complex; it is a tactic to prove that what the communists want always happens, no matter how long it takes, that there is no hope in opposing their will. The point in debate is only a symbol, and what it represents is the inevitability of communist world victory, in accordance with the teachings of dialectical materialism, which is their faith. All this, too, is part of brainwashing.

The visit that was made to Red China in late 1954 by British Labor Party leaders was exploited by the Reds as part of this hopelessness-inevitability line. Former Prime Minister Clement Attlee and his tousled rival, Aneurin

Bevan, walked through the cynically named Model Reform Prison at Peking without seeing or talking to the inmates. Absolutely no contact was allowed between them. A number of American and British prisoners and eminent Chinese were inside its walls at the time, having endured mental torture for months or years. This visit to their prison by these VIPs — very important persons — was made the subject of the so-called discussion meetings that are obligatory everywhere inside communist countries. The Reds interpreted it as obvious proof that there was no sense any longer in these prisoners hoping that they could obtain help or sympathy from the outside. Every bit of first-hand evidence I had been accumulating for years from the victims of brainwashing had gone to show that this is how the minds of non-communists and anti-communists are cracked by the Reds. How many minds finally collapsed when presented with this additional piece of Attlee-Bevan evidence is anybody's guess.

Foreign correspondents knew at the time that one of the inmates of that prison was an American girl named Miss Harriet Mills, who had gone to China on a Fulbright scholarship, and who had remained when the Reds came, confident that good will would be her passport. That was her downfall. She was one of the longest occupants of the brainwashing prison. A fellow prisoner who had been released told me of seeing her handcuffed, always with a young Chinese attendant. After a lengthy period, they saw her being led to the "education department" of the prison. They thought her "mind reform" had progressed sufficiently for the Reds to give her some little job, such as teaching English. She could not do so without co-operating to some degree with the authorities. No matter how slight, it could be used as the start of a new sense of belonging, to replace the old. Shortly after the visit by these VI Ps, her spirits seemed to change. She sang Red songs and her nerves were peculiarly high pitched. Whether this was elation or hysteria is academic. Her prison "education" continued for two more years.

What should be incontrovertible is that a normal good willed individual, who had never been taught brainwashing, cannot avoid being influenced by this inevitability-hopelessness line if left behind bars for a period of years, fed only half-truths and lies, and made the subject of every subtle form of persuasion. The Reds fit their most diabolical pressures into familiar settings. They make their meetings frequently look and sound like a student huddle or a parlor discussion back home. They slickly pick on the liberal tenet that there is some right and some wrong on all sides and that nothing is wholly white or wholly black. With this as an area of agreement, they pass on to the easy assurance that as good and bad can be found everywhere, "both sides" are therefore the same. The "purge on both your houses" line is useful to them there, exploiting the victim's impatience with his own side, building up this opposition to his own people and their culture and morality.

Once this is accomplished, the Reds again switch to a new tack. They use the area of agreement already reached to lay stress only on the Red argument. They work then on persuading the prisoner to rid his mind of the "bourgeois poison" he had been carrying about of seeing good on all sides! That is patently ridiculous, they point out to this weary mind. Having exploited that liberal maxim to put their argument across, they have no need for it any longer and dump it. Their patient then is taught that there is good only on one side, that the other is "all bad" and the enemy. When an individual reaches this upside-down stage in his theorizing, he can then be freed with confidence that his cure and convalescence undoubtedly will take a long time, as in any serious illness, and that in the meantime the Reds can benefit from his neurotic repetition of their propaganda.

The Reds hold other tricks in their hand.

Threats and Violence

Threats are another concoction generously added to the brainwasher's brew. They are limitless in conception and cunning. What must have been routine — so many POW's from Korea told me of it happening to them — was the mock execution. A "stubborn" man was led into a field and made to kneel. A Red guard stepped up and pressed the cold steel of a pistol against the recalcitrant's temple. Sometimes he was asked once more if he would cooperate, other times the trigger was pulled at once. Usually there was no bullet in it. But it was like the game of Russian roulette. Every once in a while, to make it more exciting, the pistol did have a bullet in it.

Another time, newly captured prisoners would be lined up facing a ditch. They would hear the enemy officer clicking his pistol. Every one had heard of men being shot that way from behind and their bodies let fall into a common grave. The thoughts that went through one particular young man's mind at that moment were a mixture of stoicism and stupor. He told me so himself.

Instead of being shot, he noticed from the corner of his eye that the officer was passing up the line behind the fellows, turning them around and then shaking their hands. Although neither the young man nor the officer, who was probably just following orders, understood it that clearly, this was symbolic rebirth. The soldier who told me it happened to him was Claude Batchelor. "I never got over it," he said. The relief he felt must have been akin to gratitude, almost as if the man had saved his life.

What must have been routine, too, for so many victims of brainwashing, civilian and military, have told me about it, was for the examiner to slap his pistol meaningfully on the desk in front of him or for his assistant to thrust a gun into a man's neck from behind while the questioning proceeded.

Sometimes the interrogator would speak sweet reasonableness to a man, while letting him discover from someone else that his friend who hadn't cooperated had been thrashed or killed. The prisoner would be handed a cigarette and be treated like a chum, then suddenly hear his buddy in the next room screeching with pain for refusing to answer the same questions he was being asked. A number of prisoners are usually put together in a cell. When one's cellmate is carried back like mince meat or when only his clothes are returned in a small bundle, the threat to the others is plain enough.

In this category belongs the beating and kicking to death of an officer who took the Reds at their word when they said everyone should be frank. He expressed his opinion of a Red peace petition in strong words and was taken at once to the interrogation chamber. He died a few days later of the beating given him. Everyone in his POW hut then "voluntarily" signed the petition.

Discussion is another of the words to which the Reds have given new meaning. The verb had no object in the painful sense the Reds use it — you just discuss. To the Reds, discussion means going over the same thing again and again and again until your eyes swim and you feel as if you are dancing the European waltz by spinning to the same side for hours on end, unable to stop.

Major General William F. Dean, in his memoirs written after his three years as a prisoner in Korea, tells of being left in an auto in front of a police station while his escort officer went inside. "I shall never forget that town," Dean writes. "All the time we sat there someone was screaming inside the jail. This was someone being tortured, and whatever they were doing to him continued intermittently until we left, an hour later."

The communists heard those screams and could have moved him out of earshot if they had wished, or they could have interrupted the torture for a while. They did not want to. That was part of the treatment being given their highest-ranking prisoner, for whom they had great ambitions. He was to become the American von Paulus, the U.S. equivalent of the Nazi Field Marshal who was captured at Stalingrad and afterwards reappeared as a Red front. That Dean beat down such plans was a glorious tribute to his stubborn, old-fashioned character, which kept his mind on the simple truths by which he had been raised.

No hand was actually laid on him, any more than on Dr. Hayes in Kwei-yang. Neither had any way of knowing that the Red brainwashers rarely used such physical measures against those whom they had picked for key propaganda roles. The American military personnel in the Korean POW camps who were conspicuously used in the germ-warfare campaigns were not physically maltreated in the old-fashioned manner. No holds were barred, meanwhile, in the atrocities inflicted on those for whom no special role was intended, except to serve as a horrible warning for others. "I've been in the military service for years and I'm used to physical combat," one tragic figure said. "If they had hit me once, just a slap, I'd have come out of it. But they never touched me. I couldn't understand what they were up to. By the time I found out, it was much, much too late."

By letting Dean sit outside the jail, listening to the dreadful screams within, he was being informed of his probable fate if he crossed them. The communists arrange it so that these pressures that leave indelible marks on a mind aren't noticed at the time or seem to arise naturally. The Red emphasis is on those unsuspected factors of everyday living and speech. They are part and parcel of the planning, for brainwashing is devised to take advantage of each such opening.

Until his capture. Dean had not a clue to Red mind attack. He was maneuvered into doing some things he never would have fallen for if he had been properly briefed. He had only his convictions to guide him. When everything else failed, like Hayes whom he had never met, these constituted his tower of strength. They are what saved him, too.

Captain Ben Krasner, the American merchant-marine skipper, held a prisoner for eighteen months in Canton by the communists, tersely explained this in a letter he wrote me shortly after his release. You were "hit in the mind, where the bruises aren't too apparent," he wrote. Not a hand was laid on him, either. The psychological tortures thought up by the Reds had something mad about them, as if they followed prescriptions written by a doctor who had gone insane. Take the case of the foreign missionary who was led into a courtyard each day in China, his hands manacled. He was put into a big water jug, the kind used where plumbing is unknown, in which he could just fit while squatting. Water then was slowly poured into the jug. He never knew where the level would stop. Sometimes at his ankles, and he would wait for more. Sometimes just to the tip of his nose, so he had to strain hard to keep his head out, even so swallowing some. This dragged on for a month and combined with other pressures was responsible for him going temporarily crazy.

Violence was an additional element in brainwashing. The most bestial was the concealed form, hardly distinguishable from threats. Threats and violence go together. Along with the pressures that infected a mind from within, growing like a tumor, were those inflicted from the outside. Outright bloody violence ranged from head-smashing and a kick in the groin — the haphazard blows delivered in uninhibited rage — to modern laboratory refinements of these ancient tortures. The latter have immensely more deviltry to them.

The refined tortures of dynastic China were revived, often with psychological frills in the modern laboratory manner. The "tiger's chair" is well known. A man is tied face upwards to a long bench. Rocks are thrust under his legs, more and more fit in, forcing his knees to strain against the tight knots until the joints are pulled apart. The pain is increased or decreased progressively by stones being pushed in or taken out, as the watchful interrogator desires.

A variation is simply to tie a man down tightly so he cannot budge, then to rest a heavy stone on him and leave him for a long period. Sometimes pig bristles are used to agonize a "stubborn" person's sensitive parts. In "flying an airplane," the victim is hoisted by the thumbs, then doused with cold water to revive him whenever he passes out.

In the "diamond-mine treatment," he is forced to crawl back and forth on a plank covered with bits of broken glass. Sometimes he is roped and rolled back and forth over a plank studded with sharp nails.

Innumerable variations of the "ice bath" were used in Korea. In one version, the POW was stripped from waist down and put outside in sub-zero weather with his feet in a big basin filled with water that soon froze. The drop of water torture was revived. A U.N. soldier would be tied to a corner and questioned while a drop of water plopped on his head every minute for hours on end. At intervals, the examiner's assistant reached over and curled a lock of hair around his finger and pulled it out by the roots.

Men's faces were slapped with a wet towel, a comparatively mild penalty in itself, except that the poor chap's hands were tied behind his back with wires, cutting off the circulation.

The broad use to which threats and violence were used with the hopelessness-inevitability line as a backdrop was demonstrated in the controversy over the rights of Chinese and Korean prisoners of the U.N. to refuse to return to communism. The most effective tactic to force co-operation with the Red underground was the threatened punishment of loved ones left behind on the mainland. I began hearing about families seized as hostages a year before the dispute became world news.

Ghastly pressure was put on the POW 's by both sides. The U.N. was "embarrassed" by the desire of captured Red soldiers to want to stay on our side, the House of Commons was told on May 21, 1952, by Selwyn Lloyd, speaking for the British Government. He said "every endeavor was made to persuade as many as possible to agree to return." The U.N. Command, he blandly said, wanted "as few people as possible" to refuse to go back to Communist China. Widely quoted by the Chinese Reds, this fit neatly into their brainwashing pressures, along with the abandonment by the U.N. of supervision over POW enclosures to Red agents. Foreign correspondents, whose dispatches would have forced a change, were barred from the area.

Eighty thousand prisoners of the U.N. "have governed themselves, demonstrated as they wished — even arraigned and executed some of their fellows, while their guards dared not enter," said the British-owned *South China Morning Post* at Hong Kong on May 28, 1952. No more effective manner of hammering the threat of Red omnipotence into the heads of people could be imagined than such facts.

This unbelievable strain on minds that wanted to be free reached its climax at Panmunjom, where the men were brought for their fateful choice of sides. They were placed under the supervision of neutral authorities who made it clear to the world that they believed these men ought to be forced to return to Red China. Indian troops were brought in under Lieutenant General K. S. Thimayya, an inflexible and honorable soldier who nonetheless held this view so strongly that after the proceedings were over, he participated in an official Indian Government documentary movie on the subject in which I saw and heard him express the hope that the principle of "voluntary repatriation" would never become a part of international law. "I am dead set against it," he said in an interview, calling it "a frightful precedent." No matter how sincerely the Indian troops might have endeavored to fulfill the neutral role their country demanded, this attitude could not help but provide invaluable brainwashing material for the Reds. Released prisoners of war told me they were deprived of blankets and other accommodations until they found out what had been guaranteed them under the international agreement and posted this up on the bulletin board. Every subtle influence that could push them toward abandonment of the Free World to which they had come was used against them!

The showdown came in the examiners* huts, when the men were asked whether they wanted to return to Red China or stay on the side of the free people. One door led to the former, the other to the latter. "The most pitiful thing of all is that the prisoner stands alone," cabled Robert Alden to the *New York Times* from Indian Village, where these "painful scenes," as he labeled them, took place. He described the questioning of a typical Chinese. "The guards are holding him down. The communists are sneering at him while they talk. The neutrals sit stolidly ignoring the prisoner's pleas . . . the desperate man's eyes sweep the hostile room looking for some sign of friendliness."

After thirty minutes of this, he "is desperate, hoarse and gasping for breath like a drowning man. Though the day is cold, beads of perspiration stand out on his face. . . .

"These were painful scenes to witness. . . . The prisoners refusing repatriation were taken from their comrades and pinned to a bench by three Indian guards. Just a few feet away, seated behind a blanket-covered table, were the Red explainers, puffing at cigarettes and talking."

What greater assistance could a brainwasher ask? Witnesses told of typical scenes — a man would stand up as if drunk, waver from side to side, stare pleadingly from face to face for a gleam of sympathy, and then in a trancelike state stumble from one gate to the other. A man couldn't get a straight answer to his questions. Panicky, he couldn't tell which door led to freedom and which to slavery. He heard only the language of diplomats and double-talk. Plain talk was forbidden. Each time he approached the door to the Free World, the communist's commanding voice would stop him. "Comrade, that is not where you want to go . . . comrade, are you sure where you want to go? . . . Comrade, the other way ..." This would continue until, in exhaustion, the poor man would tumble through the latter, where everyone knew full well he desperately did not want to go.

Even so, there were not enough such cases to compensate the Reds for their over-all failure. They were unable to bring to bear that last ounce of pressure — sheer power — needed to crystallize such a situation into a spontaneous — "voluntary" — reaction favorable to communism. So the

Reds broke up the whole proceedings. The Free World, through the iron will of simple people, had been given a glorious victory.

The history of the POW camps in Korea constitutes one of the most enlightening chapters on how current events are manipulated as part of the brainwashing pattern, against which the nations of the Free World are just as responsible for keeping their guard up as the lonely lad in a Red prison.

Yalu Madness

The Yalu is a river between Manchuria and Korea on whose banks I spent an idyllic week with my wife when World War II was having its birth pangs, close to twenty-five years ago. The Reds set up POW camps on the Korean side in the early 1950s. These were crude brainwashing clinics. A typical case in which no threat was uttered, no violence was used, is still as clear an example of the combination of threats and violence for brainwashing purposes as I have ever come across, a modern atrocity from which Edgar Allan Poe would have recoiled.

A sergeant was being questioned in a hut one day beside the Yalu. By then he was a bony, terrified youth, about twenty, hardly resembling the stocky fellow who had dropped out of the warplane in which he had been a gunner. They had trapped him a couple of days later when hunger drove him into a Korean hut. He had been given *kimche* — pickled cabbage — by a friendly family. But meantime their little daughter had run off to tell the communists without letting her parents know.

Why had she done so? She was the victim of just as gross a betrayal as he. These kids had adored the foreign soldiers when the war began. Americans gave them the tastiest sweetmeats they had ever eaten — candies, chewing gum, and chocolate bars — they got a treasure trove, too, in colored pencils and notebooks.

Then one day all the children in the neighborhood were called to a people's discussion meeting, just like their elders, where they were told that the wicked Americans were giving out poisoned candies and explosive toys, even dropping them from airplanes for luckless children to pick up, and that many boys and girls had already been killed. The youngsters were horrified that people could be so evil. They could not imagine their elders lying to them about it, especially after one "able Party member" got up to give vivid descriptions of the agony in which their little brothers and comrades were supposed to have died.

The children resolved voluntarily, just like the grownups, to never touch a thing given them by these hateful white people, and to remember them with loathing all their lives. I saw the colored horror comics and illustrated story books in which these lessons were graphically illustrated.

The children were proud, too, to be told at the same meeting how they could help their country. "Watch out for enemy agents and spies," they were told. "Listen to what everyone says, even your parents at home and especially when friends come for a visit. Listen, and when you hear anything suspicious, report it at once to the police. This will make child heroes of you."

That was one of the main reasons escape was so difficult in Korea. That was how this young soldier came to be trapped. He had little stamina left anyway, and a sore wound on his ankle from a shell splinter.

A shot through the mud wall warned him he had been cornered. There was nothing else to do but surrender. They knocked him about a bit and took away his shoes. With rags on his feet, he was marched over the flaky, thick snow for two nights before he was brought to the first command post. A series of night marches continued from then on for a month.

His foot hadn't been frozen when he was caught, but was frozen now as he stood in front of his interrogator. Not only his foot, but his left hand. They had left him for nights on end in freezing huts. His wounded leg had stopped hurting. Now it was ugly and swollen but didn't hurt, even when he stuck his finger in it. Only it left a hollow that scared him. His frozen hand had turned blackish, too. They were so discolored, he was scared to look at them.

He had been undergoing frequent interrogations for some weeks already. He had told them much more than the name, rank, and serial number specified by the regulations. He was positive he had not leaked out anything the enemy didn't know. He would give up no secrets that might hurt his buddies or his country.

He had been given some literature to read. He knew it was Red but he had never seen anything like it before and was curious. One magazine in particular puzzled him. They said it was an American magazine, put out by Americans at Shanghai. He read names such as John Powell, editor. The magazine was called the *China Monthly Review*. What he read seemed reasonable in most places, but he resented some of the statements and some articles gave him an unpleasant feeling that they were lies. He knew nothing of communism or China, so felt at a loss in making up his mind. He had more important things to fret about, his own survival and how to keep his trap shut under the persistent questions.

They gave him some weird pamphlets to study on the subject they kept bringing up, what they called Marxism-Leninism and the ideas of Mao Tsetung — "Mousey Dung" as he and his buddies called him. He noticed that fellows who had a good memory for that kind of stuff got a little more chow and warmth. If this paid off, he saw no harm in remembering a little of it, but he would be damned if he'd take any seriously.

Meanwhile, his hand and foot didn't get any better; they got worse. Slivers of terror ran up and down his spine whenever he glanced at them. There was no doubt about it; they were frozen, and bad. He had to get to a doctor, somehow. The dreadful word *gangrene* coursed through his head, making it swell with fear. A finger came off. Just like that, a finger came off. He had to get to a doctor.

He was taken for interrogation instead. The man wasn't too hard on him. He seemed a sympathetic guy. He gave him one look and said he better get to a hospital fast if the rest of his fingers and foot were going to be saved. There was no doubt of it now; gangrene had set in.

The lad felt full of hope when he saw the sympathetic look as the interrogator stared at his poor sick foot. He had to save that! By God in heaven, he had to save that! He heard the man talking. "I am so sorry, comrade, but you look like hell!" He felt sure he saw compassion in his eyes. The examiner said nothing for a minute — they often did funny things like that. The POW now felt sure, gilt-edged surety, that he was figuring out a way to help him. He filled the silence with sweet anticipation. He was going to get treatment. He would be warm. He would not lose any more of his fingers ... maybe just one more. His leg would be saved.

"I sure have to send you to a hospital, comrade," the examiner said, breaking his silence. The curious juxtaposition of American slang and this new language made him never feel sure of what they were saying. He clung to every word now, squeezing more of that precious hope out.

"We'll have to act fast," the interrogator was saying. What a fine fellow; how grateful he felt to him. He had a feeling this man wasn't one of those fish faces. You never knew what they meant. "You have to help me send you to a hospital," the man was saying. "So many of our soldiers, the same as you, and our good peasants and villagers who only want peace, are being horribly burned and injured by your barbaric napalm bombing and so many are being infected by your germ warfare that we have no beds available. Your embargo on drugs, contrary to all the rules of war, is another handicap. But we are going to find you a cot in some hospital."

This last was all the lad heard. If he heard any of the rest, it was only his subconscious that took it in.

"But you'll have to help me do it," the fellow said again. "Every military service has its regulations. You know that. Before the people can spare you a hospital bed, when so many are in need themselves, they must know you are deserving of it. This is really a simple matter. You have been given a short pamphlet with some editorials from our *Liberation Daily*, explaining the wonderful role that people's discussions take in our new society.

"You know what discussion is; you have it in your own country. Of course it isn't people's discussion yet, but you can help make it so. Anyway, it shouldn't be too difficult for you to grasp.

"All we ask is that you read and study this, and that you do so willingly, and come voluntarily to your own conclusions. We know you understand right from wrong. When you have studied it, you will have a new grasp of the people's role. When you sincerely show sympathy to the people, they will return it a thousandfold. Their generosity is as wide as the heavens. The mercy of our great leader, Mao Tse-tung, is as broad as the universe. Then they will spare you not only a hospital bed, but give you the best treatment we have.

"Now be a good guy and go back to your quarters and study. Remember, I am going to send you to a hospital. Remember that I can't do it if you don't help. This is a people's democracy. So hurry up and do your lesson."

The lad went back to the semi frozen hut he was occupying along with about thirty-five other prisoners, determined to get that lesson learned. Never was he so determined to learn a lesson before. He lost a second finger that day; it came off, just like that. Terrorized, with almost frozen tears in his scared eyes, he studied. He would go to a hospital ... he would get the best treatment.

He was full of confidence when he appeared before his interrogator a couple of days later. He had almost memorized the page. The test was even pleasant, for it wasn't in the dread question and answer form he had resented so much in school. This was discussion, a man-to-man discussion. "What we want is your standpoint," the interrogator explained. "We don't care much about names and dates and all that sort of rubbish. What we want to know is how you stand as regards the people."

What a fine fellow he was I He felt lucky having him as his interrogator. He was like a father to him, although only a little older than himself. He would do anything in the world to please him.

"We are especially anxious," this man was saying, "that you grasp the fundamental truth that labor created everything. That is what evolution means. Labor does all and is responsible for all. Once you grasp that, you are automatically on the side of the people."

"Sure I'm on the side of the people," the youth blurted out. "I understand now, how like the book says, labor made the world, labor did everything. I am on the side of the people," he repeated pleadingly. "Now can I go to a hospital?"

"Once we can be sure of it, you'll be on your way," the interrogator said.

"This isn't communism," the lad thought to himself. "Even if it is, what's wrong with it? Don't we believe the same thing? Say, he hasn't even mentioned communism. What's all this scare about communism, anyway?"

"The people are very tolerant and generous," the interrogator went on. "They will consider you one of themselves as soon as they know you are deserving. Then you will be put into a hospital. You will be given the best treatment. Of course, you must understand we have so very little, even for ourselves, but we are happy to share what little we have with our friends. We don't give to our enemies, of course. We don't have enough for that sentimentalist rubbish.

"You seem to have learned your lesson well. But are you sincere? That is what the people want to know? Are you sincere? That is what I must guarantee to them. That is my responsibility, and if I fail and you are untrue to the trust given you, I will get into very serious trouble. I will have proven that I don't have enough knowledge and faith in our cause to be able to convince you, a simple son of a working class family. That would be a crime!"

"Don't worry about me!" the lad exclaimed, concerned now that he might be letting this grand fellow down, who was sticking out his neck for him, trying to get him a bed and a doctor when they had so little themselves, it was pathetic. That damned blockade! He'd be having all the medicines he needed if it weren't for that. And they call us civilized. Why had he been sent out here anyway? "Tell me that," he said to himself. He felt light-headed. What had he been saying? Had he been thinking or talking aloud? Who had been talking? He had just finished — what — and he couldn't remember.

"Please, God, get me into a hospital!" He knew he was saying this now, silently to himself, praying. "Please let me do the right thing. Please save my fingers."

He lost the end of an index finger that day; it came off, like the others, without pain. Dead flesh. Dead flesh on his pink body. Good God, get me to a hospital, quick!

"Sure, I'm sincere," he said aloud, making sure it was aloud, not just thought. The interrogator reached over and lit a cigarette for him. How had that cigarette got into his mouth? Oh yes, that wonderful guy, who somehow reminded him of his dad, had given it to him. Imagine, a slant-eyed gook reminding him of his own father! He loved that fellow! He was going to send him to a hospital, with fine doctors and beautiful nurses and all the medicine in the world. What a wonderful country. . . .

"The people are good-hearted and generous, but their eyes have been opened wide by their suffering and they can't afford to take chances," the interrogator was saying. "The people can't just take your word for it that you are sincere. They have to be sure of it. They have to have it proven to them."

"How do you prove it? How do you prove such a thing as being sincere?" the lad pleaded. "Tell me, I'll prove it to you."

"Really it's very simple," the interrogator went on. The lad puffed almost hysterically at his butt. He mustn't miss a word, his life depended on it, and here he was feeling so airy and faint. Damn his eyes! Wake up and listen!

"You have studied some of our dialectical materialism. That should have taught you that we believe facts speak louder than words. You must prove your sincerity. I am anxious for you to do so. Then I will be able to send you to a hospital, but you must help me."

"What must I do?" He had impatient tears in his eyes now.

"We don't want you to do a thing that you don't want to yourself, voluntarily."

What was he saying now? His head kept buzzing. Had he fallen asleep. No, by God, he'd stay awake. How he'd like to sleep, just to sleep for a whole day, for a week, forever. No, not forever. He had to live. He had to stay awake, so he'd save his remaining fingers and leg.

His poor, poor charred fingers. His leg with the hollows where he felt it. "Tell me what to do and I'll show you," he said aloud.

The interrogator's voice was firm now. "Sincerity is proven by action. Anything that will show you are on the side of the people, all people, our people and yours, for we're all brothers, all except those who are misled by Wall Street and the warmongers. All you have to do to prove your sincerity is to tell us something that will help the people, or keep harm away from them."

"What, tell me what?" the lad begged. "What do you mean?"

"Anything that will show you are sincere in your gratitude to the people who are saving your life for you, although you killed their brothers and sisters by dropping burning napalm on them and bacteria to make them sick."

"Huh?" said the lad weakly. "I didn't do anything like that. I'm a gunner."

"What difference does it make whether it was you or some buddy of yours. Aren't you all one?"

That was a tough nut to crack. Maybe he was guilty. Anyway, he would prove his sincerity.

"You can prove you are on the side of the people in many ways," the interrogator was patiently explaining, all over again it seemed. "There are plenty of opportunities all around you. Maybe some of the reactionaries who haven't had the learning advantages you've been given are stealing the people's food, hiding it for some escape attempt. That is against the people's interests and you can prove your mind reform by telling the people about it. That way you could save those men from crime. That's just one example how you can prove your sincerity."

The youth was alert now; funny how he felt his mind clear. If ever he needed a clear mind, God, he needed it now. "Help me, God," he said to himself. What the fellow was saying sounded all right, but there was a catch in it. If only he wasn't so dreadfully tired.

"There are other easy ways," the interrogator was droning on. Sometimes a word came out clear to him, other times it seemed to fade away. "You might know something about your airplanes that could help the people. You would prove your sincerity by telling it to the people."

That did it! He'd buy none of it. He'd be damned if he would. He steeled himself inside; he'd die first. Let them take their rotten medicines, their quack hospital, and they knew where they could stick it. He did not say it aloud, he knew better than that. He just thought it.

"Now you go back to your quarters and think about this," the brainwasher said. "We don't want you to do anything you don't want to do willingly."

The bastard was able to read his mind! The lad cringed. The enemy knew every move he made, every thought that went through his head. Those Reds knew everything. Oh God, whom could he trust? He wouldn't break. He wouldn't rat on his buddies. Of course he knew who was hiding food. He wouldn't let his country down. He knew other things, too. They'd never get them out of him.

The next morning after he woke up out of a short sleep that was as complete as death, he was horrified to find he had lost a toe. He had lost a toe! Gangrene had settled in his foot, too! The realization came to him for the first time that he might have to lose both his good arm and his sturdy right leg.

Panic, sheer panic, concocted out of fear and hysteria and a growing sense of being completely helpless, without friends, with nobody who gave a hoot about what happened to him any more, here or in heaven, coursed wildly through his veins.

That was how he found himself a little later before his interrogator once more. He must have been in a sort of walking sleep, he felt afterwards. He must have lost control of his mind. Anyway, he had no idea what he said. He couldn't remember a word. He is sure he couldn't have spoken coherently. He believes he just fainted. He got to the interrogation chamber, and everything got vague and misty, until after the amputations.

He lost both his good left hand and his sturdy right leg.

This, in capsule form, is what happened not once alone but plenty of times, in different degrees. Those men lost their hands or their feet out of violence, just as much as if their inquisitors had picked up a meat ax and hacked off their limbs. This was violence in the refined manner of dialectical materialism.

Drugs and Hypnotism

An ideology so ruthlessly materialistic as communism would be at variance with its own philosophy if it failed to make use of drugs and hypnotism. In special cases, when the mind is particularly strong willed so that death would come before submission to ordinary brainwashing tactics, drugs and hypnotism have been used.

Originally there were two words for this new strategy of mind attack. One was *brainwashing* and the other, *brain-changing.* The former referred to pressures just short of the atrocity of overt interference by medical science with the functions of the brain. Brain-changing meant alterations in thinking brought about by the sort of treatment hitherto identified with a doctor's prescription or a surgeon's scalpel.

The idea was simplicity itself, merely to remove a human being's memory of some specific incident and then to insert a new and different memory in place of the old. That is even a more repulsive conception than the most devilish trickery of primitive witchcraft. A highly educated person who bends medical discoveries to the practice of mind attack is incalculably more evil than any savage using potions, trances, and incantations.

The word *brain-changing* became obscured as brainwashing began to embrace all the available pressures that could be utilized to bend a man's will and change his attitudes fundamentally. *Brain-changing* specifically refers to the complete job in all its wickedness.

Cardinal Mindszenty underwent a brain-changing. That was how his vigorous mind was bent. A man's memory can be physically eliminated, if at all possible, only at the price of permanent damage to the brain. In such a brain-changing, drugs have to be used to destroy the natural alertness and strong character of the individual, and hypnotism must be employed, too, to help in breaking down resistance. Information obtained through the most persistent inquiry by every possible channel reveals that drugs and hypnotism were used on the cardinal.

The extent to which these additional pressures have been employed by Red China is not known. China still lacks the specialists that are at the beck and call of Lubyanka Prison in Moscow, but is known to be working to overcome this inadequacy, with the help of Soviet Russian advisers.

I was told about the use of drugs by at least two victims. One was Robert T. Bryan, China-born American lawyer. He was a prisoner in Shanghai's Ward Road prison for sixteen and a half months. He heard the wailing of tortured fellow inmates and saw their corpses being stacked into trucks. After ten months of softening up, the last five in solitary, he begged "for the privilege of indoctrination," summoning all his knowledge of Chinese characteristics and communist lingo. He put on a flawless act of conversion and helped maintain his stamina by keeping his mind busy thinking up ways of making it appear genuine without really giving the Reds anything tangible.

Five indoctrinators worked over him in relays for sixteen days. He was shaken out of his sleep at any time of the day or night so that the poisons of fatigue would be diffused through his whole system. After this course, he was given four weeks of "thought examination." The Reds hoped to accomplish two things by that. They would make him go over his studies so strenuously that they would be driven into his subconscious forever and they would be able to detect any flaws in his "standpoint." Afterwards, just to make sure, they gave him a month of re-examination when a committee of three specialists in ideology probed his mind.

He self-confessed for hundreds of hours during these sessions. He told them, 'Tm a changed man." He made more confessions than he can remember, sometimes up to a hundred pages. Unless he did so, they told him he had no hope of release. Each time, they came to him with further demands. This is the usual Red tactic, in everything from an international conference to a prison session. They finally demanded that he admit to being a spy.

This he point-blank refused. The fact that there was no truth in it was irrelevant. Neither was there in the other charges. He feared that with such a signed document they would execute him, and by the help of fellow travelers abroad, appear justified. "No, I won't," he firmly said. They beat him, handcuffed him behind his back, and put him in his cell for seventy-two hours. When he still doggedly refused, he was taken to another room, where his trousers were removed and he was hoisted onto a table. A hypodermic needle was jabbed into his spine. What it was he had no idea, but one of the indoctrinators later said he had been given "true words serum."

He felt light and blacked out, awakening in his cell next day with a terrific headache. He told me this happened twice. Afterwards, he was shown a document in his handwriting, signed by him, although he had no recollection of it. They must have dictated it to him while he was under the influence of the drug. He was shown the final confession they sought. Fortunately, they wanted it for domestic propaganda, and after publicizing it, let him go.

"I never for a second took anything serious that I wrote for them," he said to me. "I was putting on an act. They never convinced me of any part of their line. I was able to resist their indoctrination because I knew enough about the mechanism of communism not to be fooled. I had been a Municipal Council lawyer in Shanghai for fourteen years, and prosecuted many Reds. What would have happened to me if I hadn't known? Well, that would have been a different kettle of fish."

Another instance of the use of drugs was told to me by Lieutenant John A. Ori. While a POW in Korea, he one day noticed a white powder in his food. He thought it was salt, and was delighted over anything to give flavor to his watery sorghum. When it tasted sweetish, he thought it maybe was sugar. As soon as he finished eating, he was led away for interrogation.

"I found myself talking and talking," he said. "I was hardly able to control what I was saying. I talked a blue streak. I concentrated as never before to keep the secret I knew they were after."

About a week later, he saw some more of this white powder mixed into his food. "I was fagged out, else I would have connected it with my loose tongue," he said. "When I was taken out this time, I knew there was something fishy about it. They put the heat on, and I couldn't stop talking. I tried to talk about everything except what they wanted. Maybe the Chinese hadn't enough experience with this dope. I would not have escaped so easily in Soviet Russia. I became woozy, and the last I remember is the floor slowly rising to meet my face. How long I passed out I don't know. When I came to I was terribly exhausted, but the effect of the drug was gone. The truce negotiations were nearing an end, and maybe they became more cautious. Anyway, I didn't see any more of that white powder."

Such cases of drugging have only a temporary effect and carry little or no personal convictions with them. They belong to the softening-up process and are intended to make a patient obey an order unthinkingly or to act against his better judgment. Drugs weaken a man's resistance and so constitute a valuable auxiliary in any such effort as hypnotism.

The exact role that hypnotism plays in brainwashing is much more difficult to trace than any other element, even drugs. A man knows when he's hungry or tired, when he's tense, under threats, or has been beaten up. But he can have undergone a great deal of hypnotism without having a suspicion of it. We have a very limited knowledge of the subject generally because it was not taken seriously until recently, when some doctors and hospitals began experimenting with it and a few dentists began to use it as a substitute for laughing gas.

The trance, or hypnotic state, is well known everywhere. The description of their reactions by many victims of brainwashing pictures exactly the same condition. What appears indisputable is that a form of trance state has been widely induced in Red China by repetitive interrogation and political learning within a controlled government. Fatigue and confusion demonstrably create the same state the hypnotist strives to achieve.

We know little enough about individual hypnotism but less about mass hypnotism. Characteristics of a mass hypnotic state are frequently noted inside the Red borders. Such demagogues as Hitler unquestionably had some mass hypnotic influence. A demagogic environment has been duplicated inside the iron curtain, particularly in China. The system of government is so devised that the people have to go through hypnotic-inducing seances, disguised as study sessions and indoctrination courses. Thus the people are maintained in a hypersensitive condition, weakened by undernourishment and fatigue.

Almost every POW I spoke to who had any intensive degree of brainwashing, and certainly civilians such as Dr. Hayes, described a constant pressure on them that was identical in essential points with what can be witnessed, compressed into a much shorter space of time, at any hypnotist's demonstration.

Confession

The extraordinary Red stress on confession betrays the extreme importance they attach to it. The constant use of the words *reform* and *rebirth* in connection with it gives it a curiously medieval connotation. Something intrinsic in communism makes this confession phenomenon indispensable to it; it can't exist without it. The same confession rite has to be pursued in a simple village in the deep interior of China as in a Party meeting in Kiev or in a POW camp concealed in a twisting Korean valley.

The way the communists use the word recalls its original meaning. In ancient days a prisoner of the Roman empire said, "I confess to the rule of Rome." This meant submission to both its religious and secular control. In the Middle Ages to *confess the Latin rite* meant, "I agree with the sum total of the dogma presented to me." The dictionary shows the word is derived from the Latin *con* and *ficio*. This meant "to be in conformity with."

Although that interpretation has been lost during the intervening centuries, it is exactly in this psychological sense that the Reds have revived the word. The meaning in confession then, as the Reds now use it is agreement with the rules laid down and hence submission to the existing hierarchy. The implication in every confession i* submission to the domain. That is the framework in which the communists enforce it and what gives it a dominating role in their strategy.

The Reds have made it the most vital part of their control mechanism. They do not have to tell people about this reflex attitude of submission in each confession. They merely insist that everyone perform this rite and go through the motions frequently enough for it to become second nature and ultimately part of the person's mentality.

"They had us up all the time making self-criticisms and mutual criticisms and confessions," the returned POW's said. They joked about the trivial, silly things they had to confess. They didn't realize — how could they? — that what was of primary importance to the communists in the POW camps in Korea was not the sincerity of conversion but the much more practical goal of submission to their authority. What the Party wanted was obedience — submission.

Each time a U.N. soldier stood up and used the words "I confess," his Red masters were confident that in the back of his mind a tiny trace at least of this intrinsic content of the word would filter down, even if only subconsciously. Each time he repeated it, they were certain a little more of this content was being rubbed onto his mentality. The communists actually heard him saying each time, in their doubletalk, "I submit," getting himself accustomed to the thought.

Confession and "learning" constituted the daily routine of all brainwashing chambers. They are two sides of the brainwashing coin. This word learnings like confession, has a particular meaning to the Reds. By learning they mean communist indoctrination alone. The word has a new written character in Chinese, although its pronunciation is the same as the old word, which still remains in use in its ordinary sense. The subtlety in this hardly needs pointing out. The only way this difference, which is of such fundamental importance, can be indicated in English without going into a tedious explanation each time is to put the word inside quotation marks whenever this new Red meaning is meant.

The communists well know the corrosive effect of repetition on a man's mind and reactions. Chinese children in unison repeat the meaning of a new word, the character for which is a symbol. For all their lives henceforth, the meaning and the symbolic sense go together. Communist group meetings are largely conducted by that method of teaching. That is why nothing is more opposed by the communists than the freedom to be silent. Everyone in a people's discussion must speak up. Everyone must express the communist point of view in his own words. Then he must rephrase it and continue doing so endlessly, and listen to others do it for hours on end. The subject for repetition might be only a slight detail in Red dogma, but like children reciting a new word or phrase until they can never forget it, everyone must repeat this tiny bit of dogma until it becomes etched in his thinking, becomes spontaneous. No wonder the released prisoners from brainwashing chambers anywhere — whether or not they come out influenced by the communist ideology — talk in a peculiar long-winded way for so long. The lingo has been drilled into their heads.

The elements that go into brainwashing are intended to make the mind receptive to "learning" and to browbeat it into confession. "Learning" and confession are parallel rituals, for as the victim absorbs Marxist teaching, he is obliged to rid himself of the "burden" and the "poisons" of his old ideas by confession, "cleansing" his mind himself, achieving "mind reform." That is brainwashing for the masses. In a more intense form, it is brainwashing for prisoners. The line between the two in a communist society is gradually being eliminated.

The last thing captured U.N. troops expected when they were thrust into the dilapidated and disease-ridden POW camps established by the Reds in caves, mines, and huts in Korea was to come up against a school atmosphere. The study chamber was anywhere from a freezing Korean house to the bare exterior. A lecture lasted at least four hours. The POW 's usually wore thin fatigues and were always cold and hungry. Many died in the sub-zero weather, but the remainder had to stick it out. Attendance was announced as voluntary, except that those who failed to show up were not fed. Those who failed to join in the discussion were beaten up, some to death. The fiercest penalties were reserved for those who failed to confess, but when the chips were counted after it was all over, those who had given in easily got as bad treatment, even worse, than those who resisted the most.

When the courses started, the fellows took them as a joke. The highlight was always confession. Nothing was too trivial to become the basis for a confession that had to be contritely uttered in front of one's group or before the entire assembly. Everyone had to listen grimly and discuss it in all its irrelevant, far-fetched ramifications until it became a tremendously important issue. When one's mind became drowsy over the dullness and aimlessness of it all, you had to force yourself to pay attention.

A complicated mechanism for the manufacture of confessions had been built up by the communists over the years. Proof of the utter unreliability and untruth of confessions did not seem to upset them. As far back as 1930, a group of accused Soviet engineers headed by a Professor Ramzin confessed to a plot to set up a counter-revolutionary government headed by two men who had died in exile years before. A witness told of arriving by air to visit Trotsky in Norway on a day no planes arrived, and another man said he conferred with Trotsky's son in a hotel that had burned down years previously. On several occasions, when a defendant denied his guilt, he was hustled off the dock until he was better prepared for public display.

Yet the system was still adhered to religiously when the Reds set up their government in Peking. One of Mao's first acts was to start a nation-wide "mind reform" program that was brainwashing with its "learning"-

confession complex. He extended it into the POW camps as soon as they were set up in Korea.

The Reds hammered the point that the captured U.N. soldiers were war criminals, not mere prisoners. Each was a sinner against the Marxist faith. The communist theologians assumed that anyone who had lived in a non-Red environment was "poisoned" by the "sins" of his society. He had to repent and "make amends to the people." Through confession, repentance and atonement, the POW was told that "the peoples of the world will forgive you." They could find out how to do this only by the "learning" procedure, of which confession was the climax, leading to a new birth into the communist "paradise."

So everyone had to confess. If a man couldn't think up an actual wrong, he was gravely told that anything would do, so long as it had any basis in fact or semantics. Everything in this new world became so topsy-turvy that such distinctions lost all meaning. In their browbeaten condition, a man would suddenly lose his nerve and go before his indoctrinator or group and needlessly confess to stealing food. Could submission have been any more pronounced? He might have filched a bit to appease his hunger or with a slim hope that he might need this nourishment some day if some rescue plan was being put into effect or he tried to escape. He would lose his nerve and confess and be punished, perhaps by being thrust into the hole, an open pit in the ground, or squeezed into a "meter box," a box one meter wide, long and high, with handcuffs and leg irons. Death was not infrequently the reward for such voluntary confession.

"Confess, for we have already proved you a liar," was one of the constant cries of the brainwasher, and a man would worry himself sick trying to unravel what wasn't even a knot, but only a fake rope trick.

The confession pattern seemed to appeal to certain types of individuals. Confession had a symbolic sense for a man with high moral training. Others who were exhibitionists or appeared to enjoy flagellating themselves went for it in a big way. Like most everything else in the twisted communist society, it attracted the very naive and the abnormal mentalities.

The brainwasher's insistence that a man rid himself of "bourgeois poisons" was like mumbo-jumbo. Only when a chap had been brainwashed this way did he fail to see that far from "helping the people," he was only betraying his buddies and his country. Clarity of mind was needed to see through this, and the whole Red drive was to make a brain foggy instead.

How could a chap with only a few years of education and little or no Sunday school, who had gone directly into the military as a raw recruit, who found himself in Korea a few months later and in a POW camp a few months after that — all before his twenty-first birthday — see through such sleight-tof-hand when people at home were daily falling for card sharks, quack doctors, and communist fronts in spite of all the warnings given about such sharp practices?

Yet such was part of the personal story of many. One such was Claude Batchelor, the Texas country boy who broke away from the wretched group which said it didn't want to go home and who is now serving twenty years, reduced from life. When I interviewed him before his trial, he was filling reams, it seemed, of foolscap pages with "thought conclusions," "thought criticisms," and all sorts of modern magic picked up from the Reds. He was criticizing himself in the confession manner. The heap of pages he filled should make instructive reading for psychiatrists.

The communists have made confession the medium for their principal propaganda drive among their own subject peoples. They first determine the conclusion they wish to put across, then they select the details which add up to this fake hypothesis. Their problem then boils down to finding people with experience approximating these details as closely as possible. By befogging the minds, they endeavor to convince them that they fill the bill!

Once they locate such prospects for confession, and it is not difficult in any large number of persons to find every kind of experience, the rest becomes a technical problem for the brainwashers. When a man's beaten mind desperately grasps for familiar facts, he is led into confusion and hallucination. That is when the Reds extract their fantastic confessions. They concentrate a man's mind on certain details, some of which may be perfectly true, and once accepted, they rearrange them into the pattern they wish, to provide the new, false conclusion they are after. This is their technique, in all its utter and evil simplicity, like a black mass.

This was a subject I decided to take up more completely with a psychiatrist.

Chapter Nine - The Clinical Analysis

Dr. Leon Freedom

Dr. Freedom has a medical name for brainwashing. He called it "corticovisceral psychiatry." During our extensive discussions, I asked him for a bird's-eye picture of the process, the simple along with the complex. "How does it look inside a doctor's clinic?" I asked. After all, his field was neuropsychiatry — the working of the nervous system, with its base in the brain.

In reply, he traced the road that every human being follows in life and showed the numerous points at which the brainwasher — he called him the corticovisceral psychiatrist — was able to interfere in the normal path, putting up a roadblock or directing the patient onto a new route, leading him off in an entirely new direction.

"The only way to get a rounded picture of this situation," he said, "is to look upon it from the viewpoint of a single individual, call him Hamid, Rudolf, or Lim — it is immaterial who — for everyone develops the same way. We must begin by understanding the basic facts about this typical person, because it is exactly with those factors that the indoctrinator works.

"We start off with the obvious premise that every human being thinks, reacts, and behaves. None of us differ in that, but the way we do those things makes up our character and determines the kind of person we are. The Reds apply their pressure on these simple, fundamental traits in the isolated individual.

"The indoctrinator carefully differentiates between various types of people. One type inspires obedience and is bound to be a leader. The reticent type can sit in an office for six months without his colleagues knowing his name. The mild type is as gentle as a bunny rabbit. There is the hard, cantankerous type who is sometimes vicious or even evil. The worry bird is full of doubts about whether a job has been properly done. The impulsive type wants to do everything right then and there, and the apathetic, listless type isn't aroused one way or another by anything.

"These different kinds of people all have subconscious needs. Sometimes they are unaware of them, but aware or not, these needs are always subconsciously present. They are expressed by thoughts and feelings while working or at a party, or in bed, dreaming. Conflict arises in everyone between these responses that a man knows he has and those of which he is unaware or which are suppressed. Nobody actually realizes what is going on in his own subconscious mind. The brainwasher is trained to increase such conflict and to manipulate these responses.

"Every man has a great many basic needs. He requires affection and approval. He has biological needs, which are instinctive, for food, shelter, sex, warmth, and clothing. People are gregarious and cannot endure being isolated, so every man has social needs, too. Also, he requires a sense of security.

"All these needs obviously cannot be completely satisfied at the same time. How a person deals with his unsatisfied needs determines whether they develop into a frustration. A correct, tolerant approach maintains a healthy balance in life.

"Frustration brings about a sense of defeat, which is one of the traits the brainwasher seeks to arouse. He knows what a very useful tool defeatism is to communism. Either frustration or sense of defeat leads to resentment. Doctors and psychiatrists try to remove resentment because they know how dangerous it is to the mind. The indoctrinator, on the contrary, exerts a great deal of energy inciting and aggravating it, for out of resentment he creates hostility.

"This is one of the most important responses that he constantly seeks to bring out. Only one short step separates hostility from outright hate. Communism puts very great emphasis on hate. Without a foundation in hatred, communism would perish. When the brainwasher has succeeded in foment-ing hate, he is well on the way to achieving his main objective, which is al-ways some pro-communist activity. The customary reaction of a person fos-tering a hostility or a hate is to project it outside himself. The communist psychological planners decide the direction that this projection takes. The importance of this cannot be exaggerated.

'In projection, a person attributes to others the ideas and the impulses that he has himself, or which he thinks others hold toward him. The individ-ual who blames another for his own mistakes is using this projection mecha-nism.

"Anyone who has picked up frustrated or resentful feelings in his normal environment is that much easier for the brainwasher to handle. He is already softened up to that extent. The purpose of the Red screening process, with its exhaustive prolonged questioning, is to locate just such persons. When found, all the indoctrinator has to do is to keep working away at the hostile feeling already in the individual.

"The brainwasher aims at arousing hatred and then projecting it against a target chosen by the Politbureau. The individual may have nothing against this person or group, but it becomes his enemy willy-nilly. The brainwasher's task is to focus the specially fanned or artificially created hate on the man's own friends, society, and country. They, not himself, are to blame for his troubles.

"Inside himself, a person who is succumbing to what the communists call mind reform' feels upset over what he senses is the misdirection of his pent-up emotions. He feels guilty about it. The rise of this hostility and hate, too, especially when aimed against his own side, foments additional feelings of guilt. They provide the brainwasher with a further opening, and he seizes every opportunity to stir up this witch's brew of disturbing emotions.

"Guilt feelings are aroused also in other ways. Failure to meet a standard of achievement or conduct is a very frequent guilt stimulus. Practically eve-ryone has not fulfilled all his boyhood hopes. The brainwasher seeks to dis-cover these very normal failings so as to take advantage of them and to hammer them into a guilt complex. No matter how guilt arises, it is equally useful to the indoctrinator for projection purposes.

"In order to rid himself of a guilt feeling, a person's natural tendency is to project it away from himself. This is just what the brainwasher has been waiting for so he can step in and decide where it will strike.

"Notice how all these responses are like gears, shifting successively from one mind-corrosive stage to the next, each more unsatisfactory than the pre-ceding until, in mad desperation, the man dashes his head against any wall that the Reds put in front of him.

"The brainwasher, during his entire contact with the patient, attempts to sow doubt into his mind. No matter how strong a person may be, the mo-ment doubt settles in his mind, it leads to tension. Tension is related to fear.

The guilt complex also brings about fear. This is still one more point of attack for the indoctrinator. Fear has given communism some of its most astounding victories, often at little or no cost in blood or money.

"Fear is the expression of an unsatisfied need for survival and security. The first reactions to fear are nervousness, tension, apprehension, and depression. Instead of relieving the situation, they make the need for security and self-protection even more acutely felt. A deadly spiral is set up and the brainwasher keeps it spinning round and round, faster and faster, until the man breaks down.

"Out of fear comes the desire to retaliate. This is the reaction toward which the brainwasher has been working all the time. Once aroused, he has only to project it against whomever the Reds want to strike. What is especially interesting is that this desire to retaliate does not have to be projected against others. A person can aim it against himself, as he usually does when he is unable to direct it against someone else. Then he punishes himself, giving himself up sacrificially in any rash venture that the communists suggest. He eagerly plays the martyr.

"The indoctrinator uses all these elements in arousing and exploiting tension-creating responses, which are clinically known as psychosomatic or corticovisceral responses. These come from such sensations as hunger, pain, rage, and fear.

"In manipulating responses, the brainwasher strictly follows the Pavlovian line, considering body and mind as an integral unit. He goes on the Pavlovian assumption that any outside stimulus can be made to create any desired mental and physical reaction if enough emphasis is put on it, and especially if this can be done inside a controlled environment.

"He uses a physical means to induce a mental response, and vice versa. When he can produce such a reaction, the indoctrinator has little difficulty in projecting it in any direction he wishes.

"Sheer physical responses are most handy for him here. Consider one of the most recognizable. When induced by fright, a man's legs stiffen, his hair stands up, his skin becomes moist and his mouth dry. His heart beats fast. This response spreads to his intestinal tract with results that everyone knows. In such a state, the body prepares for fight or flight. More red blood cells are pumped into the blood, to carry an extra load of oxygen or fuel, and to produce more coagulating substance which is needed to heal possible wounds.

"At the same time, the brain's customary process of receiving and sending messages is short-circuited, which brings about a purely emotional reaction. There is no time for reasoning. All delay has to be avoided in order to meet the supposed or actual emergency in time.

"Artificially induced pressures, such as a state of chronic fatigue, deprive a man of the strength to combat repetitious suggestions until he starts to doubt his own thoughts and convictions. When he reaches this state, he begins to live in a realm of fantasies and false beliefs. He becomes wax in the hands of his brainwasher who knows, of course, exactly what he wants from him.

"What happens in each instance is that a symbolic significance has been transferred into an organic behavior. When tension cannot be relieved by a verbal expression, behavior has to find an outlet, and it expresses itself this way. The brainwasher achieves this by a treatment that is very much like injecting small doses of poison into a man's bloodstream at intervals. He tampers with a man's make-up this way at different stages in the development of the case.

"In capsule form, the whole process is a series of pressures, including arrest or house detention, isolation from outside sources of information, interrogation, endless and repetitive assertions by teams of psychological workers, fatigue, malnutrition, exhaustion, autosuggestion and, finally, the emergence of obsessions, hysterical states, and delusion states, in which confessions are freely given and the subject can no longer distinguish his beliefs from reality or properly recall his past fund of information."

Dr. Freedom stressed that the traits which were deliberately encouraged by the brainwasher were the same as those he himself diagnosed in his clinic as responsible for illness or mental upset. The Reds were using the highly specialized knowledge of medical science to take balanced minds and to make them unbalanced. This approach, and this alone, was their contribution to modern thought.

Every psychiatrist is familiar with the attitudes and stresses that have settled into a person's system until he becomes a medical or a mental case. Dr. Freedom's research confirmed that the communists created such unhealthy conditions in order to project the resultant hate and desire for retaliation in the direction decided by the Red planners. This was the exact opposite of the efforts of medical science in the Free World, which were directed toward discovering the source of a patient's mental disorder. The psychiatrist tries to trace this by the path it came. He may find that it stemmed from resentment, and that this emanated from a feeling of inadequacy and inferiority, or of anxiety and insecurity. In this manner, the psychiatrist uncovers the unsatisfied need that has made a man sick. Brainwashers do exactly the same, only in reverse order, setting up destructive responses so as to upset a person's mind for the purpose of exploiting him for political reasons.

"The methods devised by the Free World to combat illness are used by the communists to create it," Dr. Freedom repeated. "That is why brainwashing can only be properly understood and dealt with as man-made illness."

The most diabolical intrigues of the past never descended to such dark, unstirred depths. There is something repulsive and against nature in it. This is not easy for the normal mind to grasp. Once realization dawns on a person, he is revolted by it. The tendency of the good-willed mind is to cast off such shocking information by the safety valve of disbelief. Pavlov referred to this sort of reaction as the "inhibitory process." The all-too-frequent, very human response is, "I just won't believe it." Pavlov called this type of reaction, "conditioned inhibition." He was dealing with the reflexes of animals, but the comparison with humans is perfect. By bringing all those unpleasant facts out into the open, the evil that is inherent in communism becomes glaringly apparent.

When exposed to the light of day, people instinctively would want to fight it, if only out of a sense of self-preservation. That is why a totalitarian state can only survive by maintaining an iron curtain, what Dr. Freedom calls a conditioned or a controlled environment.

The Reds themselves have thought up nothing in brainwashing, or in any other phase of psychiatry. Dr. Freedom emphasized. "All that they have done is to take what free science has developed and use it in a manner that would ordinarily be considered mad," he said. "There isn't anything original about what they are doing, only in the way they are doing it. Their single innovation has been to use what they copy in a diabolical order. Their objective is solely to make minds sick, not healthy, to create frustrations and to fan them into hates, so they can be projected against their own subjects and the Free World."

Self-Analysis

Some of the most inspiring words I heard were the reactions of Dr. Freedom upon hearing some of the brainwashing cases I had come upon. When I was anywhere in the vicinity of Baltimore, I would hotfoot it to his home immediately. At such times I would go painstakingly over my notes with him.

One such unforgettable incident was the case of the Negroes who had resisted Red flattery and force. At once after my interviews with Bob Wyatt and Russell Freeman, I visited the Freedoms. On both occasions we stayed up very late discussing them. The Freedoms were as thrilled as I.

"Left to themselves, with only the barest formal education to fall back upon," Dr. Freedom told me, "these Negro citizens had struck upon devices that were clinically perfect. They couldn't have been improved upon! They didn't let themselves be led astray in all sorts of intellectual by-paths full of sophistry and traps. They made up their minds that they were not going to listen to that kind of talk. They had a perfect reason. They went down to bedrock and kept their minds focused on underlying truths. They never let themselves lose sight of these.

"One such fundamental fact was that the Reds were at war with us. As this was true, they held to the obvious conclusion that the communists could not be meaning us any good. They noticed the way they were being fed the communist arguments and saw that what it boiled down to was force. The fact that they used force to put their ideas across meant they were lying. These colored prisoners simply had sense enough to come out of the rain!

"Another fact they didn't lose sight of was that the Reds were certainly not going to give them any more out of life than they already had in their own society. The enemy was persuasive and seductive, as well as vindictive and untruthful, so the problem these prisoners faced, once they reached these conclusions, was how to keep themselves from being seduced in spite of themselves.

"They well knew how weak a man's resistance became when he was hungry and tired, worn out through and through, with his mind in a fog. They had to find a way to remind themselves at all times to be on their guard, not to be taken in by an unexpected piece of candy or a sudden increase in rations, not to listen to flattery. They had to be most alert at those moments especially when they were least able. So they struck upon a device that was psychologically a stroke of genius.

"The simplest and surest way to remind yourself not to listen to something is to interfere with your listening apparatus. A child instinctively puts his hands over his ears when told something unpleasant. That is what they did, in effect. Using dirty needles to puncture their ear lobes, causing minor infections, and the piercing with anything handy, which led to swellings, were the best possible things they could have done. They could theoretically have had the ear piercing done by the finest surgeons on earth, in the most up-to-date hospital, with the most hygienic instruments possible, so they would suffer no discomfort whatsoever. But then they would have sacrificed the whole purpose of the operation, which was to remind themselves not to listen. They did not allow themselves to be distracted by incidentals from their end purpose. Fortunately, they hadn't the facilities and were handling themselves on the basis of their long acquired hunches.

"As long as the infections persisted, they had a constant reminder, 'Don't listen; beware!' As long as they remembered, that was all that was necessary. They needed a symbol of resistance, too. This could give support to the reminder. What better symbol could they have picked than the cross, which means succor and help? So long as they remembered the symbol, they didn't have to have real gold crosses, as their sophisticated brethren would have required. Anything could replace the symbol, even bits of straw. They did not, as unfortunately happens so frequently, begin to accept the symbol as the objective, instead of being the constant reminder.

"They were their own best psychiatrists. The tragedy and lesson in it is that they had to resort to such simple devices to protect themselves. America and humanity generally should be very proud of those men. They have shown what can be accomplished, even behind the curtain."

I also discussed with Dr. Freedom the weird emphasis that the Reds put on confession. They borrowed it from religion for purposes of politics, but used it in a way that put it into the psychiatrist's field.

Dr. Freedom said confession was analogous to a psychological catharsis — a mental purge. This explained the Red stress on what they called self-criticism and mutual criticism, always within the group structure. Out of this, he said, came what psychiatrists term *resistances, transferences,* and *counter-transferences.* The entire process was similar to the familiar clinical practice known as *free association.* By it, the individual's defenses are removed, his resistances overcome, and his various complexes revealed. By uncovering forgotten or buried experiences, the psychiatrist discovers the basis for his patient's approach to problems and his attitude regarding them. He then removes the psychological dynamite from the complexes, which could explode if kept compressed.

I had frequently noticed how interested brainwashers were in a man's thoughts while asleep, his dreams. "Why were you restless, what were you dreaming about?" were standard questions when a subject did not sleep well. As privacy is taboo under communism, guards were ordered to report such unconscious reactions. Psychiatrists know that dreams are important as a source of much information. The nightmare is one phase, disclosing hidden desires and secret fears. What was in effect dream analysis was still another road the Reds took into a man's private thoughts. Nothing was permitted to remain private under communism if the Reds could find a way to intrude.

Dr. Freedom pointed out that the various types of Red meetings were actually "clinical sessions in which the symbolism of complex situations, which were emotionally charged, were talked over again and again. That gave a sense of relief, and confidences and secrets were easily ferreted out. Confessions gave relief by unburdening the patient of fears, guilt complexes, and shame.

"All this gave the Communist Party a constant flow of material for use in blocking future conduct — for purge trials and control measures generally. When an individual was strong in his feeling of guiltlessness and did not feel shame, the communist brainwashers methodically set out in their ruthlessly practical manner to create the guilt sense and shame, using any available means to do so."

The Red POW camps were simply large clinical laboratories in which the prisoners were dealt with as patients and as mental cases. Whole populations are also treated in this way, which is why the Reds need their bamboo-iron curtain. Visitors and other contact with the outside would impede or wreck the course of treatment laid down for these captive peoples. The "cure" is made when people's minds are changed. The objective is to alter their natures, to bring about that robot creature endowed only with instincts, the "new Soviet man."

That gross parody of medical practice requires fear to make it work. The eternal distrust and suspicion met with in all Red society, as Dr. Freedom pointed out so graphically, are fear elements. All autocratic and dictatorial societies are based on fear. They are all controlled societies. These reach their peak in the totalitarian regime.

Fear permeates everyone in such a society, from the ruler down to his most abject subject. The Reds arranged their environment in such a way that fear is always present. Never has a more complicated political structure been erected than the communist, layer on top of layer. An equivalent control mechanism had to be devised to defend it from within as well as from outside: total conformity in thought as well as deed, a psychic penetration of the mind. Otherwise there could be no dependable Party discipline, the fundamental safeguard for communism. Equipped with the advantages given by modern science, the Reds have adopted the latest psychiatric methods in order to achieve mind control. Whereas psychiatry strives to free the individual's mind from fear, the Reds use the same methods to inject selected fears into the mentality of their patients. They use what they have learned about a mind's defense mechanism as a weapon to invade the mind.

The psychiatrist recognizes the natural recourse of people to God in time of emergency. The Red indoctrinator strives simply to get onto that road and replace God with the Party. The psychiatrist seeks to expose and eliminate repressed emotions, to release a weight such as an inferiority or persecution complex. The Reds endeavor simply to divert all this to their own use. Instead of curing the complex, they create it if it isn't there already, so the natural search for an outlet can be diverted from normal channels to trust in themselves. That is why the world has witnessed an organization that started out as a political movement degenerate into a fanatical faith. This was inescapable once the total approach was determined upon.

Victims of brainwashing, including returned POW's, frequently told me about their brainwasher going into a tantrum, becoming almost panicky in his insistence on a confession. The inquisitors were under the same pressures as others to accomplish the task set for them, to fulfill their work quota. If they failed, they were severely penalized, as any other worker in this dog-eat-dog system.

The communists justified this by saying that failure to complete an assignment showed lack of Marxist understanding. If an examiner were truly sincere in his materialistic faith, the Red argument goes, he would be successful in persuading his prisoner of the communist truth, and then the man would naturally do the correct thing — confess whatever crime had been trumped up against him.

I could not help being struck by the demonstration of fear the brainwashers themselves gave in their anxiety to expand the field of fear in their victims and use it for Red purposes. The insistence on confession, as described by its victims to me, seemed to fill some need in the brainwasher, too, as well as satisfy his Party superiors. The prisoner's confession seemed needed by the brain washer to relieve his own mind! I brought this up with Dr. Freedom.

He declared this is the natural result of such proceedings. The disillusioning assignments given to Red functionaries, conflicting with the simple beliefs and ideals with which many of them had been lured into the Party, create agonizing conflicts in their own mind. Whom can they discuss these with? Nobody! Everyone is in the same boat. While some harden themselves, very much as a criminal does, others find no peace.

Fear permeates both sides in the communist confession ritual. The man who stands up and confesses does so out of fear, and the inquisitor needs to hear it to quench his own fears. Both are in the same plight. The communist hierarchy depends on these confessions just as much to lay aside its own searing doubts. Only this way can they lift the weight of guilt and fear from their own minds. When such confessions are not forthcoming, they have to be exacted, even at the cost of concocting crimes out of thin air. Their tremendous burden of guilt can only be removed by everyone else taking the blame, absolving the top. Only by listening to confessions by all these others can they lay aside their own fundamental lack of assurance, and remove from their minds for a while the haunting contradictions that plague them. Confession is a drug to them; the more they take of it, the more they need and the more sadistic they become, transferring the blame for their own evil deeds to those poor, confessing scapegoats. The circle is vicious to the nth degree.

The fake crime the authorities insist on must be confessed with concreteness. Where evidence is lacking, it is manufactured, for nothing must stand in the way of this bizarre rationalization. They doubt, and the more they do so the more they have to dope themselves with fake confessions. That breeds even more doubts, and more confessions have to be squeezed out to quiet the hysteria in them. The man who makes the faked confession is a less tragic character than the officials on whose behalf it is exacted. The former's plight is less complex; he can see an end. The latter cannot; they have to be fed more and more confessions to ease the gnawing at their insides. The totalitarian state depends on confessions to cleanse its own guilt from the record and to proclaim its own innocence.

The need for artificial evidence to justify confession has given rise to a complicated brainwashing mechanism. Yet however constant, unceasing, and plausible the confessions sound, they always are inadequate, the subterfuge never fully satisfies. Confession becomes a desperate form of play-acting, each side having to go through the show with poker faces so as not to break the spell.

When the softening-up process in brainwashing is successful and is accompanied by sufficient indoctrination, the whole act can take place within the person of the accused. He can be his own make-believe character, rationalized by Red dialectics which hold that everything in nature is in flux, including truth. Only change and struggle are recognized. Only their own communism can defy this natural law of theirs, only communism remains stable and unchanging according to their doctrine. That is where the faith comes in their quack religion.

The sole stability, they teach, is in the eternal verity of the communist cause. Using this as the sole standard, they judge all truth and falsity. Under this hypothesis, they consider as truth only that which upholds the communist line; everything else is untruth, lies! The good and the bad are similarly defined by them. The good is what advances the cause of communism. The bad is what hurts communism. No exceptions are recognized. No religion has ever been more fanatical in its adherence to dogma.

In this framework, individual guilt is a minor matter; what weighs heaviest on a man is his guilt as a member of a collectivity. He is guilty for the sins of his forebears and for all the wrongs committed by his kind. The limitless-responsibility theory has him hemmed in. He loses a sense of individuality in time or space. Confession becomes easier that way, and voluntary, too, of crimes he never committed, of crimes that never took place. Whether they actually happened, in the form confessed, becomes irrelevant. What is relevant is his need to cleanse himself of this heavy burden, of original sin, the sin of having belonged to a bourgeois society, of having forebears who were not communists.

Any crime, existent or non-existent, can become the handle for a communist rebirth in this earthly faith. Cleansing for it requires confession. This is mysticism pure and simple. An infinite amount of wearying, circuitous thinking is required to reach such a mental state, for otherwise it would be recognized at once as crazily off the beam. A child could see through it if expressed in simple language. Even this is feared, so the child has to begin indoctrination — brainwashing — from the cradle, to get the inherited impulses from a non-communist past out of his subconscious. Communist training starts when the child begins schooling. From then on he must learn to speak this new, mystic tongue. Plain words and straight thinking must arouse a sense of naughtiness, to be avoided as a temptation of the devil, the bourgeois devil. This gives communism its superficial appearance of puritanism.

The Red priest and his congregation must put themselves into a virtual trance for this in their churchlike service that they call a "people's democratic discussion meeting." That is the immediate objective of communal brainwashing and is why every man, woman, and child under communism must experience it. That is why they have to undergo flagellation and self-humiliation and self-abasement. Intricate ceremonials have to be gone through to make the mind light and bring about this trance state. What it actually brings on is utter submission, the goal of the whole confession phenomenon, the key to the communist program for world expansion, to which everything is subordinated. Confess is the magic word which, like an electronic push button, operates the gears of the whole control mechanism.

Each time a U.N. soldier stood up and used the words "I confess" in the Red POW camp, and each time a missionary or merchant did so in a brainwashing chamber inside the communist belt of countries, the mystic Pavlovians of high communism knew that he was saying, "You're the boss." Each time he repeated it, he was rubbing a little more of that psychological content of the words "I submit" into his mentality. In Red double-talk, he was being made accustomed to submission without knowing it. That is the framework on which communism imposes confession of captives and comrades alike.

National Neuroses

If brainwashing can make a single individual neurotic, what about the inhabitants of a village, or a city, or even a country, when subjected to these same pressures? There is no doubt any longer that this type of mind attack is being waged against entire populations, not only against a few foreigners trapped inside Red borders and on nationals regarded as "backward elements" by the Reds.

The only possible conclusion is that a long-range program is being pursued which, if left unhindered over a long period, will make whole populations just as neurotic as a single individual.

I presented this problem to Dr. Freedom, leaving in his hands a pile of translated communist statements and literature about "re-education" and "mind reform," which ranged from official declarations to picture-story books, fiction, and drama.

When next we met he was very grim. "The documentation you left with me confirms how the communists fit everything into a broad strategy," he said. "All or most of the techniques used therapeutically by neuropsychiatrists and psychiatrists for the rehabilitation of mentally ill patients are employed by the communist hierarchy to produce hysterical and obsessive delusional states in the populations under their domination."

The identical process of brainwashing, as imposed on civilian or military prisoners, is being applied to the inhabitants of whole villages, towns, and cities by "group discussion" and "learning" meetings, frequent demonstrations, parades, and an endless chain of so-called patriotic campaigns. Group leaders, corresponding to "block captains" for neighborhood festivities in the West, make sure that everyone participates, until each area is molded into the desired form. Individual treatment is reserved mainly for "backward elements" who lag behind in their "conversion."

The Chinese as a race are undergoing mind treatment inside a Great Pavlovian Wall. In the new collective approach, that which medical science recognizes as causing neurosis in an individual is being applied on a nationwide scale. It is imposed in a subtle way on the peoples of China specifically, and on the inhabitants of every communist country. They are undergoing what the disciples of Pavlov callously term "mental hygiene." The process is a parody of "group therapy," the treatment of patients in a group instead of individually. This developed out of World War II, along with putting patients back on their feet within a few days after an operation, at first because time was pressing and doctors were scarce and later because this was found more healing. A New York psychiatrist named Dr. Wilfred Hulse, who served in World War II, told me how group therapy for mental crackups started out of necessity at the Battle of the Bulge. If it could be utilized to repair minds on a wide scale, the Reds saw that it could also serve to break them.

A saturation treatment is being given to communist society. The routine of each day and night is so arranged that the people simply cannot escape from the sight and sound of communist propaganda pressures. The spoken and the written word are injected into every conceivable phase of working and leisure time. Writings are prescriptions, not stories. Entertainment is sugar-coating for mind pills.

The list of characters in a Chinese communist play about indoctrination processes, entitled *The Question of Thought,* when removed from its dramatic wrapping, could be included in a physiologist's textbook as representative of the varied types in modern Chinese society. The play has curious similarities in structure to Cardinal Wiseman's drama *Fabiola,* written almost exactly a hundred years before. The identical emotions are awakened, only the emphasis in Fabiola is in one direction, while in The Question of Thought it is in the opposite. Both were written in the pattern of the Christian morality plays that began about the year 1200.

In *Fabiola* all strata of life in early Rome are represented, including rich man, soldier, farmer, slave, peasant, and civil servant. In each of these two plays, in accordance with the contrasting standards of their societies, the virtues of honor, integrity, chastity, modesty, and courage were opposed, in the persons of the cast, to the vices of cupidity, arrogance, pride, timidity, unctuousness, and falsity. The reason for the almost hysterical enthusiasm evoked by these plays was that they fulfilled the desire of human beings anywhere to identify themselves with what the environment considered good and triumphant, in a cause presented as ideal, and in the person of a hero or heroine.

The characters in the Red drama were deliberately made neurotic by persuasion, autosuggestion, duress, and imitation. Peasants and workers were lured by double-talk and double-think into the exact opposite of what they knew in their hearts was good. This is why communist literature is not entrusted to a single individual to write, but is produced by collective authorship in a controlled committee framework. In this way, each sentence can be gone over again and again by "able Party members" to make sure that it contains the exact psychological effect desired by the communist mind manipulators.

"These techniques are obviously the result of profound study by Soviet planners into national characteristics, based on Pavlovian principles that the nervous mechanism is the chief link in all processes occurring in the organism, and that the organism's conditions of life constitute the determining factor in its behavior," Dr. Freedom explained.

The same set of psychological techniques are used against the young, the middle-aged, and whatever segments of the aged the communist hierarchy believes are worth salvaging. They are applied with particular intensity to the very young and the teen-agers. If this manipulation of minds is able to continue unhampered, within a comparatively few years a "new youth" will be produced with blind spots in their minds, making them oblivious to anything not acceptable to Pavlovian symbolism.

"This will create a nation of hysterically inflamed people obsessed with the idea that they have to destroy us before we destroy them," Dr. Freedom warned.

Such a form of fanaticism, which in the case of the individual has already crossed the dividing line that separated it from mental unbalance or actual clinical insanity, is being induced on a national scale by the Reds, with a world scale the ultimate objective.

This calculated creation of national neurosis is incontrovertibly the greatest threat ever posed against human society. A people with such a streak in them cannot listen to reason, for they are conditioned into simply not hearing it. Ordinary logic can have no effect on such a body of men. They, like the individual neurotic, require a cure, something fundamentally different than the give and take of a New England town meeting.

Additional confirmation of the paramount importance with which communism regards the mass-scale Pavlovian approach is provided by the extensive training courses and experimentation being conducted by Soviet Russia and Red China. In China, the exchange of prisoners of war in Korea was followed within a few weeks by a series of Pavlovian study sessions. The setbacks and successes obtained by brainwashing in the POW camps were studied, so that the next time prisoners are seized the indoctrinators will have an improved technique to go on, based on what they learned from past experience.

A large Pavlov conference by physicians, physiologists, psychologists and biologists was held at Peking in September, 1953. Kuo Mo-jo, an archaeologist who had been preaching Marxism since 1925, gave the opening address. He was a government official exclusively engaged in propaganda work at home and abroad. He had no role in a conference of medical people, except to set its psychological warfare tone. The official Chinese communist news agency reported that these medical practitioners attended classes where they were taught "the universal truth of Marxism-Leninism as applied to Pavlov's work," that he was a "militant materialist" and that his theories were "permeated with the thought of dialectical materialism." The forum voted, in the usual unanimous manner, that it was necessary to learn Marxism-Leninism in order to understand Pavlov.

The delegates "participated in the experimental work on conditioned reflexes conducted by the specialists in psychology of the National University and the China Union Medical College," the dispatch said. "A tentative outline for the study and discussion of the Pavlov theories was drawn up," to be participated in "by the entire scientific circles of the country."

Five months later, in February, 1954, the *Kwangming Daily*, frequently used as the Government voice in scientific matters, reported that "university teachers and scientific and medical workers in more than twenty major cities are systematically studying Pavlov's theories on the activity of the higher nervous system. Since eighty prominent Chinese physiologists and other specialists in this field took a special course in Pavlov last year, its study has spread to Shanghai, Tsingtao, Lanchow, Mukden, Harbin, Canton and other cities. Laboratories on conditioned-reflex work have been set up in medical institutes and hospitals to develop Pavlovian research."

Editorially, this semi-official publication declared:

"Pavlov's theory on the activity of the higher nervous system has given a scientific basis for man's capacity to transform the world by his consciousness of the world. It destroys the idealistic theories which have dominated physiology for a long time. Pavlov's theories have become the foundation of the natural sciences." The paper also called on China's physiologists, psychologists and medical workers to put Pavlov's theories into practice.

Clinical treatment is conceivable for a limited number of persons, but how does one treat a sick country? Professional organizations in the medical and psychiatric fields in the Free World can have no more important task than to tackle this problem.

"The perversion of therapeutic techniques by political authorities of the totalitarian countries is a phenomenon of such tremendous importance that it requires exhaustive study in order to counteract and defeat it," Dr. Freedom emphasized.

What was startlingly evident was that, under official stimulation and compulsion in the Red bloc of countries, such over-all study was already being given to the subject for a war against men's minds. If the same attention is not given to it in the free nations for purposes of defense and to keep intact the beneficial purposes of science, their people will be as vulnerable to its pressures as were those luckless and unwarned young men who were made prisoners of the communists in Korea.

Chapter Ten - How It Can Be Beat

Mental-Survival Stamina

Communism, by applying Pavlov's findings to old ways of influencing minds, appeared to many people who consider themselves coldly realistic as having hit upon a strategy that was unbeatable. The Reds discovered that science, like fire, could be used more easily for destruction than construction, and have chosen to use it that way.

This gave rise to a defeatist state of mind which expressed itself in such questions as: "Every man has a breaking point, so there's nothing you can do about it, is there?" This attitude was frequently given a respectable cloak by being called "objectivity," "neutrality," and even an "independent point of view," but it was defeatism and part of the deliberate softening-up process under communism.

The communists endlessly repeat their hopelessness-inevitability line by argument, implication and example. Whether in a Soviet prison or at an international conference, it is always present. Like a medieval poison, it can turn the moral bloodstream into water.

The communists, with calculated modesty, attribute their victories to dialectical materialism, as proof of the hopelessness of opposing their will and the inevitability of their ultimate triumph. Their dialectical materialism boils down to sheer materialism that wears a mystic cloak and proclaims the gospel of constant change through unceasing struggle, with the eternal, inflexible truth of communism as the only measurement for verity and good. This political theology admits no conclusions except its own. That is what communism means by science. The moral appeared to be that the Reds got what they wanted sooner or later. They possessed the patience, ruthlessness, and one-track mind necessary for a successful delaying tactic. "Be wise to yourself and join a winner while you still have the chance," they kept saying, in language adjusted to every mental level and social stratum, to all who had not submitted. They never ceased reiterating this, like a magic formula.

When the lengthy list of elements that went into brainwashing was put down on paper, one after the other, it represented such a formidable array that it did look, superficially, as if the Reds had come upon a winning combination. The impression increased so long as one's mind could be kept focused on just those points. If it were really true that any response could be obtained by using any stimulus, from a soft caress to a shouted word, as the neo-Pavlovians taught, there simply appeared to be no stopping it. The problem that it presented was so new and sinister that it tended to paralyze opposition.

My attention at first was concentrated only on what brought about the breakdown of the mind, because it was only this that was at first apparent. This was the fundamental control strategy on which communism based its entire aggression and mind-remolding program. The immediate question was what it was and how it came about. Out of the experiences of those who underwent mind attack, the pattern for brainwashing slowly revealed itself.

Indoctrination, persuasion, explanation, publicity and public relations, education, examination and re-examination, criticism and self-criticism — each of these only cover a single facet of brainwashing. Clergymen indoctrinate. Schools educate and re-educate. Successful persuasion normally indicates a better argument. To assume that any one of these words or labels was a synonym for brainwashing only concealed its sinister content and helped the Reds continue to wage their mind attack against an unprepared foe.

What first struck me in the communist attitude was their great fear of the word, as if it might destroy them. Joseph Z. Kornfeder, an American who graduated from the College of Political Subversive Warfare at Moscow and was one of the first to break away from communism, discussed it with me. He described mind attack as "the most sensitive nerve of international communism." He said the only Red defense would be to hush up the subject, because even to deny the idea would be to bring attention to it. Anyone who heard the details, even if he were skeptical, could not help but recognize brainwashing once it was attempted against him. "A sensitive nerve has to be left untouched; anything that rubs against it hurts," Kornfeder added. The damage would be so much the greater if the details about it could get to the people who live inside the communist countries.

How correct he was gradually became evident as more and more victims of brainwashing began to tell what they had undergone. Without my noticing it for quite some time, a second pattern of brainwashing began to take shape out of these many interviews. Each person I spoke to, when he explained what had been done to him, referred at the same time to his own struggle against it. I took notes on what each person said had helped him to resist. After a while I noticed a similarity. Indiscernible in the beginning, a technique of mind defense, of how a mind could be protected, began to take shape.

This knowledge, disseminated and emphasized throughout the world, particularly in the satellite states, can pull the rug out from under brainwashing and wreck communism's most potent weapon. Those who suffered under brainwashing as well as former high communists and psychiatrists all agreed to that. Awareness of how it is perpetrated can bring about its ultimate defeat. Knowledge of it is mental vaccination.

Colonel Schwable, who confessed to germ warfare, said: "I would have given my soul to have known those facts." He told me how he had spent several days, almost around the clock, writing a paper about military medals because the Reds had promised to let him leave his isolated Korean house and return to the regular POW enclosure as soon as he did it. "If I had known their whole idea was to wear me down, I would have made the job last months," he said. When he completed it, all fagged out, the Reds ignored their promise and began pressing him for the germ-warfare confession. "When they brought up bugs instead of military secrets with which I was loaded, I sighed inwardly with relief," he told me. "If I could keep them talking about bugs, I said to myself, they wouldn't get to the war secrets I knew. No military secret ever slipped from me. But how did I know that it was bugs they were really interested in? I couldn't take bugs seriously, and couldn't imagine anyone else doing so. I thought I was putting something over on them."

What was evident out of the experiences of the brainwashed was that two men could undergo similar pressures under the same set of circumstances and one would crack and the other not. But why was it that the man who seemed to possess most of the advantages was frequently the one to break? He could be better educated, huskier, even of a higher status in life. Yet he cracked. Another chap, who didn't appear to have a ghost of a chance, retained both his honor and his life.

What made one man capable of being an inspiration to his comrades and a frustration to the Reds, while another who should have held out equally or better succumbed to Red pressure and became a rat?

Then I began asking, "How were you able to survive as well as you did, while others in a better condition broke down?" In brief, the question was, "To what do you attribute your survival?" The replies showed how a mind could defeat the most subtle pressures ever devised by a witch doctor or a corticovisceral psychiatrist. The details given to me built up to this new pattern of mental-survival stamina.

No discovery could have been more thrilling. If brainwashing can take a fine mind and make a parody of it, the safeguarding of such an intellect is one of the basic problems of our age. Its solution is necessary to enable free society to win out over the police-state concept. Give it any label — cold, ideological, propaganda, or psychological war — it is nothing more or less than the ancient conflict between the influences that dehumanize and collectivize people and those that develop individuality and free will. The new Red warfare is based on mind attack. Military terminology describes it perfectly. Such terms as *artillery attack, diversionary attack, air attack,* and *gas attack* have become familiar. Mind attack is a natural extension of all these.

Indeed, the attitudes of people have always been the real target of any attack. The result of every battle is decided by how men react mentally. The Reds subordinate all other weapons to this new strategy, abandoning all considerations of honor, decency, and religion, except when those, too, can be used specifically as weapons in mind attack.

Hitherto, society has given its youth what is known as physical-survival training. Our young men are taught as boy scouts, in school and in the army, how to endure physical hardships. Our boys are taught to take care of themselves if lost in the woods or on a deserted island. They learn which berries are nourishing and which are poisonous, and how to protect themselves against beasts and savages. An aviator is taught how to stay alive if he crashes into the jungle or on an ice floe.

Nowadays our men must learn something else as well. They must be given mental-survival training. They have to learn what to do if they are lost in an ideological jungle. They need to be trained to survive under this new man-made menace of mind attack. The camp crafts that young men previously learned must be expanded to cover these new emergencies. Never again shall it be said that a product of free society died of starvation because he could not stomach unaccustomed foods such as *kaoliang* — the sorghum of North China. Never again should our youth worry themselves sick over the double-talk of a trained propagandist because they are unable to distinguish between words and motives. In mind war, a man must be prepared for false friends and deprivations of all contact with his own kind. Never again shall a free man suffer the pangs of isolation while in the company of other human beings simply because their skins or their cultures differ radically from his own.

Forever hence, he must know the traps that are set up for him by mind attack, traps that are devised with less compassion than those built to capture a wild beast. He has to know that each kind of attack has its appropriate weapons. The tools of a successful artillery attack include guns, ammunition, soldiers, and observers. The tools of mind attack include food, fear, fatigue, and deception. He must be prepared for these. He must be trained in the defenses against the planned disintegration of his will. He must know how to handle the tools that can guard the well-being and integrity of his mind.

Free society must teach each man and woman that this is everyone's business, for everyone is the target of total war. There is no front and no rear in mind attack.

I was given a multitude of answers to my question of what constituted mental-survival stamina by persons of completely different natures and professions, from widely different cultural areas of the world. Their replies varied in detail but were alike on essential points. This similarity was the most significant point about them.

The elements that gave a man moral strength were just as definable as those which gave him physical strength. Out of the experience of all these brainwashed persons came a practical and a satisfying pattern for survival against mental pressures. Such survival knowledge can ultimately destroy communism, internally and externally.

These elements can be named and listed. They are:

Faith, convictions, clarity of mind, a closed mind, purpose, keeping one's mind busy, confidence, deceit, high jinks, adaptability, crusading spirit, group feelings, being yourself. Certain of these labels, standing by themselves, would give too broad or misleading an impression, such as a closed mind and deceit. Within the framework of maturity and dissemblance these two are trimmed to fit within our democratic way of life and still remain practical. They are all bound up in integrity which gives them their direction and potency.

Each requires detailed description.

Faith and Convictions

Missionaries and other men and women attached to religious organizations naturally leaned on their faith for support while under mind attack. What was not generally expected, however, was that hard-boiled laymen would do the same with equal fervor, reaping the same beneficial results. In this skeptical day and age, such a finding sounds unrealistic and meets derision and resistance. Yet for me to report otherwise would be to misrepresent what they had told me.

The people I interviewed were mostly down-to-earth, practical men who could not be swept off their feet by emotionalism. The Shanghai lawyer and the Budapest engineer, the top sergeant from Korea and the automobile salesman from Detroit, were men of the world. Still, they declared that the most important elements in their survival were faith and prayer. So did the majority of those who went through Red brainwashing.

They credited strong convictions, too, with playing a decisive role in their struggle for stamina. Those who did not emphasize prayer and faith laid great stress on convictions as an indispensable, strength-bestowing quality.

The convictions that protected a man were contained in his way of life, expressed through a code of conduct in which he could put steadfast faith and to which he could give his fullest loyalty. Whatever shape convictions took, if they constituted a way of life and were scrupulously followed, they set up roadblocks to mind attack. The code did not have to be of any particular kind; it could be ethical, social, political, patriotic or religious. Religion frequently was expressed as a way of life rather than as a specific dogma. Patriotism, simple faith in one's own country, was one of the basic convictions. So long as a code was rigidly adhered to, one set of convictions served as effectively as another. The weakness lay in their lack, not in their types. The secret was in knowing what one believed and why.

Men who relied on form alone, such as the mere repetition of religious passages without thinking of their meaning, only helped defeat themselves by adding to the Red fatigue pressure. There was no substitute for real awareness when a man was completely on his own. He had to know what he was doing.

These three words — prayer, faith, and convictions — were closely linked in most minds and were often used interchangeably. At least one of these was mentioned in every case when a man thought back over what had given him his main support.

I asked Robert A. Vogeler one day what qualities had helped him most. His case was the first to bring home to the American people the fact that brain-washing was something more than an intriguing word concerning others, never themselves. He had been held incommunicado for eleven months. He was grabbed by his leg when he attempted to hurl himself to death down a steep alleyway inside the prison compound. Later he made the usual confessions to the usual fake accusations and was given the usual long sentence. He was released when the U. S. Government agreed to meet the blackmailing demands of Red Hungary.

What pulled him through, Vogeler said, was firstly religion and secondly faith. "What's the difference?" I asked, for in this realm of attitudes the dictionary is only of limited help. Each person chooses his preferred connotation and gives it his own special emphasis. "I mean faith in what I had been brought up to believe in," he said tersely. "In the dignity of the individual, the rights of man, and the American way of life generally."

His deep-set, narrow eyes and dark eyelashes gave him the look of a skipper or a pilot. "My father was a Protestant, my mother was a Catholic, and I became an Episcopalian as a compromise, I suppose," he mused. "I have never been much of a churchgoer. But while I was suffering in that communist prison, it was religion that was the main source of my strength."

"What do you mean by religion?" I asked. He had carefully thought this out in prison. What had kept his spirit up, he said, was not the eye-for-an-eye approach. "That has been tried for ages and has never worked, but has always led to some new attempt at revenge," he explained. "The faith that held me up was the philosophy of the Crucifixion, of rebirth."

He tried, during his long days and nights of incarceration, to recall exactly what the New Testament said about this. He gave himself the task of bringing back to his mind the verses he had learned as a boy in Sunday school. He made a practice in prison of saying grace whenever he ate, no matter what sorry pretense of a meal was put before him.

He keenly felt the lack of a Bible and kept asking for one. Six months after he began his prison term, when the communists were no longer worried about what might maintain his moral strength, they let him have a copy. He set himself a routine, picking certain pages to read morning, afternoon, and night. "I believed in that part of religion which teaches that every experience has a reason," he said. "I knew that my sufferings had to have a reason, too. Knowing this, I understood that I had to survive and would survive to give this reason meaning and fulfillment."

As a consequence, Vogeler came out of the Red prisons no longer just a practical businessmen, but a man with a mission. His experience under communism had broadened him into a crusader for freedom. I often came across this phenomenon in the men who had climbed down from the Calvary of brainwashing. They had acquired a new perspective and had been taught a new sense of values.

Bob Bryan, the Shanghai lawyer, answered the same question with the words "prayer and faith." I wondered why he hadn't said it the other way around. Wasn't prayer founded on faith? But he was not discussing the theory of religion, only his personal experience. In a prison a man finds himself praying and he does not stop to think how this came about; he accepts it.

I visualized the big prison where some of my old friends had suffered during the Japanese occupation of Shanghai, where the communists were now engaging in atrocities of the mind. Once its doors had locked behind a person, he was strictly alone.

"Do you mean to tell me," I asked Bryan, "that while you were being tortured, isolated from all who might help you, forced from one confession into another, drugged when you tried to balk them, you actually gained staying power by the mere act of prayer?"

The forthrightness with which he replied defied challenge. "Prayer gave me the strength to keep my wits about me," he said. "Otherwise I never could have done it."

"Exactly how did it help you?" I persisted, not because I doubted what he said, but because theory alone could not have helped him at such a critical time; it had to be something specific. And so it was. He told me how prayer fulfilled a definite function, defeating the communist isolation tactic. "No matter how much the Reds insisted that I was wholly abandoned, out of reach of any aid, I was able to demolish their whole argument by prayer." The thickest prison walls could not hold back his prayer. "When I was most in need of support, prayer gave it to me. Prayer made me part of an invincible force."

Additional clarity on the role of prayer in time of stress was provided by Dr. Hayes, who mentioned the comfort and staying power he derived from the prayers of others. As a minister of the Gospel he knew that many persons were including him in their own prayers. These, and his own, gave him the sense of belonging to what could not be vanquished. "The certainty that other people, many of them strangers to me, were thinking about me and praying for me, made me feel completely confident of the future," he said.

The element of conviction, which was such a tremendous factor in preserving stamina, requires separate consideration. Without convictions, a man was soft clay in the hands of the Reds. I heard of no case where anyone without convictions was able to resist brainwashing in an effective manner once the communists began to apply the heat. Extra proof came from an entirely different direction, from those who had capitulated miserably. They had invariably been lacking in strong convictions. Whether they were well educated, well proportioned, wealthy, or of high position, the result was the same as with anyone else who lacked convictions.

Claude Batchelor was a tragic example of this lack. His lawyer asked me for a deposition, which I wrote after prolonged sessions with his client in the modern prison at old Fort Sam Houston. I summarized my conclusions in two paragraphs. Indeed, only one phrase was needed to tell the whole dismal story: "A lack of settled convictions and with no depth of feeling given to him by home, church, or school."

Not once in the many hours I spent with him did Batchelor allude to positive convictions. The words "I believe . . ." seemed no part of him. He was a handsome, tall lad with clean-cut features and a patient manner. What had he been taught at home, church, and school?

Personal convictions are interpreted in as many different ways around the world as there are customs and traditions. Each civilization produces its own, although the objectives are the same. When such differences in approach are not understood, we mistake strength for weakness and weakness for strength. The most revealing example of this was given to me by a Chinese woman named Mary Liu.

She had been in an unrivaled position to know what was happening behind the scenes. She sat in at meetings from which all foreigners, even sympathizers, were excluded, when so-called spontaneous accusations and demonstrations were being rehearsed as if for a theatrical performance. She was in a position to relate the whole inside story and to show what provided mental-survival stamina inside this bizarre environment. She revealed the existence of convictions where least expected, in a form that inevitably escaped the attention of the West. She exposed what could be a fatal weakness where the Reds seemed safely in control, as in China. Hers was the most dramatic and encouraging life story I had ever come across in more than a quarter of a century of interviews. Only a few words of it can be related here.

Mary's credentials could not have been more convincing. She carried them in her physical disabilities and in her conquest of them. Her background must first be understood.

Somehow, when hardly more than a baby in Nanking, she had been left out at night in freezing weather and when brought back into the house was already suffering from severe frostbite. In the China of that period, on the eve of the establishment of the Sun Yat-sen republic, girl babies were frequently abandoned to die outside city walls. Not much care was given to them under the best of circumstances. If they lived, well and good; if they died, it was welcomed as the will of heaven. Fortunately, Mary was finally sent to a mission hospital. One hand and the fingers of the other, as well as both lower legs, had to be amputated to halt the spreading gangrene. The American surgeon carefully saved the stub of one thumb, a foresight which helped her grow up a normal child, able to wield pen or brush, chopsticks or knife and fork. She was naturally graceful, but this grace was predominantly of the spirit, which was the unbeatable in her.

The missionaries took her in and brought her up, educating her in their schools. She graduated from Ginling College and became the editor of a woman's magazine published in Shanghai by the Protestant denominations.

Equipped with artificial lower limbs, she refused to accept any other aid. Buttressed by faith and convictions, she looked on life as a grand opportunity for service. This approach to life focused her mind outside herself on all the wonderful things she could do for others, and was her greatest stabilizer. Glancing through her Bible one day as a child, she found a verse that has served her ever since as the foundation for her mental stamina. The words were Paul's: "And he said unto me, My grace is sufficient for thee: for my strength is made perfect in weakness." A thrill coursed through Mary as she read this, for it seemed to have been said with her in mind. Her life confirmed this passage in its deepest sense.

She was visiting Hong Kong, outside of China, when the communists took over Shanghai. She promptly returned there, confident that of all people on earth, she had the least to fear from the Reds. If they were the slightest bit sincere in their sympathy for the handicapped masses, she was their best symbol of victory over impossible odds.

But the unimaginative brainwashing machine saw in her only a symbolic example of the isolated, unconditioned man they feared so much. They could not spare her and survive themselves. They set to work to remold her mind and rid it of its Promethean individuality.

As their pressures increased, Mary contemplated escape by suicide and slept with deadly pills by her pillow. The Reds prevented even this by making her lifelong associates responsible for her. Their lives were now in her hands.

She was a token of the unconquerability of the individual, no matter what the obstacles, even when deprived of hands and feet. The Communist Party saw this power in her and was afraid. She was maneuvered into a corner where she had to accuse the people who had saved her and who had made it possible for her to live her wonderfully useful life. She had to declare that black was white, good was evil, and that the Americans who had helped her were selfish in doing so. She had to say, in effect, that they had only sought to use her as a tool for cultural aggression.

Mary had been unable to believe that such a travesty could be seriously insisted up>on for her, too. She had to go through with the farce, but in doing so, she developed a counterstrategy. She did only what she was absolutely unable to avoid doing, accusing only those outside of communist reach, who had already died or were abroad. She laid careful plans to escape abroad, so as to make her experiences known to the religious organizations of other lands, particularly in places such as India, to warn them in time against allowing themselves to become pawns of Red policy, as she had seen happen in her own country.

By going through with an act, the Chinese is able to fool his indoctrinators and in this way to "gain face" and needed time, which the Chinese have always recognized as a form of power. The maintenance of status is a distinct "gain of face." Part of the communist strategy is to humiliate the Chinese so that he "loses face." This face, which we call prestige, and "face-saving," are power elements.

The communist regime knows that vast numbers of people are waiting for the moment when open opposition will be practicable and have a reasonable prospect of success. This is why there is no semblance of trust between the Reds themselves and why every communist country has to be kept under unceasing purges.

Mary was not arrested, but neither was she a free woman. She was not able to resign from her job or move her home. She could not do anything normally associated with freedom, except continue going each day between her editorial office and flat. Even this was a travesty, for she was deprived of any work to do. All that was left on which to spend time was the ritual of self-criticism, mutual confession, expiation, and purge. She walked an ideological tightrope, exerting all her energies to maintain her balance.

At one grueling self-accusation meeting, while the Reds were insisting that she denounce those whose selflessness and affection had aided her, a new conviction, that was part of her blood heritage, came over her, filling her with composure and assurance.

"I felt certain, at that moment, that I would outlast Mao Tse-tung," she told me.

Her reaction was typical, as I learned from many other Chinese. Many throughout the nation, who also were undergoing varying intensities of mind attack, were strengthened by the same startling conviction. They absorbed vital staying power from it.

"Did you actually mean that you were sure that you, Mary Liu, would out-live Mao Tse-tung?" I asked. "Weren't you thinking figuratively?"

"Whether I was thinking figuratively, I leave to you," she replied, "but when that thought came to me, it was in the form I've related to you. I knew that I would outlast Mao Tse-tung. That is exactly the feeling that came over me. Let others interpret it; I can only say how it felt."

She agreed that she thought of Mao not so much as an individual, but as the symbol of communism. She now knew, too, that while she represented in her own being what was essentially Chinese, Mao represented an unnatural and tyrannous ideology. He would topple, as had all those others who had gone counter to the race culture of China. She lost her fear of the indoctrinators who stood over her. Her only problem was to play for time.

This was conviction and it also was faith. The ordinary people of China express it in the simple formula: "An unjust ruler loses the mandate of heaven."

Mary recognized that this was a struggle for ultimate survival. "Stamina to a Chinese is essentially a long-range strategy," she explained. Certainty as to where the greater staying power lay, provided by religion and convictions, gave her the support that enabled her to endure her many tortured hours and eventually to make a thrilling escape into the Free World.

Although the conviction that Mary explained may sound very Asian, its roots are in human nature common to all races. Only its dress was Asian.

Clarity of Mind

Clarity of mind is a vital element in mental survival. A clear mind cannot be brainwashed. Every case I investigated only confirmed this the more, whether of someone who stood up nobly or who crumbled pathetically. They proved that before a mind could be brainwashed, it first had to be put into a mental fog.

These cases showed that the first requirement of a clear mind was rational thinking. One of the most important lessons to come out of brainwashing was the simple, Aristotelian principle that A is always A, and that when it is B, it is no longer A. Once the communists could convince a man that A is also B, if only for a second, they had succeeded in driving a wedge into his clear thinking which inevitably split it right down the center. Intriguing discussion over what is reality and what is illusion was all right in a classroom or a parlor back home, but not with a brainwasher who was playing for keeps. In the brainwasher's chamber there was no room for theorizing.

When under mind attack, an individual could not loosen his grip for an instant on what he knew and believed. Otherwise, the resultant indecision and hesitation gave the indoctrinators exactly the openings they were seeking.

Clarity of thought cannot exist in a vacuum. The mind must have facts to go on. Some of the easiest and most disconcerting Red conquests have been of very intelligent young men with little or no education, certainly without any instruction in the wiles of communism. The intelligent but uninformed individual, particularly if a high IQ gave him a natural capacity for information, was easily confused by half-truths and by being cut off from access to the facts that alone could clarify the situation. His mind was like an empty pail; all the Reds had to do was fill it. From confusion to a false conviction was but one step.

Another push-over for the indoctrinators was the indecisive mind, especially the falsely academic kind that always sees some valid point in the other side's argument. One of the main reasons for the intensive preliminary questioning by the Reds was to locate just such individuals. They saved the communist brainwashers a great deal of time and work.

The indoctrinator's purpose in using torture and terror was to make a man groggy, so he couldn't think straight, or to force him by sheer pain and fear to do as the Reds wished. But unless a man's clear thinking was destroyed at the same time, the communists were unable to rely on him. His signed statements could be publicized and his confessions employed to incriminate others, but he himself could not be trusted beyond these immediate objectives.

His submission could be a ruse. Once the pain and the fear had passed, he was likely to be overwhelmed by resentment, and when the opportunity arrived, become an uncompromising enemy. He had to be kept in prison or inside the controlled environment of a Soviet country. Slave-labor camps are considered by the Reds as the only profitable spot in which to keep such people.

The Reds know, too, that they cannot trust a person who submits at once. The POW's in Korea who gave in easily were often more badly treated than those who resisted the most, and they frequently lost their lives in the bargain. Instead of reaping the gratitude they expected for their betrayals, the Reds considered them dangerously unreliable. After squeezing all they could out of such weaklings, the communists tossed them aside to die.

Clear thinking can cure as well as prevent mind deterioration. The brainwasher is perpetually plagued by doubts as to whether a man is really convinced or has only bowed to force. "You are not being sincere, comrade," he constantly repeats. How can he be sure that clear thinking has really been "cleansed" from his victim's mind? The study course devised by the Reds to deal with this dilemma is like animal training rather than schooling. So long as the student is able to keep his mind clear, he retains his freedom of choice. The entire procedure by the Reds is to root out all trace of choice.

Brainwashing is not only used against foreigners and selected nationals, but is imposed on whole populations in the Soviet bloc, everywhere from Russia to Vietminh. Obviously, it has to be modified immensely for such widespread application. The Reds do not have anywhere near the trained personnel for such a program. The overwhelming majority of the communists themselves have only gone through a softening-up process. Inside the power framework of communism, this is all that is required as long as people have no alternative but to do as the Politbureau wants. If they talk and act as if they were truly indoctrinated, they are just as useful to the Reds.

Those two tiny words, "as if," are power elements. When a person can be made to perform as if by his own free will, even if he hates it, the result is the same. A great proportion of these individuals, as time goes on without hope being restored, try to justify their surrender by finding excuses for it, convincing themselves that they are not living a lie and that the Communist Party has as much right to chastise them as a parent has to punish a wayward child.

The Red hierarchy is obliged to select its underlings mostly from among such people. They are the "active Party members" and even the indoctrinators. I met some of them among the Chinese Red Army troops who had gone over to the side of the Free World. A surprisingly large number had been Communist Party members. They told me how they had joined the communists as young men, accepting Red claims and promises at face value. The cynicism and cruelty they had to indulge in as they advanced in Party trust conflicted with the idealism that had brought them into communism. They became confused and a creeping disillusionment spread through them.

Their helplessness to do anything about it rankled within them. They crushed these dangerous thoughts down into their subconscious, which turned them into conscienceless automatons and neurotics. They became grim and unhappy Party workers.

Every Red country is full of such people. While trapped within the Red apparatus, their guilt feelings are projected against the anti-communists who fall into their grasp. They become the crudest indoctrinators and the blindest theoreticians, full of suppressed bitterness and hates. Their only outlets are the scapegoats who fall into their hands.

Chao Chin-yun is a case in point. He was still in his early twenties when I met him in Formosa, after he had won his desperate fight in Korea not to go back to Red China. His determination never to return was tattooed into the flesh of his arms and chest. He told me how he had been a petty political officer under the communists. They had recruited him simply by picking him up as they passed through his village. He believed what they told him and rose steadily in their trust. He was immensely proud when he was given the responsibility of conducting people's trials in Szechwan Province. Each day, he received instructions from a Red superior who pulled the strings from behind the scenes. He cited the case of a youth named Tan whom the Reds felt could be very useful, but who, with peasant intuition, rejected all overtures. The Party heads bided their time. When a hand grenade was thrown into a barracks one day, causing a little damage and no casualties, they seized upon the incident, planting a rumor that Tan had been seen passing there just previously.

A mass meeting was called at which this was brought up. Tan was accused, transforming the meeting into a "people's court." Chao got a thrill out of manipulating it so that Tan was found guilty and the people began shouting, "Kill him! Kill him!" Chao thereupon adjourned the meeting until next day.

That night he visited the terrified prisoner who pleaded his innocence and begged Chao to help him. Chao told him that the only way out was for him to confess and throw himself "on the people's mercy." If he did this, and agreed to obey the communists in all things from then on, Chao said he would ask "the people" to save him. Tan readily agreed. The next day, Chao urged the crowd to accept Tan's plea for mercy, and to hand him over to the Party to deal with as it saw fit. Everything went according to plan, and as a result of this harrowing experience, Tan was filled with gratitude to the Party for saving his life. He became an enthusiastic follower, not suspecting that it had been stage-managed from the start.

Chao told me that the success of this maneuver filled him with pride and excitement at the time. He was kept too busy to think about its real significance. Only later, in the few minutes he lay awake on his cot before falling asleep after a long day's work, did he ponder such incidents. He forced himself to stop thinking about them, but had already become confused and disillusioned. When pressure from the outside, in the form of the Korean War, broke through the controlled environment in which he had been living, all these hidden thoughts surged up out of his subconscious and he seized his opportunity to escape. He became overnight a conscious foe of the communism he had been deceived into supporting.

A virtual shock treatment is needed to bring about such an abrupt change. In the case of these Chinese POW's whom I interviewed, release from their mental bondage came with a break in the controlled environment. This was the essential point.

The same was always true, whether it was a Chao Chin-yun or a Claude Batchelor. Chinese brainwashers, stationed in the Red hospital and at other points around Panmunjom, retained control over Batchelor's little coterie of men who said they did not want to go home. They were set to spying on each other in a collectivity of fear and distrust disguised as unity, to dancing the yangko and beating drums, interpreted to the outside world as enthusiasm, and to smoking hasheesh.

The prisoners were induced to edit and read each other's mail and were persuaded to announce that they did not want any more letters from home. They took the bundles of mail handed over to them and put them unopened under a cot to be distributed after the end of the negotiations, when the words of their loved ones would be too late to have effect. They were never alone, never outside the collectivity. Any slight jar would have put an end to the trance-inducing pitch of hysteria on which the Reds depended.

Batchelor told me that one night he noticed a few pages from *Reader's Digest* poking through the edges of a stack of mail under the cot. He managed to slip them out without the others seeing, and found an article by Whittaker Chambers on communism. What he read conflicted so drastically with every word he had been hearing for several years that its effect was like a hammer blow. The multitude of concealed doubts and worries that had been torturing him settled into one clear thought. He had to get away. He consciously set his mind on escape, and before dawn managed to slip out. The Pavlovian animal, when its conditioned environment is interfered with, tends to forget what it has been taught!

The Red hierarchy cannot help but suspect this, and so cannot trust its own adherents. This prospect of an explosive collapse from within drives the Politbureaus to madder and madder lengths in their internal controls. The terror they impose outside their ranks reflects the terror they feel within.

If mutual accusations and purges ceased for even a brief period in any communist country, this internal crack-up would begin at once.

Confusion, the first requirement in brainwashing, is also the initial step in communist disintegration. But the clarity of mind that can best safeguard a free man is the greatest threat of all to the communist plan.

Using One's Head

A remarkable proportion of the outstanding cases of mental survival was of men with a closed mind on communism. They shut their ears and closed their eyes to what the Reds were saying. They based their attitude on two simple premises. They knew that the Reds were telling them lies, and they knew, too, that when the Reds did tell them something truthful, it was for the purpose of harming them.

These men realized that the Reds fought dirty, using subterfuge to fool a victim. They were out to tire him out. By refusing to take anything they said seriously, a man defeated their fatigue tactic. He used plain common sense when he told himself, "I won't even listen. I don't care what they say, I just don't believe them."

The men who closed their minds found that they had hit upon one of the principal defenses against mind attack. Other men lured by the siren cry of objectivity walked into the Red trap with open eyes. By the time they caught on, it was too late. They were physical wrecks, abject collaborators, or both. What should have been obvious to them was that conduct which is normal under ordinary circumstances was tragically out of place in a prison environment.

Perhaps the strongest confirmation of the importance of the closed mind came from a man who broke speedily, providing the false evidence on which his associates were framed. Near the close of a long discussion with him, I mentioned the closed-mind factor. "Other men whom I interviewed considered communism bad and refused even to discuss it," I said. "They had a closed mind on it."

In a subdued voice that betrayed his shock, he replied, "But that is the most horrible thing I've ever heard in my life. A civilized man doesn't close his mind to anything."

He could not have better phrased the confusion that led to the undoing of himself and so many others. He had mistaken a brainwashing chamber for a college classroom and a brainwashing session for a collegiate debate. His liberal upbringing had blinded him to the fact that an open mind is useless and even dangerous when it is calculatingly cut off from the information it needs. What this man was defending, although he did not realize it, was not an open but a perpetually indecisive mind.

"Doesn't a man ever come to a decision on anything?" I asked him. "What else is maturity if it is not the time when a man has reached basic conclusions on right and wrong conduct?"

"How can a person maintain liberal principles if he closed his mind on anything?" he persisted.

I thought of those who had survived brainwashing and who told me what a great help a closed mind on communism had been to them. They were not intolerant or illiberal men. They had merely decided upon a counter-tactic to the enemy's, recognizing that this was an all-out fight in which they were engaged.

A young lady passed our table. "You surely don't really mean that a mature man discusses everything objectively," I said. "Do two men, such as you and I, discuss seriously whether it might be all right to violate that young girl? Of course not. We don't even talk about it. We have closed minds on the subject. Or do you still insist on keeping an open mind on everything?"

"Of course not in such an obvious case," he replied.

"What could be more obvious," I asked, "than a political system that makes a bestial attack on the minds of small children, teaching them to screech, 'Kill him, kill him!' at the trial of their own father or mother? Such scenes are put on the radio in Red China and piped into the classrooms to train other youngsters to do likewise. Do you have to discuss whether that is good or bad? Doesn't a mature man close his mind to anything that permits such fundamental violation of basic human qualities?"

I doubt if I'll ever forget the strange look that went over his face. "I just never thought of that," he answered. I don't know what effect this conversation had on him, but it helped confirm what I had learned about the importance of a closed mind in preserving mental integrity.

A closed mind, of course, is a radical preventative. Fanaticism can easily be confused with it, and this is not what it means. A fanatic not only closes a door in his mind, he cements it shut so it can never be opened again, and shuts every other nearby door the same way, irrespective of where it leads.   . An intelligent person closes the door when he reaches a conclusion, moving on to other problems, but keeping the key safely in his pocket so he can open it again if he wishes. If he does, it is by his own free will and judgment and not at a brainwasher's insistence.

The mature thinker's approach to communism is that it is evil, not partly evil but all evil. That is surely the only possible stand to take when under the unfair and deceitful pressures of brainwashing, when the dice are loaded against a man. I heard one woman explaining it to another this way, "You know, you're not a little bit pregnant; you're either all pregnant or not at all," and it was as simple as that. To make another comparison, consider a glass of purified water. Let the tiniest drop of poison fall into the glass and the water isn't a little poisonous, it is all poison. The amateur sophisticate is led astray by the argument that a chemist could conceivably remove the poison and then the water would be fresh again. That is exactly the sort of argument the victims of brainwashing have to guard against, as Dr. Hayes discovered. Theoretically the poison could be removed from the water, but as a practical matter of fact it would be too complicated and expensive a job and even then not certain. The clear thinker does not permit himself to be led up the garden path by this phony "new liberalism" any more than by the "new democracy" o£ the Reds. He recognizes both as illiberal and undemocratic, and the entire communist ideology as poison.

The experiences of the brainwashed showed, too, that the ability to keep one's mind busy is an ever-present element in the maintenance of mental stamina. The communists engage in a perpetual duel for the contents of a man's brain. They try to empty it of every thought that is not polarized around communism and its pressures. They seek to weary and worry it by filling it wholly with the fears and the reactions they give it. Their purpose is to drive a mind to distraction. They start off with the emotions that break a man, such as fear, boredom and desperation. They put their victim in agony by arousing an exaggerated sense of personal responsibility and guilt.

The only way this obsessive pressure can be beaten is by relieving the mind, giving it other thoughts. Anything that relaxes the strain does the trick. An American woman, Mrs. Frances Hamlin, did it most ingeniously in Tsinan, North China. The communists put her into a small room, separate from her husband, also a missionary and also under detention. They refused to let her have anything with which to occupy her mind. They knew she had an alert brain and expected the enforced idleness and emptiness to be an unendurable torture, enough to break her. They told her she would have to decide "voluntarily." Then they took away her books, pencils and paper, leaving her with only a few personal possessions and the blank walls. They waited with patience that was a mockery. She defeated them by braiding a belt entirely of human hair, her own. She took the hairs as they came from her own head in daily combings over a period of six months. She kept herself preoccupied with this self-imposed task.

She was one among many who, thrown entirely on their own resources, evolved novel ways of keeping their minds preoccupied with anything except their communist environment. General Dean swatted flies and kept score, making a game of it. Major MacGhee made a study of insect aeronautics. The Reverend Olin Stockwell, one of the earliest victims of brainwashing in China, whose Calvary started in 1950, wrote a couple of hundred poems and memorized enough of them to publish when he returned to freedom, under the title *Meditations from a Prison Cell*. Indeed, he has enough left over to fill several more such booklets!

Stockwell was in solitary confinement for fourteen months and then was hurled into an intensive course of brainwashing that lasted nine and a half more months. The Reds were confident that fourteen months of isolation for a man who had been accustomed to group work all his life and had probably never spent a whole day by himself before would make a mush of his whole mental apparatus and put him in perfect shape for "re-education" and rebirth the Red way.

They were particularly confident, too, because they knew Stockwell had lost patience with the old regime and had received their new government with a completely open mind. Stockwell had two strikes against him already, according to what all their experience had proved. Yet in all that siege against him, they were unable to win his mind! Stockwell was an example of a liberal who did a lot of rethinking of his own while in prison and who came forth with several weapons that saved him. He kept his mind busy — ^very, very busy; he closed his mind to certain basic Red approaches, and he did not hesitate to tell any tall story if it would put the enemy off its guard and release his own tension. He fought back in the spirit of the chaplain who exclaimed, "Praise the Lord and pass the ammunition." He did not split intellectual hairs about it; he just defended himself under the instinctive assumption of his early days in the Midwest that if they were fighting him, they "didn't mean him no good" and he wouldn't go along with them no how. He expressed it more grammatically than the colored boys of the Golden Cross Club Against Communism, but the meaning was the same. He had the same capacity, when the chips were down, to put his footing onto fundamentals.

During his enforced idleness, he had been anything but idle. He wrote about sixty-five limericks, then graduated into poetry, composing 128 poems, each fifteen to twenty lines long. The Reds carefully took away everything he wrote almost immediately afterwards, so he was in a continual race against time to memorize a limerick or a poem before his guard would seize it. This gave him a day or two at most. Then, as a memory aid, he thought up a catchy title for each limerick and poem and memorized those, too, and finally arranged an index for all of them, preserving it in his head because the Reds wouldn't let him take any written material away with him.

The people who must really have thought he had lost his head were his friends at Hong Kong when he finally was released. As soon as he reached a room where he could rest, he got out paper and started writing limericks and poems out of his head in an unending stream. Nobody had ever seen anything like that before, ever! He was determined to get them down on paper before they slipped out of his mind in his new, normal environment.

He gave himself such a busy schedule under isolation and later on under brainwashing that he had no time left to worry about the Reds! As he had decided not to take what they said "seriously but to dissemble acquiescence, it was all an act to him, make-believe, and his mind was simply closed to any semantics the Reds could use to change his attitudes.

"That saved my life," he told me. The troubles that usually wear a man down, such as dysentery, came and went without shaking him because he had built up so many resistances. First of all, he was too busy thinking up clever limericks. He brought his sense of humor into play here. He was able to see how grossly ridiculous his whole situation was and get a laugh instead of a tear out of it. That was as stimulating to him as a drug, without the harmful effects. Tears would have been just what the brainwashing doctor prescribed! The ability to squeeze amusement out of his plight took a lot of the sting from it.

"That was the most creative period of my life," Stockwell told me, and there was no doubting he meant it. Between the limericks and the poems he wrote a hundred devotional talks and made up several crossword puzzles, too. He was thinking, all right, as the Reds insisted, only he tricked them by not thinking about what they wanted!

He not only kept his mind busy but strengthened his convictions that way, for his poems were usually on religious themes. The limericks were on any subject that came to mind. No matter how rough or distasteful an experience, he could always trust to a limerick to put it into place. They thought that an alert brain such as his would become so depressed under isolation that it would seek a way out in suicide and took away whatever might serve as instruments for it. That inspired this:

"The guards took razor blades and knife
To keep me from taking my life.
They need not fear an end so drear
For I am still in love with my wife!"

He had always kept clean, and sudden deprivation of facilities for cleanliness would be sure to put him into the doldrums, the Reds thought. Instead, he wrote:

"If you would be prison-wise
You must learn to economize.
One basin of water surely had oughta
Wash floor, shirt and face contrariwise."

And:

"Three months without bathing you stink
And clothes once white are now pink.
But don't bother your head, the jail it is red,
So sure they'd turn pink, don't you think."

How was dialectical materialism going to beat that? It just didn't have a chance except by a treatment that would have been brain-changing and sheer atrocity, which would have required much more costly and specialized attention and would have ended up by making him utterly useless to then^ anyway.

"Were you really able to memorize all that?" I asked him, a bit skeptically, I must admit.

"How could I ever forget them?" he exclaimed, and for the next twenty minutes recited a half-mile of them at me!

Stockwell learned a whole philosophy of survival during his isolation. Besides his other defenses, he fell back most strongly of all on his convictions, his faith. Whatever confusion there might have been in politics, which wasn't his field, he made up for it in his faith. The greatest strain, he discovered, was uncertainty, not knowing from hour to hour what would be next, although for hundreds and hundreds of hours nothing came next; but it might have and sometimes did, and this could become maddening, and was for many people, especially those unused to solitude. He overcame this by faith that there just had to be a purpose where there was so much suffering. Whether his penance vile would endure a day, a year, or a decade, he was willing to take it because he was thoroughly convinced "something worth while would come out of it in the end." He kept his vision focused on that end. The hope-lessness-inevitability line came up against a stone wall in him.

"I learned in prison," he told me, "that we must accept tragedy and turn it into something worth while and make it meaningful, and that tragedy seems made just for that purpose. You can always do it. The only suffering that is impossible to bear is that which is not meaningful, that seems without a pur-pose."

He changed what seemed deadly to what actually was vital and creative by a healthy attitude! He had never written poetry before, except a few lines at school. He had never had the time and the stimulation to delve as deeply into his philosophy as in prison. Out of his isolation, Stockwell made an oppor-tunity to seek out the factors that really made life meaningful.

Stockwell's experience, too, demonstrated how extremely important it is for a man in captivity or caught in a corner to feel sure that he has friends outside remembering him and on his side, doing what they can for him and praying for him. Stockwell stressed the contribution that prayer made in his case. The Reds seemed to realize this and would go into tantrums of frustra-tion over it. "You can't pray here," the guards would shout at him and at a hard-boiled little Chinese general named Shan Chuang-yi, who had been in prison already two years and who continued reading his Buddhist scriptures with the utmost composure.

The two were alone together once for a few brief minutes and Stockwell was struck by how sturdily the old general was holding up. "Without some kind of a religious faith, nothing holds life together," the soldier said to the missionary.

The brainwashers learned that Stockwell's wife was at Hong Kong and taunted him, saying, "All her prayers won't get you out." Stockwell didn't ar-gue the point; he was satisfied that the prayers of his wife and friends were enabling him to sustain himself during his imprisonment, and that was an accomplishment in itself.

Stockwell learned another lesson. He told me that merely to accept suffer-ing was not sufficient to maintain stamina. "You have to learn how to use suf-fering," he said. Others who had been brainwashed expressed it to me in dif-ferent ways. Some called it a "sense of mission" or just having a purpose.

What it crystallized into was taking the offensive and not being satisfied to rely just on the defensive.

That was a curious thing for a missionary who was very liberal in his political thought to have learned in prison, the hard way. Actually, like so many Americans, he had never been a softie; he was just trying to be fair, but when the chips were down, he wouldn't budge from what he knew. He knew that there was something mad and evil about what he was facing and that if he made believe it wasn't so, he'd be licked. So he humored the Reds as one does any insane person. "I lied like a trooper," Stockwell said frankly.

A description of the clever and simple devices that people thought up to relieve their minds under brainwashing would constitute one of the most heroic chapters ever written in the history of man's slow but sure advance toward civilization. The person who did not find a way to keep his mind busy underwent a self-torture that was at least as corrosive as anything the Reds could do to him directly.

Another indispensable element in mental survival was confidence. A prisoner who possessed it was able to accomplish the seemingly impossible by mobilizing every bit of his physical and mental qualities, concentrating them upon a single objective, with results that seemed miraculous. Every human being has untapped resources of mental and physical powers. Confidence can summon them into action at a moment's notice. With them, a person can accomplish what he never suspected he could do.

Confidence can stave off defeatism. The man who doesn't know when he's licked frequently turns defeat into a glorious victory. History is full of instances. The Reds have made a subtle art of this by a stalling, dragging-out process accompanied by attrition and a constant return to the fight from some new, unexpected direction, under a different name or disguise. The more hopeless a situation appears, the more resounding is the eventual victory. Confidence can make such a victory possible and at the same time keep a man's mind alert against tricky Red attacks. Overconfidence is simply blindness.

Confidence has a touch of mysticism in it, made practical. Sometimes it comes very close to fatalism. Japan-born Arthur J. Breen, whose grandfather was one of the founders of Doshisha University, was in Peking when the Reds came in. They put him in prison for two years, much of it in solitary. He said he noticed Chinese holding out under conditions which would have cracked almost anyone else. "What kept them going was the fatalistic streak in them," he said. 'Tatalism, the way they felt it, was a form of hope, a kind of confidence. When you're fatalistic that way, you don't worry any more. You're able to keep your mind off your miseries. That's the biggest part of the fight."

He compared fatalism to hope "shrouded in dark clouds." What it boiled down to, he said, was simply "not giving in." I had frequently noted the similarity between confidence and fatalism among military men. Surely both qualities merge in the very usual reaction, "Why should I worry? If a bullet hasn't got my name on it, I won't get hit." Curiously, men who had that sort of feeling frequently seemed able to get away with more than others. If it weren't so, soldiers like Douglas MacArthur wouldn't have lasted through their first baptisms under fire.

The most important thing is anything that keeps your mind off the threats and horror of a situation, concluded Breen. He had spent much of his life in Mongolia, where he had been a guide for Sven Hedin on that explorer's second expedition. A lean, haggard, and tall man, he looked the part. He had only been six months out of prison when I met him, and his reactions were still fresh, although it was obviously too much of a strain for him to talk for any length of time on the subject.

Confidence possesses other qualities, too, as my interviews made very evident. Confidence did not mean recklessness, although it equipped a man to take a chance which he otherwise would not consider. Frequently, lightning advantage has to be taken of the slightest opening if a guard is to be outwitted or any bold stroke attempted. Anything that detracts from clear-headedness converts it into mere deviltry, which usually leads to disaster. A daring action must be made deliberately, without panic. That is where confidence — or this kind of fatalism — comes in. The same spontaneous co-ordination a pilot requires for an emergency landing is called for.

Out of the experiences of the brainwashed, another survival element conspicuously shown was adaptability, which is the capacity to roll with the punch. The man who uses it feels out his enemy's tactics, fitting himself into them and manipulating the situation to his own advantage. The communists concentrate on trying to beat him down. His objective, irrespective of whether he is a businessman arrested in peacetime or a soldier captured on the battlefield, is to preserve his physical and mental integrity. If he can keep thinking offensively, his defenses fall into place naturally and he is able to adapt himself to the enemy's twists and turns.

Bob Bryan and John Hayes and a great number of others who had intimate knowledge of the Chinese mind managed to do so.

So long as such an individual kept his objective clearly in his mind, while watching for an opening, he was frequently able to find a safe hiding place inside the framework of the enemy's terminology and procedures. He fit his thought processes into the brainwasher's pattern of thinking, using the enemy's weapons against him. In doing so, he was only turning the tables on the communists themselves. One of the main approaches of the Red propaganda worker is to infiltrate himself into the thought patterns of his foe. A keen observer, a Frenchman named Henri Vetch, whom I first knew twenty years before in Peking when he was a young bookshop proprietor, expressed this very graphically for me. I met him again just after he had been released from prison, where he had been sentenced in connection with one of those fake plots with which the Reds come up every once in a while, this one being a conspiracy to lob a mortar shell over the wall of the Forbidden City just when

Mao Tse-tung was passing on the other side, thus killing him. Henri had observed brainwashing at close quarters. "The Reds get furthest with Americans by using their own idealism against them," he told me. "By forming their arguments in the idealistic manner familiar to you Americans, they give you a guilt complex and find it much easier to provoke you into confessions that way." Surely there should be no scruples about using this same tactic against the Reds.

Henri did so in a particularly baffling way for the indoctrinators at the Peking Model Reform Prison, where he served two years of a ten-year term. He made a deep study of the most ancient books of China, especially the *Book of Changes,* and interpreted them extensively as the true fountain of communistic theory and almost everything else. His judge became so infuriated at times that he did an Indian dance around him, slapping and kicking him. Henri carefully wrote out an appeal, accusing the brainwasher of being untrue to the old Chinese principles of Mao Tse-tung, and came up with so much double-talk on it from these classical sources that the Reds had to dispose of him some way, either by execution or expulsion. Chou En-lai at that moment was trying to wean France from the West, and so Henri was expelled from China. Henri had calculated his timing and had figured out that they did not want to kill him.

Victims of brainwashing who are not acquainted with the enemy's traditions nor with communism cannot be expected to operate that way. But the American POW's watched the changing Red tactics and changed their own accordingly. When a policy of indiscriminate collective punishment was being followed, the trick was to lay low and play a waiting game. When the enemy put on what it called a "lenient policy," individuals were encouraged to go ahead and try anything they thought would rattle the Reds. The fact was never lost sight of that harsh or lenient, these were only tactics in an unchanging strategy.

Cutting Them to Size

Deceit permeates the whole communist approach, and when a prisoner was able to use it successfully against the Reds, it had a stimulating effect on morale. The greatest Red deceit was their claim to omnipotence and omniscience. They deliberately set about making their victims feel that they were being faced by supermen who knew everything and could do anything. When a prisoner managed to make the Reds themselves fall for a deceit, he was able to bring them to earth with a thud.

Bob Vogeler told me how he managed it. The communists acted like animals toward him, making animal demands, and so he said, "I decided to throw them a bone from time to time to chew on." He had no hesitation in telling them falsehoods if this succeeded in calling them off him for a while.

In the meantime, he kept his mind busy thinking what to tell them next. He found them falling for his fanciful tales, and so began to lose respect for their ability. They could crack like anyone else! "They insisted they were invincible but I proved to myself they weren't," Vogeler said.

He had to think up his tall tales carefully. When they did catch on at times, he managed to make them think he had made a natural mistake. He used real names but sometimes misspelled them so as to make what he said seem credible. "I'm not a good speller," he told them. "That's how it sounds to me. I'm not always right." He managed to get a particularly obnoxious Red *agent provocateur* into trouble by inserting his name in an incidental manner in a statement. Vogeler's stamina went way up after that. Numerous POW's from Korea told me about using the same tactic. Every time it worked, morale was given a big boost. The main achievement was to cut the brainwasher down to size.

Use of these infiltration tactics, from deceit and dissembling to adaptability and rolling with the punch, was every bit as legitimate against the communists as against an opposing general in the field. The Reds do not differentiate in their ideology between peace and war; they recognize only communism and the enemy, which means everyone else. They are engaged in what they teach is a death struggle between communism and all other systems. They believe that this conflict can be waged anywhere, at any time, under any guise, and that anything which weakens or destroys noncommunists and anti-communists is a legitimate weapon.

Deceit or dissembling belongs in the list of survival elements. Deceit against the Reds is justifiable not only on the basis of it being a war tactic — a war at least against the sanctity of a man's mind — but because a streak of insanity runs through communism, as it did in Hitlerism. In Edgar Allan Poe's "Dr. Tarr and Dr. Fether," the inmates of an insane asylum change places with the wardens. That short story reads as if Poe were describing a twentieth-century brainwashing establishment.

I noticed in my interviews that practically everyone who got out of the Red trap had to operate, wittingly or unwittingly, as if he had been cornered by a madman waving a dagger in his hand. Anyone who tries talking logic at a time like that is a corpse. The fanaticized assailant has to be humored and outmaneuvered. Some would readily use the word *deceive,* others prefer to call it *dissembling.* The Reds insisted on a kind of logic that was perverted and untrue, as their theory of unlimited responsibility amply showed. Those who were able to take advantage of this twisted Red philosophy as a cover and to help manipulate themselves to safety by it certainly had every reason to do so.

High jinks was the most appropriate name I could find for a stamina-giving element that brought the full force of humor into action alongside several other stimulating elements, such as deceit and adaptability. Crazy Week was high jinks at its best. Stunts of that sort were particularly effective in sapping Red morale, at the same time raising that of their victims. The indoctrinator was left wondering whether he was being flattered or insulted and, while he had a humiliated feeling over it, he wasn't able to do a thing because it would have made him lose even more face.

In one typical instance, an American POW was summoned by a brainwasher who tried to inveigle him into a political trap. Instead of tiring his mind over it, the POW diverted the whole discussion by using an off-color slang expression which hardly anyone understood. The brainwasher, taking the bait, asked him what the phrase meant.

"What!" the American exclaimed. "You don't mean to tell me you don't understand that!"

No, the brainwasher answered awkwardly, he didn't.

"Everybody knows what that means," the POW said, shaking his head as if stunned. Then he broke into a smile, saying, "You're kidding me, aren't you? You know what it means."

The indoctrinator repeated that he didn't. The American stared at him, a look of pained disillusionment crossing his face. "How can you teach me anything if you don't even understand plain English?" he asked. The humiliated brainwasher never did get around to bringing up the real reason for summoning the prisoner.

The temptation is very great to confuse such repartee with wisecracks, especially by Americans. But they are poles apart. Wisecracks arouse instant retaliation. A wisecrack is obvious, laying a man open to the accusation of showing a "hostile attitude." The punishment for that in Korea was incarceration in the hole. If a man were lucky, this would mean the low part of a Korean hut, where the flues are situated; if not, it meant a pit in the ground with a few logs shoved over the top for a roof.

One of the most powerful elements for mental survival is to have a purpose. Nothing can snatch a man from total defeat or death faster than to have a purpose. The explosive discovery of a purpose in what previously had seemed to be only futile suffering kept men in the Death March alive, eager to see the fight through, where a moment before they were almost praying to die. That's what John Dunn achieved, a miracle of generalship that rang like a bell on that freezing day through those men's souls.

When a man's nerves are strained to the utmost and all effort appears meaningless, he can squeeze out renewed endurance by giving his suffering a purpose. Former prisoners of the Reds told me how a purpose could become an obsession that a man lived by. His fixation could be escape or revenge, the gathering of vital information, or anything else that makes life meaningful again, so that the men will cling to it tenaciously. The purpose must be genuine, something worth going through suffering to achieve, for it to be truly effective. Many a prisoner kept whole that way. Whether he had the patience of a Job or was as ornery as an old coot made no difference. If he came up with a good reason to go through his ordeal, he had made it endurable.

Any purpose is a help, but the evidence I have gathered shows incontrovertibly that the purpose which has a broader perspective than one's own self provides the greater survival stamina. Indeed, it becomes two elements in one, because individual survival then becomes necessary not for itself alone, but for the wider purpose to be achieved.

Herb Marlatt, when he suddenly realized that the knowledge he was obtaining this very hard way was something his country had to know to save itself, was immediately given two reasons to go through with his sufferings and survive. Yes, one objective was to continue to exist, but the other objective was to convert his suffering into something meaningful to the nation from which he had sprung.

Call this additional purpose a sense of mission or a crusading spirit, and it becomes another element in our list. Without it, men like Dr. Hayes would have seen no sense in going on. What for? To linger in life for a few more years when one is already well past middle age? When people are dying all around one, death appears a trivial matter. If only one's own self were concerned, it would be trivial.

If anyone doubts the decisive importance of this crusading spirit in survival, let him talk to some of the civilians or military personnel who have gone through brainwashing. What remained most firmly in one's mind after release from brainwashing was the crusading spirit. Those who possessed it had been among the most successful in frustrating their brainwashers.

Back in the Free World again, I found them seizing every opportunity that came their way, going out of their way to create opportunities to fulfill the sense of mission which had given their ordeal a purpose. In some form or other, this crusading spirit was to arouse their fellow citizens to an appreciation of what the free society provides its people and to a realization of the menace to humanity in the new totalitarian concept of brainwashing. Some called their crusade patriotism, others called it religion. Many gave it no special name, but busied themselves like beavers propagating the lessons they had learned when face to face with the faceless horror of mind control.

There was yet another direction this crusading spirit took. Men like Hayes deliberately set themselves to the task of winning the enemy. They grasped the very simple fact that the brainwasher was a person like anyone else, that the people under communism were human like any other people, susceptible to the same basic emotions, vulnerable to the same fundamental appeals. They were frustrated and unhappy men, sick, trapped, or fooled into evil. So long as they were infected with the communist virus, they were dangerous. But they might be cured. Most of them are not truly communistic, but are prisoners and hostages of their own system. Men like Hayes sensed that communism was very, very vulnerable, and what made it most vulnerable were the human beings to whom it entrusted its madhouse ideology.

What gave a crusading spirit such extraordinary potency was that it took the man away from the mere defensive and put him on the offensive, itself a stimulating change in outlook.

Group feelings belong to this list of stamina-producing elements. No communistic tactic is more relentlessly pursued than the rooting out of group connections, no matter how innocent of political content, so that no other outlet is left except that which communism itself provides. Anything that preserves group sense defeats this tactic.

The mad Red fear of any group that exists outside his own controlled environment permeates the whole communist society, in or out of prison. Thus, Boy and Girl Scouts, Girl Guides, the Salvation Army, and weekly luncheon clubs such as the Rotary were considered subversive and truly dangerous to the rigid Red structure, for they encouraged people to think as individuals. All of them were suppressed with as much vigor as any non-Red groups in the POW camps.

Such group life as the prisoners were able to maintain or develop was therefore a disastrous setback for the brainwashers and a source of great strength for the POW 's. The Masonic group that remained undetected, the Golden Cross Club formed under the eyes of the Reds, and the underground that the POW 's gradually brought into existence, constituted elements of vitality.

Group feelings never could be crushed entirely in the religious field. When Sam Davis, the British "Chaplain of the Church of the Captivity," as the POW's called him in North Korea, was thrust into solitary confinement for "holding Bible class without permission," the men defiantly gathered anyway and sang so loudly that he would have had to be stone deaf not to have heard. Tough top sergeants as well as businessmen told me of the effectiveness of prayer in making them feel part of an unconquerable body, beside which communism was puny, indeed.

The Reds divided the prisoners into small study groups, the easier to control and indoctrinate them. A group spirit grew up whenever the men devised ways of outwitting the brainwashers, making a farce of "learning." The sense of mutual companionship this gave was all the stronger because it sprouted in such a normal, healthy way.

A virtually irrevocable rule, an element on which the success of all the others often depended, was the simple one of being natural, of being yourself. Some of the elements listed are already part of the character of any brainwasher's victim. These he should have no hesitancy in assuming and should even rely on them as his safest refuge. Others just do not fit a man's character. A missionary needs no urging to recognize the strength-giving qualities in the crusading spirit. A China born lawyer can fit himself into the hair-splitting technicalities of the Reds. An ordinary military officer must depend on stark convictions and the clarity of mind that warfare demands. Each can benefit from all elements. But each must never allow himself to go out of character, for that is fatal. Of course, here too, the rule has to be made with the provision that exceptions prove a rule, and adaptability should sometimes force a change. The rule nonetheless remains, as it has been down the ages, to be yourself. That means true integrity.

These are the elements that have proven themselves, under the challenge of brainwashing, to be able to lick it. The pattern for mental survival as it disclosed itself out of the communist ordeal has more elements in it, more flexibility, and is susceptible of far greater interplay than can be found in the Red pattern for the destruction of men's minds. The person trapped by brainwashing, whether a prisoner from abroad or the unfortunate inhabitant of a country behind the bamboo-iron curtain, has plenty of weapons from which to choose.

Chapter Eleven - A Matter Of Integrity

The world by now has received ample proof that nothing emanating from a Red source can be believed. The ideology of the Communist Party — by teaching that truth is what conforms to its changing political line and that good is what helps the party — excuses any lie, atrocity, or aggression so long as it is pro-Red in intent. That is the inflexible standard. None other is recognized. Words and deeds that normally are regarded as deceitful and evil constitute routine procedure under communism.

Evidence of this strategy of lies appears anywhere one happens to be. There were two glaring examples within a fortnight while I was writing this concluding chapter in Singapore. In one, a woman appeared on the platform at a mass demonstration and, holding up a baby, cried out that neither she nor her child had been allowed to see or accompany her husband who was being deported to Red China. Subsequent information showed that she had refused to go with him and that it was not their baby, anyway! The baby had nothing to do with the case except as a callously used instrument for Red propaganda.

Material I have gathered on the horrible murder of Gene D. Symonds, a liberal American correspondent in Singapore's Red riots of May, 1955, includes appalling details of communist atrocities. In one such, a human torch was made out of an Asian detective. The anniversary issue of the communist-run World Federation of Trade Unions magazine has just come to me with the photo of this man before he died, showing him covered with blood and oil. Only the facts have been turned completely around. The caption has him "a Singapore worker attacked by police when on picket duty."

But such travesties o£ truth should no longer surprise anyone. They are local reflections of far bigger lies. The germwarfare hoax and the faked doctors' plot in Moscow have no parallel in history. Never before has any government or official body descended to such depths of criminal libel and corruption of morality. Every facility at the disposal of Moscow and Peking was used at home and abroad to accuse the U.S. of waging bacterial warfare over huge areas of North China, Manchuria and Korea. In the doctors' plot, outstanding Russian physicians confessed to a hideous use of their profession to cause sickness and death among top men of the U.S.S.R. The case appeared airtight. Witnesses testified to every detail. A woman doctor received the Stalin prize and was nominated to run for high political office for her testimony for the prosecution. Then, after Stalin died and before his succession was straightened out, the same government ministry that had announced the news issued another routinely worded communiqué saying it was all false, there had been no plot at all, every word of it was untrue!

This same falsification is constantly being confirmed in everything the communists do, big or little. Certainly, on the basis of overwhelming evidence, no confession reported by the communists can be believed, no matter how overwhelming the evidence appears. In each of their hoaxes, the Reds have painstakingly manufactured the evidence along with the confessions.

Of course there have been lies told before and by governments, too, but never, by the greatest stretch of imagination, has anything ever come near this policy of planned falsehood that underlies the entire official and unofficial Red structure. Whereas normally the truth is told and the lie is the exception, in the lopsided Red world, the lie is*the customary procedure and the truth is the exception. Red statistics have been thoroughly exposed as having only a propaganda relationship to real measurements.

This poses a new and an unprecedented problem. The responsibility of free society is to let all the people in the world know these facts, at home and abroad and on both sides of the bamboo-iron curtain. The Reds have been proven deliberate and consistent liars by their own mouths. When people realize this simple fact, which is so enormous that its implications escape the average man, the confession trick will be deprived of all its propaganda value to the Reds. People everywhere will sensibly meet every Red pronouncement of a new confession with a horse laugh. This knowledge of Red cupidity, when properly disseminated, will make the confession technique boomerang, removing one of the main props of brainwashing. Even its psychological value as an insidious manner of putting submission into the subconscious minds of their people will be radically reduced. The makebelieve in the brainwasher's chamber will become that much more difficult.

The confession problem is universal under communism. The military phase of it is receiving the main attention at this time because of the sudden need by military forces to deal with it, as brought to a head in the Korean War. Actually, like health problems, this is just as much or more a public issue. Incalculable numbers of human beings residing inside the communist bloc are being forced to go through with this vicious act. Whenever a foreigner is available and the Red secret police feel some advantage can be taken of him, he is arrested and given the treatment. The only way to pull the rug out from under this tactic is by world-wide exposure of it.

In dealing with the mind, as with the body, each individual is a case by himself, requiring individual attention. No specific set of rules can be devised to apply the same way to everyone. This is just as true for those who go into an infected area as for those who come out. Each mind and each physique differs slightly from every other. The safest guide in this morass is to adopt the kind of approach health officers make. The situation is almost identical. Rules of mental hygiene are just as applicable in this field as are regulations for physical hygiene.

A special problem has arisen in the military sphere as concerns information that might properly be given to an enemy interrogator and whether a soldier should or should not be permitted to confess. What appears obvious at once is that this problem has nothing to do one way or another with the plain fact that no statement from communist sources can be believed and no confession made inside the communist environment can be given any credence by any reasonable body. That is a simple fact. The only time the truth can come from communist sources is when it suits their propaganda purpose.

Irrespective of military policy in any part of the Free World, that should be evident. Each military service, in addition, in relation to its own situation and objectives, must just as obviously define policy for its own personnel. As with everything else, it simply has to take reality into consideration if its decisions are to hold when the test comes.

The only answer that can logically be made to this question is that the soldier should certainly be trained for any contingency that he may meet. Confession at times can be used as a weapon against the enemy. The objective always should be resistance and the destruction of the entire Red basis for mind atrocities. As in any other sphere, a line should be drawn and every normal effort made to meet it. Nobody should admit a single detail under Red pressure, but if facts have to be given under pressure, imaginations should be ready and trained to provide the sort of misinformation that will lead the brainwasher far astray. This should be just as much the tactic to be followed by anyone, from refrigerator salesman to professor of mathematics, who happens to fall into the coils of the brainwashers.

The civilian nowadays can have as important or more important strategic information in his head than a military officer. Comparatively few of the people actually engaged in scientific fields that are important for defense are in any military service. So long as the Reds indiscriminately seize anyone in pirate fashion who happens to be within their reach, any individual with vital strategic data should keep out of the danger area. I should not think that a civilian with a strategic secret should have any less responsibility to keep it from the communists than a soldier. The war on minds is against civilians just as much as the military; it is a total operation.

209

Surely the least that can be expected of a soldier is that if seized he keep always in mind that he remains under military discipline while a prisoner, not ceasing to be a soldier, and that part of the responsibility that goes with this is to suffer wounds and to die if need be. The battle does not end with a man's capture. Nowadays, that is often where it really begins! The communists have arranged it that way.

The most important Red purpose in brainwashing is not its employment against foreign enemies but against the populations of communist countries themselves. They are always suspect to the Red hierarchy, actually its main enemies. In that area lies the field of battle where the main fight has to be waged and where the spread of knowledge, providing mental vaccination, can be of most good. In no other field is the offensive so much the best defense as in the ideological. Decent humanity has not the right to permit people to be caught in a controlled environment and to be made into guinea pigs for ultimate dehumanization under a perverted Pavlovian technique.

The war against men's minds has for its primary objective the creation of what is euphemistically called this "new Soviet man." The intent is to change a mind radically so that its owner becomes a living puppet — a human robot — without the atrocity being visible from the outside. The aim is to create a mechanism in flesh and blood, with new beliefs and new thought processes inserted into a captive body. What that amounts to is the search for a slave race that, unlike the slaves of olden times, can be trusted never to revolt, always to be amenable to orders, like an insect to its instincts. The intent is to atomize humanity.

That is the ghastly form which the conception of the "new Soviet man" has taken. Secrecy and the darkness of a controlled environment are required for it to work. Wherever this secrecy is denied to the Reds or the controlled environment penetrated, brainwashing cannot succeed.

Surely there can no longer be a trace of doubt that brainwashing is sheer evil. The fight against it is the culminating issue of all time, in which every human being is a protagonist. There can be neither escape nor neutrality where such responsibilities lie.

There can be neither front nor rear, for the great lesson that came from the brainwashing chambers was that while every man has a cracking point, every man's cracking point can be immensely strengthened. That is the job of home, school, and church. The mother, teacher, and pastor are in the front lines in this ideological conflict, and every word they say to their sons and daughters is important to the struggle, for character more than anything else will determine the outcome.

Truth is the most important serum and integrity the most devastating weapon that can be used against the totalitarian concept. Facts can demolish the entire fake communist paradise. Nothing should be allowed to interfere with the task of getting those facts across to the people who need and can use them.

The men who went into battle in Korea against the tanks and minds of the communist forces had not been given a hint regarding Red brain warfare. That is what gave the communist brainwashing machine the expectation of easy propaganda pickings among the captives.

Only an informed people can shoulder their responsibilities effectively. When free men know both what they are fighting against and what they are fighting to preserve and enhance, they are unbeatable, stronger than any strategy.

What is absolutely essential is that the full facts be given to all our people, for mind warfare is total war. This approach can make our struggle for the mind the crusade it should be. Never since man received reason beyond the instincts of animal kind has there been a more important issue. In the fight to give man forever the opportunity to develop, every possible weapon must be utilized on the field of battle, which is everywhere. There is no "behind the lines" any longer.